EATING UP ITALY

'The most intensely greedy, fragrant and sensuously written travelogue I have ever read.'
NIGEL SLATER

'Elizabeth David meets Jack Kerouac – around the table and on the road, this is a brilliant insight into Italian gastro-culture.'
GIORGIO LOCATELLI

'Fort's book, which is beautifully produced, is a reminder that the cuisine of Italy is infinitely varied, changing as it does from season to season.'
PAUL BAILEY, Sunday Times

'Eating Up Italy is an effortlessly sensuous read from start to finish, intelligently laced with thought-provoking observations and insights.'
JOANNA BLYTHMAN, Scotsman

'This is the most tantalising account of Italian food you're ever likely to read, written with a brio that never flags from first page to last.'
VANESSA BERRIDGE, BBC Good Food

'Matthew Fort's Eating Up Italy is a rattling good read and a greedily observant gastro-travelogue.'
PHILIPPA DAVENPORT, Financial Times

'There are many refreshing things about Eating Up Italy. One is the studied avoidance of everything that is clichéd about Italy's image abroad… This is not a conventional guide book (we are not meant to revisit the restaurants or even places Fort goes to) but it is an invitation to see and taste Italy in a different light… What emerges is a mosaic of regional and inter-regional diets under threat, but surviving and even renewing themselves, in a globalised world where the rural way of life will soon be something of the distant past.'
JOHN FOOT, Guardian

EATING UP ITALY
Voyages on a Vespa

MATTHEW FORT

CENTRO BOOKS

Centro Books 200 East 90th Street, New York, NY 10128
www.centrobooks.com

Publisher's Cataloging-in-Publication
(Provided by Quality Books, Inc.)

Fort, Matthew.
Eating up Italy: Voyages on a Vespa
by Matthew Fort.
p. cm.
Includes index.
ISBN 1-933572-02-7
978-1-933572-02-4

1. Cookery, Italian. 2. Italy--Description and
travel. 3. Italy--Social life and customs.   I. Title.

TX723.F668 2006
641.5945
QBI06-600311

Book Design and Cover by
Viqui Maggio

www.centrobooks.com

Printed in USA
August 2006

1 3 5 7 9 10 8 6 4 2
Centro Books Original Trade Paperback

CONTENTS

ACKNOWLEDGEMENTS

Half the world seems to have made some kind of contribution to this book. First and foremost are my publisher, Louise Haines, who had the courage and percipience to commission the book, and the patience to wait and wait and wait for it; and my agent, Caroline Dawnay, who has never ceased in her encouragement, support and understanding.

Then there are those who have kindly read, and re-read and re-read, the various versions of the manuscript, and who were perceptive, constructive and encouraging in their views, notably my brother Tom, John Irving in Bra and Henry Porter. Bob Granleese made many pertinent suggestions. If this book has any merit, much of it is due to them, and to my editor Anne Askwith.

I owe a great debt to my sister-in-law, Mary, who acted as project manager for the various stages of my odyssey, pointing me in the direction of this restaurant or azienda and that, finding me hotels and giving me guidance. With another brother, Johnny, Mary followed my progress, providing encouragement and enthusiasm every kilometer of the way.

I might never made the journey at all had it not been for the early backing of Derek Johns, Clare Blampied of Sacla and Mark Price of Waitrose, all of whom provided practical and sage support; and I certainly would never have met a tithe of the people, cooks, producers, growers and eaters, who made the various stages such a marvel of pleasure without the support of the Slow Food Movement, and the people who make it the extraordinary organization it is. Many – Giusseppe Antonini Attonio Attorre, Manfredo Fossa, Augusto Lana, Gianfranco Manini, Vito Puglia, Gilberto Venturini, Walter Zaga – gave unsparingly of their time, passion, wisdom and contracts.

Through them I met others who showed a kindness and generosity which I can never repay: Silvia Cappello and her family, Giacomo Bennelli and his, the Gaetano family of La Carolee, the Cicchi family in Ascoli Piceno, and Laura Borgognoni in Ancona.

Above all, I thank my wife and daughter, Lindsay and Lois, who encouraged me to go, put up with my long absences without complaint, and waited patiently for my returns. Without their love and reassurance this book would have no point.

NOTE

Italian cooks are not so obsessively concerned with precise measurements in recipes as the British tend to be. Expressions such as 'a handful of' and 'the right amount of' abound, and cooking times seem non-existent. This stems partly from the natural confidence of people who cook on a daily basis, and partly from the fact that no two cooks can agree on ingredients, let alone the proportions in which they should be added to a dish. I have tried to formalize the recipes that I have collected without losing the character of the originals. I may not have succeeded in every case, but it seems to me better to respect a living culture than opt for arid exactitude.

NOTE FOR U.S. EDITION

The recipes in this book have been converted to U.S. measurements (for the intrepid cook). We tried for exactitude, but family recipes leave a lot to interpretation. We hope you try some of them and if you do, please visit our website, *www.centrobooks.com*, and tell us how you fared. We ask that you please use caution, since many of the recipes call for a glass or two of wine. And if you find wine listed in the ingredients and not in the recipe, all we can say is "Saluti."

For Lindsay

EATING UP ITALY
Voyages on a Vespa

1
WHETTING
THE
APPETITE

MELITO DI PORTO SALVO
REGGIO DI CALABRIA

*Crostino di pane di grano con pomodoro,
peperoncino e origano*

The biscuity gold slice of toast was heaped with tiny cubes of cardinal-red tomato, shiny with oil and juices, and flecked with dark green particles. The crostino was explosively crunchy, with a slightly malted flavour. The tomato was clean and sweet, its flavour sharpened by the exhilarating intensity of the dried oregano, the warmth of chili rising up through fruit and herb.

First came the *antipasti: neonati*, minuscule fish no bigger than a toothpick, fried to crisp little nuggets; a couple of slices of burly *prosciutto di Calabria*; fleshy, acrid black olives; and some chewy hanks of *melanzane sott'olio*, *aubergines* preserved in oil; tomato, chili and oregano, on *crostini*. The biscuity gold slice of toast was heaped with tiny cubes of cardinal-red tomato, shiny with oil and juices, and flecked with dark green particles. The *crostino* was explosively crunchy, with a slightly malted flavour. The tomato was clean and sweet, its flavour sharpened by the exhilarating intensity of the dried oregano, the warmth of chili rising up through fruit and herb.

Next there was the *primo piatto, tagliolini* with tiny artichokes and fennel braised to an amber, emollient, vegetal softness. It had a sensuous, sybaritic luxury, slithering down my throat. Another plate, the *secondo piatto:* a random selectionof very fresh grilled baby cuttlefish and fat prawns, their caramelised, marine sweetness cut by the sharp acidity of lemon juice. Finally a salty, sharp young *pecorino* and a couple of early nectarines, full of juicy sweetness that trickled down my chin.

An agreeable sensation of repletion suffused my being from the tips of my toes to the remote corners of my brain. This was what I had come for. Each mouthful was a reminder of the essential plainness, and grace, of Italian food. There were no extraneous sauces, no distracting garnishes, no mint sprigs or dashes of fancy oils. The flavours were clean and clear. The beauty of each dish lay in the quality of the ingredients, and in the understanding with which they were cooked. I mopped my chin and finished off the last of the red wine, which tasted of chemicals and damsons. Lunch was done. There was time for an espresso.

'I think you need a glass of *bergamino* as well, *signore*,' said the waiter.

'*Bergamino*?'

'The *liquore* from the *bergamotto*.'

In my ignorance I had always assumed that oil of bergamot, a staple for a thousand perfumes, eau de toilettes and

aftershave lotions, not to mention the fragrant, vaguely medic-
inal *liquore*, came from a flower. Indeed, the fragrance of the
flower, *la zagara*, filled the blustery breezes here in Melito di
Porto Salvo, the southernmost point of the southernmost coast
of mainland Italy. But it was the large, rounded, lemon-yellow
fruit that was the basis of a substantial industry in the area,
with a *consorzio del bergamotto* based in nearby Reggio di
Calabria and a tightly controlled group of producers.

Prominent among them was Signor Enzo Familiare, whom
I met later that afternoon. He was a short, handsome man of
around seventy, I guessed, with the lively manner of an elderly
leprechaun. We wandered among the ranks of immaculately
maintained trees in his groves tucked away off the main road,
just outside Melito. As he pottered from one tree to another, he
caressed their trunks or let the leaves trail through his fingers,
speaking about them all the time with the fond indulgence of a
kindly uncle. Words gushed from him. I watched his lips. I listened to his voice. I understood perhaps one quarter of what he
was telling me.

'The name "bergamot" probably comes from the Turkish *beg-
armudi*, meaning the Lord's pear,' Signor Familiare said. 'The harvest is over for the moment. Picking the fruit lasts normally from
November to March. The tree also grows in Central America, but
there the skin of the fruit is not as productive or as fragrant as
those that grow only on a narrow strip about one hundred kilometres long between Villa San Giovanni and Gioiosa Ionica and
between the sea and the slopes of the Aspromonte a few kilometres inland.' Bergamot, he explained, was *'un incidente felice della
natura'*.

A happy accident of nature – it was a cheery way of describing the anomaly of this oddball member of the citrus family produced by spontaneous genetic modification. No one seems to
know exactly how the first bergamot came about, although one
account I had come across claimed that during the eighteenth century a tree was discovered growing in the gardens of the
Archbishop of Naples which bore fruit that looked like something
between a lemon and a grapefruit. Naples has an impressive

record in the annals of miracles, but, if true, the sudden appearance of the bergamot may be counted as among the most enduring.

The qualities of the genetic freak were quickly recognised after its discovery, and during the eighteenth century a substantial industry sprang up to exploit it. In those days the essential oils were painstakingly extracted by hand, the skin of the fruit being striated to allow the oils to ooze out on to a sponge, which rested on a stick over a bucket. Little by little the oils would then drip out of the sponge into the bucket – a process that sounded soothingly ruminative. Needless to say, those days are long gone, and today the extraction is done by the quicker, more reliable, but less romantic machine, with the *consorzio* in charge of ensuring quality control. It takes two hundred kilos of fruit to make one kilo of essence.

Even Signor Familiare admitted that the gastronomic possibilities of bergamot were limited, although it had found its way into the food chain in the form of *bergamino* and *bergamotto*, and via them into ice creams and sorbets. It also has a curious connection with British culture through Earl Grey tea, which is perfumed with bergamot (a tea, incidentally, which is more likely to have been the product of some marketing man's imagination than the favourite tipple of Earl Grey, an inconspicuous Prime Minister between 1830 and 1834). Otherwise the flesh of the fruit goes for agricultural feed, the thick pith to make pectin and the oils to the perfume industry.

'But all my production,' he finished proudly, 'goes to Manchester for Body Shop products,' and he showed me a photo of the Body Shop's founder Anita Roddick standing among his trees.

From Melito to Manchester – it was difficult to associate the two in my imagination; but then it struck me that it is the true nature of commerce to act as a link between improbable parties and places. The association was certainly no more improbable than my arrival here from the cheery purlieus of Acton, a less than fashionable suburb of London. I wondered what other curious conjunctions this odyssey through Italy would bring me.

I have been in love with Italy for most of my life. It's an affair that began in 1958, when I was eleven, and we took a family holiday at Cervia on the Adriatic coast. I remember little of the cultural side of things – the endless churches and monasteries around which we were dragged, or the celebrated mosaics and frescos that seemed to clutter up every available surface. On the other hand, I can still taste the ice creams with which we were bribed every step of the way, and visualise the vast cold buffets, complete with swans sculpted from ice, that appeared in the dining room of the Hotel Mare e Pineta at lunchtime each Thursday, and the grapes, slices of melon and segments of orange coated in light, friable caramel that we bought from a vendor on the beach who cried out *'A-ro-via gelati e vitamine B-B'*, brushing away swarms of wasps as he wandered past.

I consummated the affair as often as I could thereafter, but perhaps its intensity was maintained by the short duration of my visits. A question always lingered in my mind as to whether what I felt was true love or merely another Englishman's infatuation with sunlight, landscape, food, wine and people seen through the distorting glass of sentimentality and self-delusion. So this journey, from the very southernmost tip of the country to Turin, eating as I went, was to be an attempt to sort through the waffle of interior monologue. Food, in all its forms, was the medium through which I would try to understand this beautiful and baffling country. Of course the journey had a certain sybaritic appeal, too. Quite a lot of sybaritic appeal, in point of fact.

I had considered walking, or doing the trip on a bicycle, but dismissed them as being impractical. A car? Too boring, too conventional, too . . . middle-aged. No, a scooter, a classic Vespa, design icon, landmark of Italian culture, sound, sensible and slowish. A voyage of exploration on a Vespa – that was the thing. It was true that I had flunked my road test in England for 'failing to maintain sufficient forward momentum', or 'Not going bloody fast enough', as my taciturn tutor, John, had put it, but speed was not of the essence as far as I was concerned. Anyway, the Italians did not seem to worry unduly about road tests for machines under 150cc, and I wasn't going to go near anything with that kind of zip.

To make things yet more practical, I had arranged to do the journey in three sections, allotting one month to each. The first would take me from the tip of Calabria to Naples; the second from Naples to Ancona; and the third from Ancona to Turin. Why stop at Turin? Well, the theoretical justification was that this route, from south to north, described the course of the unification of Italy.

That was why I had come to Melito di Porto Salvo. It was here that Giuseppe Garibaldi landed in 1860 with 10,000 men after his conquest of Sicily. He progressed northwards up the western coast, routing the forces of the reactionary Bourbons as he went. In fact, I had taken lunch in the dining room of the Casina dei Mille, *un ristorante con alloggio*, a handsome, imposing, cream-painted house that had served as Garibaldi's headquarters.

The building had been preserved as a monument to the great man by the owner, Signor Romeo. The rooms had a certain gloomy magnificence: one barrel-vaulted, the other square; both had a red-brick ceiling complementing a brown tiled floor, and the walls of each were hung with various pictures, photographs of the great man and documents pertinent to his life. In most pictures, his distinctive dome-like forehead had an imposing nobility, in spite of the receding hair being brushed up and over. The eyes were quite narrow and slightly slanted. Much of the lower face was hidden beneath a beard, in different lengths in different photographs, but always conveying the same bushy masculinity. Even in apparent repose, he exuded tremendous energy. The force of his personality was palpable, his sense of his own rightness incontrovertible. I couldn't help feeling that, inspiring beyond measure though he was in warfare, what a pain in the neck he must have been at other times.

For all its place in history, Melito di Porto Salvo was a queer place, devoid of any charm or notable feature that I could make out. On the town's seaward side, a shingle beach, on which litter, detritus and brilliant wild flowers mingled with louche promiscuity, gingerly skirted the edge of the town. Beyond that, the flat grey sea and the flat grey coastal plain merged one into the other. The only thing distinguishing the two was the fact that, out at sea, there was no scab of indiscriminate construction of depressingly tawdry buildings. It may not be the most distinguished piece of coastline in the world, but any charm it might have had had been completely buried beneath a haphazard mish-mash of ribbon development, the consequence of bureaucratic corruption and the absence of civic control. The sad, transitory nature of the coastal plain was emphasised by the brooding magnificence of the tree-covered crags of the Aspromonte, the southernmost tip of the Apennine range, which could be seen rising up further inland.

I found it curious that, the Casina aside, no effort seemed to have been made to commemorate Melito's place in history. There was no Garibaldi visitor centre, no Garibaldi heritage trail, no shops selling replica red shirts or mugs celebrating 1860, fake powder horns or plastic muzzle-loading rifles or memorabilia medallions. In fact, there was nothing to indicate that the first practical step towards the unification of Italy, which I thought might have merited a bit of razzmatazz and celebration, had been taken here, in this unkempt, dusty, down-at-heel town.

Eventually I tracked down a monument of a kind, just off a dirt road that ran along the shore. Its place was marked by a concrete pinnacle of peculiar hideousness, which stood on a low mound covered with trashy, 1950s crazy-paving ceramics. There was a stone set into the earth with an orotund inscription, much of which was lost among the cracks and weeds growing over it. It was a desolate spot. The wind blew stiffly, hissing through the sea thistle, gorse and mimosa that grew in clumps on either side of the monument, causing the mimosas to rock their yellow heads vigorously, and any number of plastic bags trapped between the stones and haphazard detritus, rusting cans and cannelloni of concrete piping to flap back and forth.

I wondered how far Italy was really unified in any social or political sense. Its post-unification history had been chequered to say the least, but the total neglect here of someone whom I had always thought of as one of the country's true heroes struck me as very rum. Perhaps food might be a more accurate gauge of Italy's unity. Pasta, prosciutto, pecorino (the ubiquitous sheep's cheese) – those, surely, were universally recognised from Melito to Milan. Well, I would find out. I headed back up the desecrated coast to Reggio di Calabria beneath lowering skies.

<hr/>

'This swordfish,' Silvia Cappello addressed the proprietor of Baylik, one of Reggio's suaver restaurants, through a cloud of cigarette smoke. 'Is it Italian or Greek?'

'Italian,' he replied firmly.

'Are you sure?' Her voice rang with disbelief. 'It's very early for swordfish here. I think it must be Greek.'

'Absolutely not,' he countered with spirit. 'They are just beginning to catch them in the Straits of Messina.'

'Hrrummph,' said Silvia. 'I'll have the sea bass.'

She was, if anything, more passionate about food than I. Her large, grey eyes sparkled when she talked about the differing qualities of this café or that, or held forth on the provenance of pastries, or the distinctions between the multiplicity of Calabrese dishes. I had met Silvia at the Italian Institute in London, where she taught Italian to people like me. She was Calabrian born and bred and had offered to initiate me in the mysteries of her native cooking. She was in Reggio, visiting her mother and I had contacted her to take her up on her offer.

'What was all that about?' I asked, when the battered man had beaten his retreat with our order.

Silvia explained that the swordfish made their way up the Calabrian coast through the Straits of Messina to spawn. Usually they only arrived at the end of April or the beginning of May. That's why she was suspicious about the provenance of the swordfish. It was too early for the true Italian catch.

'So? What's the difference between a Greek swordfish and an Italian one?'

'As they come up through the Straits, they are getting

amorosi, ready to spawn. It makes their flesh *più dolce, più delicato, più morbido* – sweeter, more delicate, softer, better in every way.'

'Can you really tell?'

She looked scandalised. 'Of course,' she said in a manner that brooked no further argument. I wondered how many British teachers or food enthusiasts could pontificate knowledgeably on the mating habits of salmon or trout, let alone on how these may affect the edibility of the fish.

I had the swordfish, and I couldn't have told if it was Italian, Greek or Turkish. But to regard that as important would have been to miss the point. In a sense it didn't matter whether or not there was a difference. It was believing that there is a difference, believing that quality matters; that was what was important.

Silvia had abiding high expectations in all matters to do with food. For most Calabresi, indeed for most Italians, that I had met, excellence was assumed to be a common goal when it came to eating, and their critical faculties never seemed to rest. Italians discuss what they have eaten, what they are eating, what they are going to eat, with the same matter-of-fact passion that we reserve for the weather; and, in absolute contrast to the English, they criticise openly and fearlessly if they think that food or drink is not as good as it should be. The expectation of gastronomic virtue is as natural as breathing.

I learnt another valuable lesson about swordfish, which applies equally to tuna. If you cut a swordfish or tuna steak about three centimetres thick and cook it right through to bring out the flavour, the flesh dries out and becomes fibrous and tough. So British chefs came up with the bastard concept of the seared tuna. This produces a nice brown crust about half a centimetre deep, beneath which is not nearly so nice, cold, raw and virtually tasteless fish. They tried to persuade us that it was a good thing, when we knew, in our heart of hearts, that it was really pretty nasty. The Italians have been at the business of cooking swordfish and tuna rather longer, and have got it worked out. They cut the fish into slices about one centimetre thick, and cook it very fast by grilling, frying – *a padella* – in olive oil over a very high heat, and then add *salmoriglio* (which is no more than olive oil, lemon, garlic and oregano), or just a splash of lemon and a dash of salt. The result is that the fish is cooked through, which brings on the flavour nicely, and still tender and toothsome.

Reggio di Calabria was the urban equivalent to a veteran boxer, not without dignity and a sense of history, but scuffed, tatty and rather beaten up. Long, long ago, as part of Magna Graecia, Reggio had been prosperous, but the combination of earthquake, war and political and criminal exploitation seemed to have knocked the stuffing out of the place. Most of the architecture was of the general-purpose neo-classical style of the 1920s–1940s. In spite of the odd elaborate detail – wrought-iron balcony, cornice or frieze emerging from the broken plaster like that on a social security building – it had a rather Victorian feel.

But among the streets that scrambled up the hillside from the edge of the Strait of Messina were hidden glories to which Silvia introduced me: cafés – Caridi e Lagana, Caffé Malavenda, Le Cordon Bleu. They were efficient, immaculate, gleaming, with pristine display cabinets stuffed with voluptuous pastries: *cannoli*, kind of boat-shaped, pinched in the middle and stuffed with sweet ricotta; *sguta* and *cuddhuraci*, traditional Easter pastries of Greek origin; fancy cakes of chocolate or strawberries; *mostaccioli, mzuddi, brioche ripiena di gelato* – buns stuffed with ice cream; and sfogliatelle, like pastry oysters, stuffed with ricotta again and dusted with icing sugar. The variations on pastry, almonds, ricotta, candied fruit and sugar seemed endless in their refinements.

The shapes, combinations and ingredients, in particular the use of almonds, were a continuous reminder of how much the cooking of Calabria owes to the Arabs, both directly, through the control that the Moors exerted on the coastal regions in the twelfth and thirteenth centuries, and indirectly, through Sicily on the far side of the Strait of Messina. It was curious, although, on reflection, perhaps not surprising, to discover just how closely Sicily and this, the western, side of Italy, had been linked to the culture of northern Africa, while southeastern Italy, the Adriatic side, owed more to Byzantium.

For obvious reasons it would be inaccurate to blame the Moors for one of the most distinctive features of cafés and pastry-shop windows: the high-kitsch Paschal lambs formed out of marzipan, covered in white chocolate and decked out in the most fearsome colours, that filled the windows and display cabinets around Easter. These were a reminder, possibly a remainder, of the eighteenth-century southern Italian passion for the more vivid and gruesome aspects of baroque art.

Taking pity on my solitary state, Silvia invited me to lunch on Easter Sunday at home with her mother and her mother's sister. Signora Cappello was a handsome woman, with a powerful and decisive mien, and her sister, a civil servant, had a dark languor and sharp intelligence. Home was a large flat in uptown Reggio, cool and dark. The walls were hung with an extensive collection of pictures, and the furniture had the heft of old-fashioned virtue. This taste for shade seemed odd given the prevailing weather conditions, but, for most of the year, blinding light and severe heat are the principal enemies. Houses had been built as fortresses against the sun, just as they had been in Britain in the nineteenth century, when it was the fashion for them to face north for fear that too much sunlight would cause curtains and carpets to fade quickly.

I had always thought that my own family's tribal feasts were pretty substantial, but nothing prepared me for the majestic sequence of dishes of a traditional Calabresi Easter feast. This one started with *rigatoni al forno*, the kind of dish that anchors you to the table in more ways than one. It consisted of fat, short, ridged tubular pasta with meat balls, mozzarella, *provola*, cooked ham, Parmesan, *melanzane*, hard-boiled eggs and *sugo* – tomato sauce – and it had been baked in the oven.

The difference between *sugo* and *ragù* had been something of a mystery to me, but Signora Cappello briskly cleared this up for me.

'Normally *sugo* is simply tomato sauce, and *ragù* is a sauce with meat in it, like a *ragù bolognese*, but down here ragù is a bit different. First I make a *soffritto* (the great Mediterranean base flavour of onions, or onions and garlic, stewed in olive oil). Then I put a piece of beef and a piece of pork on top, then add the tomatoes. Now I let it bubble quietly for four hours or more. The meat is kept nice and moist, but also it gives up some of its flavour to the sauce. So you can eat your pasta with the *sugo*, and then eat the meat as the *secondo piatto*. It is a very practical way to cook, no?'

'Yes,' I said.

Braised lamb with potatoes came next. 'It must be *pecora* – ewe,' said Signora Cappello with the certainty of an *ex cathedra* Papal bull. 'It is more tender and tastier than *agnello* – ram.' For a moment I wondered if, like swordfish, it was *più amorosa* as well.

Then there was a salad of Romaine lettuce and fennel; *involtini di vitello*, thin slices of veal stuffed with breadcrumbs, parsley, garlic, Parmesan and then grilled; fried artichoke, which had been sliced, dipped in egg and breadcrumbs, and fried; and a classically unctuous *melanzane alla parmigiana* – 'The *melanzane* must to be female,' said Signora Cappello, which prompted a long discussion about how you can tell whether a melanzana is female or not.

My mental grip rather loosened by too much of everything, I foolishly suggested to Signora Cappello that it was inevitable that even in Italy traditional cooking and eating habits would gradually become like those of the rest of the world, manufactured and microwavable.

'Never!' she replied with considerable force.

'But,' I pointed out, 'neither of your two daughters cook. Both of them have responsible jobs during the day. So who will have time to shop, harangue the shopkeepers and cook in this way?'

'I will,' she said, in the same tone of voice as before. Unquestionably she would, but I wondered about the rest of Italy.

Finally we came to *la pastiera*, the classic Easter tart made with ricotta, pecorino, *grano* (a special wheat) soaked in milk, eggs, tiny pieces of candied peel, custard, a little *mandarino* liqueur and the beaten white of an egg. It was rich, but, thank God, comfortingly light.

Even the Calabresi don't eat on this scale very often, but in the light of this trial by calorie it struck me that northern Europeans have a rather distorted view of what we loosely call Mediterranean cooking. We have been led to believe that the Mediterranean diet is light and healthy, made up mostly of vegetables, pulses and olive oil with a few grilled dainties by way of protein. Actually, with its roots in a recent, and in many cases contemporary, peasant culture, it is hearty, hefty, filling and loaded with carbohydrates. If you have spent the day in the fields under the broiling sun, the last thing you want is a plate of tomato and mozzarella followed by a grilled sardine and salad. You want something to fill you up. And by the same token, on high days and holidays, you celebrate the richness of your larder, not its meagreness.

By the time we had finished, it was definitely the moment for the armchair, the paper over the face and the long snooze. Instead of which, Silvia badgered me into another of the great Italian traditions, *la passeggiata*, the stroll through public places, the leisurely tread along a prescribed path. This is a quite different ritual from walking in Britain. We British go for walks, mostly in the country. It's an expedition. It has an objective and a specified time frame. We even wear special clothes (usually because it's cold, muddy or raining or all three). The Italians also wear special clothes, but they are the marks of civilisation, designed for display. The Italian *passeggiata* is purely social. Normally it is framed by the end of the workday and dinner. It signifies that the tyranny of labour is over for the day, to be replaced by the tyranny of the family, but it has no purpose other than to show, to meet and to talk; in particular to talk.

That night I lay on the bed in my hotel, marvelling at the size of my stomach and the gastronomic riches I had already uncovered, and contemplating what lay before me. I began to feel decidedly queasy.

It was clear that I should have done this odyssey when I was twenty-five, or even younger, rather than fifty-five. The notion of riding a scooter through sun-drenched landscapes was essentially a romantic one. It went with a sense of freedom, adventure, personal exploration and sexual possibilities; wind in the hair, sun on the back, the road winding down to the sea, unknown delights around every corner. It fitted less easily with the trembling jowl, thinning hair, spectacles, a tendency of the stomach to flow over the top of the trouser, deficiencies of short-term and long-term memory, job, wife, child, mortgage, responsibility and all the other clutter of humdrum existence.

From the orderly safety of home, the journey had seemed so sensible, so straightforward, so intelligently structured. I had read *Old Calabria* by Norman Douglas, after all, the old goat's account of his ramblings all over the region at the beginning of the twentieth century. I had been caught up by his enthusiasm and his perceptions on the nature of place. The range of his reading and knowledge continually astounded me, from reports on depopulation in rural areas to the Flying Monk, Father Joseph of Copertino, from the etymological harvests of his bed ('which surpassed my wildest expectations') to the consequences of the great earthquake of 1908 in Reggio di Calabria. The entertaining detail, the informed observation, the odd connection, nothing escaped the energy of his prodigiously curious mind, framed in prose that was elegant, masterly, humorous, at ease with itself. True, he did not have much to say about food, but, I had thought, what an example to follow.

Now I saw all too clearly that my breezy insouciance was chronically misplaced. Faced with the reality of diversity of the country, the inadequacy of my personal resources – not very good Italian, scooter terror, and cursory research and preparation – I found the reality of my undertaking, frankly, terrifying. And it was raining. It had rained since I had arrived. It looked as if it would rain for ever. It was less of Chaucer's 'Whan that Aprill with his shoures soote The droghte of March hath perced to the roote' and more of the kind of weather with which Noah had been familiar. Worse still, it had forced me to postpone my rendezvous with my Vespa, and take to a car instead. I had had a memory of a limpid Mediterranean shim-mering like a dragonfly's wing beneath skies of eggshell blue, of cheap wine and primal flavours, of heat soaked into the bones of my body, of singing crickets and long siestas. But that April the skies were the same colour as those in Britain in a particularly damp March, and there was a stiff, chill wind.

Still on the morrow, come hell or high water, and there was a good chance of both, I would collect the scooter and head north. But suddenly a great wave of missing family, familiarity, hearth and home washed through me. It's an odd thing, but the great travel writers or explorers don't give much time to homesickness. There's not a lot of it in the works of Norman Lewis or Eric Newby or Wilfred Thesiger. Sir Ranulph Fiennes doesn't seem to give it another thought, and it never seems to occur to Redmond O'Hanlon or William Dalrymple or Paul Theroux, 'Oh gosh, I wish I was at home doing the washing up right now.' Didn't they ever feel it? Had Michael Palin never wanted to sob into his pillow when he was making around-the-world documentaries or David Attenborough wished he'd just stayed at home to walk the dog? Well, I did.

MELANZANE SOTT'OLIO CON PEPERONCINO

Eggplant in oil with chili peppers

This recipe, like those on the following pages, comes from the redoubtable Signora Capello. They are all as typical of her as they are of Reggio or Calabria, but that is the nature of Italian recipes. They are particular to a place and to a person.

Eggplants are a great testament to the power of trade and war. They owed their ubiquity in Mediterranean cooking to the Turks, who introduced the tame variety to Europe from India, where the smaller, wild variety originated. This should make about 2 one-quart mason jars. The eggplants should be the long, purple ones, and preferably female (don't ask). The inclusion of celery is a typical Sicilian touch.

Wash, dry and then slice the eggplants into thin strips. Mix the strips with the salt and leave them for 48 hours.

Wipe off the salt and wring the eggplants out very thoroughly, squeezing out as much liquid as you can. DO NOT RINSE ('or you might as well throw them away'). Chop the garlic, celery and chilies.

Arrange the strips of eggplants in a jar in layers with the garlic, celery, and chilies in between, pressing them down to make sure that there are no air pockets. Cover with olive oil, pressing down again. Store in a cool, dry place for 4 months before eating.

11 lbs. eggplants

3/4 cup salt

4 cloves garlic, chopped

2 celery stalks

2 small hot red chili peppers
(the smallest, reddest
ones -*Diavollili* -
if possible)

Extra virgin olive oil

SALMORIGLIO

Salmoriglio

There are no hard and fast versions of this sauce, which is brushed on fish, meat and vegetables after grilling or roasting. This is Signora Cappello's own version. Variations on salmoriglio *also crop up in Sicilian cooking.*

Beat the olive oil in a bowl, gradually adding the lemon juice or vinegar. Then stir in the chopped garlic, oregano and salt to taste.

4 cups extra virgin olive oil

Juice of 2 lemons or
    equivalent of white
    wine vinegar

1 tablespoons garlic
    finely chopped

1 tablespoon plus
    1 teaspoon dried
    oregano

Salt to taste

INVOLTINI DI VITELLO

Stuffed veal cutlets

Serves 12

Lay out the cutlets on a work surface. Dust with salt and pepper.
Mix all the remaining ingredients to make a stuffing, using enough olive oil to bind them.
Distribute the stuffing ammong the cutlets, roll them up and secure each one with two toothpicks.
 Grill for 10 minutes, turning from time to time.

12 thin veal cutlets

Salt and pepper

12 tablespoons bread
    crumbs

6 tablespoons chopped
    parsley

5 cloves garlic, chopped

1/4 cup grated parmesan

Olive oil

PASTA AL FORNO

Baked pasta

Serves 4

Heat the oven to 350°

Make the meatballs by mixing all the ingredients and forming small balls with the mixture.

Boil the rigatoni in salted water until cooked. Drain. Cut the eggplant into slices 1 inch thick. Fry in hot oil until soft.

Grate the provolone, slice the mozzarella, chop the ham. Cut the hard-boiled eggs into thin slices.

In a baking dish put a layer of rigatoni. Place in order: a layer of hard-boiled eggs, a layer of eggplant, and then a few meatballs. Cover with tomato sauce, cheeses and ham. Repeat until all the ingredients are used up. Scatter grated Parmesan over the surface.

Bake in the oven for about 25–35 minutes until the mixture is bubbling and the top is golden.

For the Pasta

1 lb rigatoni

1 eggplant

Olive oil

4 oz. provola

4 oz. ball of mozzarella

4 oz. cooked ham

2 hard-boiled eggs

2 cups tomato sauce

1 cup grated Parmesan

For the meatballs

1 lb ground beef

4 tablespoons white bread crumbs

1 egg

3 tablespoons grated Parmesan

Flat-leaf parsley, chopped to taste

1 clove garlic, finely chopped

White pepper, to taste

PASTIERA

Pastiera

Serves 12

Sift the flour onto a work surface. Make a hollow in the centre and add the sugar. Chop the lard into small bits and add to the flour and sugar. Lightly beat the egg, egg yolk and vanilla extract together and pour into the centre. Using a fork, gradually mix the ingredients, drawing in the flour from the sides until the mixture comes together as a dough. Knead the dough with your hands until it is soft. Wrap in plastic wrap and chill in the fridge for at least an hour.

To make the filling

Soak the flour in enough milk to moisten, with the cinnamon, lemon zest and 1¼ teaspoons of the sugar, for 15 minutes.

Put the ricotta into a large bowl with the rest of the sugar, the candied fruit and the milk-soaked flour mixture.

For the pastry

3½ cups all-purpose
    white flour

3/4 cup sugar

1/2 cup shortening

1 egg

1 egg yolk

1 tsp vanilla extract

For the filling

1 cup sifted all-purpose flour

Milk

1 pinch of ground cinnamon

1 piece of thinly pared

Lemon zest

1/2 cup sugar

3/4 cup ricotta (preferably
    sheep's)

1½ cups candied fruit, includ-
    ing cedro and pumpkin
    (substitute lemon or
    grapefruit for the cedro,
    an obscure member of
    the citrus family)

Separate the egg yolks from the whites. Boil the milk in a saucepan and add the cornstarch. Cook over a gentle heat, stirring, until the cornstarch has been thoroughly amalgamated and the milk has thickened. Let it cool down slightly before beating in the egg yolks. Add the orange flower water and *mandarino*. Fold the crema into the ricotta mixture. Beat the egg whites until they are stiff, and fold them into the mixture.

Roll out the pastry into a 12-inch pie plate. Pour in the ricotta mixture. Bake at 375° for 1 hour. Serve cold.

For the Crema

3 eggs

3/4 cup milk

1 teaspoon cornstarch

3 tablespoons orange
flower water

3 tablespoons *mandarino*
liqueur

2
KING PIG

REGGIO DI CALABRIA
VIBO VALENTIA – PIZZO
PIANAPOLI

Soppressata

The soppressata *was fine grained and the colour of roses and spicy and sweet, with aniseed coiling through it.*

I thanked the Lord that, by the time I finally opened up the throttle on 50cc of raging power on my Vespa and wobbled off through the heart of Reggio with a combination of blind bravado, blind terror and blind relief, it was 1:30 p.m., and the roads were almost clear. The Calabresi maintained the extremely civilised habit of lunching properly every day. From about noon to 1 p.m. the roads were filled with traffic, and everything closed down as people headed for home or a restaurant for lunch.

Your average Italian Vespa rip would have been kitted out in trainers, jeans, shirt and maybe, just, a helmet. Wearing a helmet had recently become compulsory, but it was treated more as a fashion accessory than cranium protection. But as far as I was concerned, comfort came before cutting a dash. I was dressed in heavy-duty brown shoes, heavy-duty green cords, T-shirt, shirt, a rather macho lightweight charcoal motorcycle jacket with pockets in all sorts of unlikely places, black leather gloves and a white helmet like the *basinet* of a knight of the Middle Ages. There was no way that anyone was going to identify me as an Italian. This was unlikely anyway, as I had no intention of travelling faster than fifty kilometres per hour, a preposterously stately pace by Italian standards.

I envied the Calabresi their complete mastery of their machines. They seemed to have no fear of hurtling down roads at speeds which I thought suicidal, or zooming up them while carrying on an animated conversation with their pillion passenger over their shoulder. They could hover like hawks, absolutely stationary, without putting their feet on the ground, just revving their engines to maintain their stability while they nattered away to one another for a minute or two before swooping away into a gap in the traffic or flow of pedestrians. Man, or woman, and machine were fused into a single unit, apparently with a shared nervous system. Perhaps they were simply born with an instinctive ability. I was not.

With a tentative skitter and then a wild leap like an agitated kangaroo, it was up, up and away, finally, at last, at very long last. The open road lay before me, new horizons rushed to meet me, a sense of adventure embraced me. It was 'the blithesome step forward . . . out of the old life into the new', as the Wayfaring Rat put it in *The Wind in the Willows*.

The sun shone for the first time. The road ran along the edge of the coast. To my right the land rose steeply to the thickly wooded slopes of the Aspromonte. To my left the sea twinkled below. I saw a traditional swordfishing boat, with its disproportionately high mast at least twenty metres tall with a crow's nest at the top, from which to spy out for fish, and its long, needle prow, thirty metres at least, from which to harpoon them. It was a detail from another age.

I roared up hill and drifted down dale. I sped round the odd pothole. I didn't feel frightened. I didn't panic. I didn't feel out of control. I didn't feel that I couldn't cope. The scooter made a noise like a demented gnat, particularly going uphill. So long as the demented gnat sound didn't drive me bonkers, and the machine could take the strain, everything would be fine.

Just beyond Nicotera, I sat in an olive grove and lunched on bread, salami, tomatoes and pecorino. The grove was full of borage, butterflies and light. The air was warm and fragrant. This was all right, I thought, liberty, lunch and loafing.

I looked out over the town back towards the Golfo di Gioia beyond. From up here the coastline was still seductively beautiful and romantic, in spite of haphazard development and container ports. Tankers, container ships and tramp steamers lay anchored in the bay of Gioia Tauro, larger versions of the Phoenician and Roman galleys, and the later Venetian and Genoese merchant ships that had once anchored there. The movement of boats is dictated by history. Present trade follows the pattern of past trade. Ships sail to and from the same safe havens, and follow the same invisible paths, century by century.

The occasional car ground past on the road. My scooter was still, its demented gnat noise stopped for a while. Its continuous state of high-pitched excitement, particularly going uphill, put me in mind of a then well-known DJ and media personality known as Ginger, and so Ginger it became. I grew dozy and stretched out on the ground.

Presently I was accosted by a toothless gnome in a peaked cap. He was the brother of the owner of the olive grove, he said, and just wanted to check that there wasn't a dead body on family property, as if dead bodies were quite a regular occurrence.

I explained that I was having a picnic.

'*Ai, mangia,*' he said in a singing tone, giving a little chopping movement with his hand against his tummy. '*Va bene. Buon appetito.*'

Presently I roused myself from my reveries, and took myself across the hilly neck of the Capo Vaticano, past olive and citrus groves and herds of sheep minded by shepherds with dogs the size of wolves, towards Vibo Valentia and Pizzo.

While Calabria is rich enough in history, much of it soaked in blood, it seemed to be short on cultural artefacts and remains. War and earthquakes had destroyed most of them. However, Vibo Valentia – Hipponium to the Greeks, an '*illustre et nobile municipium*', according to Cicero – had, it seemed, been spared the general wastage and was packed with churches and pictures of note.

There was, said the guides, the church of San Leoluca with 'extremely fine stucco work', 'a superb marble group of the Madonna between St John the Evangelist and the Magdalene (notice the bas-reliefs around the bases)' and a Madonna and Child attributed to Girolamo Santacroce. There was the thirteenth-century church of Rosario with a 'strange baroque pulpit', and the church of San Michele, 'an exquisite little Renaissance church . . . with a fine but somewhat overshadowing *campanile* of 1671'.

I can testify to the quality of the *campanile*, and, indeed, to the classical elegance and beauty of the outside of San Michele, but of the rest – nothing. Every church I passed that wasn't being done up with EU grants was shut. I banged on doors. I pushed. I prayed. No good. So, no strange baroque pulpit, no

Madonna and Child attributed to Girolamo Santacroce, no stucco work, no bas-reliefs. So much for higher culture.

But who needs higher culture when agriculture is to hand? Quite by accident, I came across an unheralded market of dazzling variety. Here were broad beans, ready podded, like tiny green opals; fat, busty fennels; early season artichokes piled in spiky ziggurats; boxes of mixed *cicorie selvatiche*, bitter wild salad leaves; a great log of tuna, its flesh purple/carmine; and tiny red rock mullet, neatly laid out like a pattern in a kaleidoscope.

The two cheery brothers with blood-stained hands who ran the Macelleria del Mercato treated me to *'nduja vibonese*, a local variant on one of the classic pig products of Calabria: a creamy, fiery sausage of pork and peperoncino or chili, in this case liberally laced with fennel seed. It was eaten, they said, with raw broad beans, bread and wine. One of the brothers then carved me a long, thin slice of *zingirole*, the brawn of Vibo, from a large bowl, the inside of which was mottled with a blue, green and cream swirled glaze, like sunlight shining through sea water in a rock pool. Curls and whorls of ears, snout and other odds and ends were set in a pale amber jelly. The *zingirole* had a dainty, delicate flavour and a gently chewy character. They made *zingirole* only in winter, he explained, when the pigs were in the right condition. It wasn't suitable for hot weather. This was the last of the season.

The pig has an almost sacred place in the food chain in southern Italy. Pig-loving traditions of Italy go back to the earliest times. The Romans, Martial and Cicero, recorded their partiality for pork products, especially those of Lucania, the modern Basilicata, a little to the north of Vibo; the omnipresent *luganica* is a descendant of that sausage. Both Norman Douglas in *Old Calabria* and Carlo Levi in *Christ Stopped at Eboli* write of the reverence with which pigs were treated, observing how they had the run of villages, and, in many cases, houses as well, until the day of retribution, of course. It was still true in Calabria that pigs enjoyed wide appreciation, even if they didn't have the freedom of the houses and village streets in the way that they used to.

In common with most of Italy, Calabria is home to a bewildering diversity of *salumi*, cured pork products – *capocollo, soppressata, 'nduja, 'nnuglia, frittuli, salato, scarafogli* and *spianata calabrese*, to name but a few. These, in turn, generate their own multifarious families through geographical associations. So Spilinga and Poro are famous for their 'nduja, Cosenza for its frittuli, Acri for its salsiccia. Each is made with very express cuts of meat and with very precise techniques, but varies according to local custom in the use of spices, herbs and wine. Invariably, however, all contain chili in varying quantities.

The most famous of Calabria's *salumi* are *capocollo, soppressata* and *'nduja. Capocollo* is the neck and shoulder of pork, boned out, packed into a pig's bladder, cured, lightly smoked and then aged for at least one hundred days. It is eaten only as an antipasto, sliced thinly like salami. *'Nduja* (apparently *'nudja* is the Italianisation of the French andouillette – a reminder that southern Italy was regularly part of greater France) is a paste of pork fat and pork meat infused with sweet and fiery chili, and other flavourings depending on where it is made. It can be spread on bread or heated up to make a sauce for pasta, typically *maccheroni. Soppressata* is an altogether more sophisticated number, and I had hopes of meeting up with a maker further north.

I said goodbye to the cheery butcher brothers. They wished me well and joy with the *'nduja* that they had given me to complement the *zingirole*. A skinned calf's head peered at me mournfully from behind them.

Beyond Vibo Valentia, astride the coast road, was Pizzo. Scrambling up and down the precipitous side of a hill that eventually dropped vertically into the sea, Pizzo might have been designed by Piranesi and M. C. Escher. The streets and alleys above its piazza formed a maze of vertical disorder. The Vico Minotauro turned off the Via Minotauro; and the Vicolo Minotauro, scarcely wide enough to allow a plump English sightseer to pass with ease, turned off the Vico Minotauro. Stairs and steps and passageways fell up or down, round each corner, opening up a series of microvistas, truncated by the corner of a house, the basement or roof. There were no cars or scooters here. Feet were the only form of transport; and, as I explored, I eavesdropped on the patchwork harmony and disharmony of domestic life, and caught its accompanying smells.

By any qualitative criteria, Italy is the world centre for ice cream, and Pizzo is its self-declared capital. The rest of the country would certainly dispute this claim, but at Pizzo there was certainly a lot of ice cream packed into a small area. I counted nine bars around the Piazza della Repubblica alone, each of which made its own ranges of ices.

The history of ice cream, in which we must include *granitas* and sherbets or sorbets, the Moors' gift to summer refreshment, is also a long and complicated one, going back to the sixteenth century, and, to be frank, only really of interest to the food historian. The point is that the ice creams in Italy have an intensity and freshness that are foreign to British and American ices, where flavour is sacrificed to sugar, cream and air.

Angelo Belvedere was something of an ambassador for the ice creams of Pizzo. He gave off an aura not of romance or woolly artisanality but rather of canny commercial *nous*. He wore a Pepsi baseball cap and a many-pocketed waistcoat. Metal-rimmed spectacles framed shrewd eyes, and he seemed no stranger to the interview – 'I am the grandson of the founder of the Gelateria Belvedere, which was established in 1901. My grandfather was *un gentiluomo molto elegante* – an elegant gentleman.' Grandfather Belvedere had a sharp nose for business opportunities as well.

'My grandmother started making the ice creams for family weddings, birthdays and christenings. She used snow packed into blocks to freeze the ice creams. It was very hard work.' Then came technology, with freezing salt and a hand-cranked freezer. Her husband noticed that locals gathered in the Piazza della Repubblica on high days and holidays to listen to a brass band, sweltering in their respectable suits in the sun. 'So he set up a kiosk on the corner of the piazza, and my grandmother, she made more ice creams and they became famous. I followed them and now my sons work the kiosk and the café.'

The latest generation of the Belvedere family used modern technology as astutely as their ancestors. The ice creams were made in small batches of a few litres at a time, and contained only fresh fruit and high-quality flavourings. I rolled my tongue up and over a hummock of jade-green pistachio and glossy, dark mahogany chocolate held in a cone. The texture was smooth and lusciously creamy, the pistachio more intense and perfumed than any nut, the chocolate powerful, with a clean, penetrating bite.

'Every producer has his own particular way of doing things,' said Angelo, 'but most of them use an industrial ice cream base as a stabilising agent, and add eggs and milk to that.' He was vague about exact proportions. 'They vary according to which ice cream you want to make. I am not going to tell you exactly what we do. There are too many sharks out there,' and his eyes glittered.

One of Angelo Belvedere's sons was manning the kiosk. He told me that the reason the *gelaterias* were so consistently good here was that they were family businesses. In Palermo or Reggio, he said, *gelaterias* change hands every ten years or so and traditional recipes are lost in the process.

'My family is an example of continuity,' he went on. 'I studied law in Messina, but in the end I came back to work here. I could never have been a lawyer. I'm an ice-cream man.' He peered down at the ice creams lined up, brilliant and glistening, in their metal trays in the freezer display – *cioccolato, nocciola, croccantino, stracciatella, zuppa inglese, cioccoriso, caffè, nutella, dolcelatte, fiordilatte, pistacchio, spagnola, melone, cassata, frutti di bosco, fragola, banana, limone, ananas, latte di mandorla.* He could have been talking a load of baloney, of course, but it made a fine tale.

After Pizzo, I turned inland, vaguely following the erratic course of Garibaldi's progress northwards through the foothills of the Sila, the next range north of the Aspromonte. The landscape became less dramatic and savage than that further south, more classical than pagan, more wooded than forested, more Lake District than Highlands. Rock roses, yellow brimstone butterflies, irises, ox-eye daisies, vetch, broom, borage and knapweed thickly populated the verges.

Not far from Pianapoli, well off the beaten track and some way down an unbeaten one, I found La Carolee. The house stood on the edge of a sharp escarpment, looking out over voluptuous, tree-covered hills. Pinky terra-cotta new paint notwithstanding, it was formidable, square, with a round tower at one corner and a courtyard at its centre. It had a squat, purposeful presence. It also had a squat, purposeful past, having been built as a kind of fortified manor house, to be defended against the bandits who roamed the countryside in the eighteenth and nineteenth centuries.

Carolee was a local dialect name for a variety of olive that grew in profusion in these hills, and the house had been named after it. A few years ago, Armando Gaetano had bought the estate from the Catholic Church, restored it, and turned it over to organic production to provide olives for the family *frantoio*, oil mill, not far away. The nominal owner might have been Armando, but responsibility was shared by the whole family, with his son, Federico, running the estate, and his wife, Maria, a small, elegant, birdlike woman, and Federico's handsome wife, also Maria, sharing cooking duties and other jobs.

Federico Gaetano was a stocky young man, with soft brown eyes and thinning hair, the curve of his cheeks carrying the blue-black bloom of perpetual stubble. He led me away among the trees, wading knee-deep through lupins and beans mixed with ox-eye daisies, buttercups and clovers, all in full flower beneath the trees, a thick shag-pile of vegetation enamelled with colours. These would be ploughed back into the earth in the fullness of time, he explained, to fix nitrogen in the soil and so provide natural fertiliser.

To anyone used to the chemical blitzkrieg methods of modern farming, the constraints of organic production seemed to require a disproportionate amount of trouble and ingenuity, but that was the way, said Federico, 'to respect the integrity of the soil and the integrity of nature'. It was difficult to know whether this was simply an article of marketing faith or a declaration of a more profound conversion to the organic way. Either way, organic methods at La Carolee produced superb olive oil, rich, spicy, deep, dandelion-gold, which they could sell at a premium. High-mindedness had a sharp commercial edge.

There are various grades of olive oil: *extra vergine*, the first oil from the press, which, according to Italian regulations, has to have a level of oleic acid of less than 1.2 per cent; the less fine *vergine*, which is made from olives that have been simply pressed, but which may have a slightly higher level of acidity, 2 per cent; straight *olio d'uliva*, a blend made by heating pressed olives, which helps extraction but affects the chemical balance in the oil, pressing them again and chemically treating the oil to lower the acidity; and finally a whole range of lesser grades of olive oil mixed with vegetable oils.

The winter of 1985 was the worst in living memory for olive producers. Of twenty-two million olive trees, seventeen million froze where they grew. Many died (although olive trees have almost miraculous powers of regeneration). Oil production dropped by 40 per cent. However, the Italians are the most pragmatic of people. Faced with a shortfall in production, they set about reducing the damage in terms of income.

To the hierarchy of oleic purity, the Italians, led by the thrifty Tuscans, began adding refinements. First came the single-estate oils in fancy bottles. Then came single-estate, single olive varietal oils. Then came, well, the whole panoply of food snobbery and marketing *legerdemain*. Since then, of course, olive oil has become one of the commonplaces of modern life. It is a culinary essential and fashion accessory. The bottle in the bourgeois kitchen is as socially defining as Nike, Nokia, Prada and Porsche. The distillation of Mediterranean sunshine and culture, olive oil occupies a central place in cultural iconography far removed from its peasant origins.

Yet, by an ironic quirk of nature, it is made in the depths of winter, between the end of October and the beginning of

March. In May there wasn't much for me to look at, except for the high drama of the olive blossom slowly turning into olives.

But olive oil production was not the only business at La Carolee. It was an *azienda agriturismo*, a farm or agricultural estate licensed to take in tourists or pilgrims like myself, or play host to vast family parties who came out for lunch and dinner on Saturday and Sunday. And lunch was not quite the modest affair that I was used to in England, and made me wonder why the British are so obsessed with the cooking of Tuscany and Umbria, which seemed limited and boring compared to the food of Calabria.

Lunch at La Carolee started off with multifarious *antipasti* –*crocchette di patate* (potato croquettes), *le braciole di carne e melanzane* (meat and *aubergine* fritters), zucchini (*courgette*) fritters, mozzarella, dried tomatoes with anchovies inside them, *melanzane sott'olio* and *soppressata*. It moved on to a *primo piatto of spaghetti con 'nduja, risotto con asparagi selvatici*, and *involtini di melanzane* – Swiss rolls of *melanzane* stuffed with pasta and baked; before we came to *spezzatino di capretto*, bits and bobs of kids' intestines, with broad beans and peas braised in a special crock in the embers of a fire; after which there was pecorino *'da vero'* – authentic pecorino; with *pastiera* and strawberries by way of a finisher. All this was conjured up out of a substantial domestic kitchen equipped with the odd piece of professional gadgetry, and organised with beady-eyed attention by Federico's mother, assisted by her daughter-in-law and a rolling cast of local ladies.

In its way, this meal summed up the nature of everything I had eaten so far. From my perspective, the food had a variety, directness and intensity that was as refreshing as it was novel. In reality, though, it was the food of poverty, forthright and filling. It wasn't that long ago, as Federico had explained, that people might have eaten prime meat only twice a year, at Christmas and Easter. So dishes were designed to make the most of whatever was to hand in a particular season, to stretch things, to make the most of the most humble ingredients – by mincing meats, creating endless variations on vegetables, by using offal and wild plants – to waste nothing, to create variety and interest by using powerful flavouring agents such as chili, garlic, tomato puree and herbs. The character of the food owed more to the quality of ingredients than to technical artifice, although the cooks seemed to share the kind of casual, natural skill that comes from ingrained tradition, an inheritance of a society that changes only slowly.

It was still a wonder that the customers could put away all this with apparent ease. Admittedly, there was a sense of leisure about the whole process. The Sunday lunchers had come to eat, and clearly took a rather Yorkshire approach to the concept of value for money. And to the division of the sexes as well: all the men sat at one end, the women at the other, with children whirling between the two. When I asked Federico about this, he smiled and said why on earth should men and women want to sit together when they were going to talk about quite different things? Judging by a ferocious dispute that broke out between one couple, perhaps separation was just as well.

The argument concerned the filling of the *pastiera*, the traditional Easter tart, one version of which I had eaten at *la casa* Cappello in Reggio. The debate touched on, among other things, the correct mixture of crystallised fruits, the origins of ricotta, the use of *crema*, or custard, and the addition of orange flower water. It started off as fairly good-humoured banter, quickly brought out jeering dismissal of the other's point of view, heated up into an intense exchange of views and finally erupted into ferocious barrages, which came to a head when the wife proclaimed with magisterial dismissal, *'Ma questo è un piatto romano!'* in tones that suggested *un piatto romano* was some particularly vile extension of the Albigensian Heresy. I couldn't help thinking that it was all rather heartening. It was difficult to imagine such passionate exchange at the WI or, indeed, an Englishman capable of holding his own on the proper filling for a Bakewell tart.

At La Carolee the notions of thrift and self-sufficiency still ran very deep. They used their own olive oil, their own *passata* (tomato sauce), their own *melanzane sott'olio*, their own *pancetta* and *soppressata*. That evening, I went up into the eves of the house with Federico, to fetch a *soppressata* and a flitch of *lardo*, the cured back fat of a pig. While wandering around this space, which was fragrant with the sweet richness of maturing pork, I stumbled over some narrow, slightly irregularly shaped bricks. I took them to be the original bricks of which the house had been built. No, said Federico. They were blocks of soap, made from mixing the pulp of the olives with caustic soda. It was very good for washing, he said, much better than the commercial stuff.

We sat down to eat the slices of *lardo*, which folded like silk over my tongue, its richness cut by chunks of raw *cipolle di Tropea*, the red-skinned onion from the coastal area around the picturesque town of Tropea. The onions were so mild – not sweet – that they could be eaten like apples. The bread was baked in a wood-fired oven by two sisters in Lamezia, and was spongy and yeasty inside its black crust. The *soppressata* was fine grained and the colour of roses and spicy and sweet, with aniseed coiling through it. With a glass of red wine, it was the kind of stuff that I could have gone on eating until there was no more.

Soppressata crops up all over Italy, but connoisseurs rate that of Calabria top of the lot. It has its own Dop (*Denominazione d'origine protetta*) designation, Dop being to food what *Docis* to wine; and Doc (*Denominazione d'origine controllata*) is to Italy what *Appellation Contrôlée* is to France, a guarantee of authenticity.

Federico was president of the local *soppressata* producers association, so he took the business of making it pretty seriously. So seriously, in fact, that he had just started breeding the traditional Calabrese black pig with which to make them. He spoke of these elongated, dark grey or mottled, hairy creatures that lived in one corner of the estate with great affection. Perhaps his affection was in proportion to the splendid sausages they made.

His *soppressata*, he said, was made from only shoulder and leg meat, which contains a good deal of fat and gelatine, which helped keep the drier leg meat suitably lubricated. It was chopped finely with a knife, not in a machine. The chopping with a knife was important because it didn't denature the meat, or heat it up, as happens with commercial sausage making, when the machinery has to be cooled with iced water, which in turn gets absorbed by the meat.

He mixed the chopped meat with 12–15 percent pork fat, red wine, chili, salt and garlic, stuffed it inside a short pig's intestine, pressed it (hence *soppressata*), smoked it and then let it age for three to four months.

This was the general recipe. Naturally every serious *soppressata* producer had his own secret ingredients, which made it so obviously superior to anyone else's. Some added paprika or pig's blood. Federico liked to mix *salsa di peperone* (home made, naturally) and fennel seeds into his. The *soppressata* was eaten on its own, and as an essential ingredient in a number of dishes such as *pitta ripiena nicastrese*, a divine form of savoury leaf.

As we munched, we were joined by Umberto, a lawyer and a friend of the family, a neat figure with an elegant intelligence. I was curious as to why the agricultural muscle and cooperation in this part of Italy, which had been greengrocer to the Roman Empire, seemed to have disappeared. Why weren't there cooperatives and associations similar to those in Lombardy and Piedmont? I asked Federico. They had been commercially pretty successful, to judge by the amount they supplied to British supermarkets.

He gave a shrug of his shoulders and a look of helplessness. Because the *contadini* – rural smallholders – don't trust each other, he said. 'If I asked Giovanni to join in an arrangement of that sort, he would ask who else was in it, and if I said Giacomo and Claudio, he would say, why should I help them? Their olive oil is only good for car engines, anyway.' But why did he say that when he could see the commercial advantages? 'Because of history.'

It was true that history hung heavy in the south. You couldn't escape its consequences. Southern Italy had rarely displayed the kind of political energy of the north. It had always been a subject region, oppressed, suppressed, exploited, put upon and sucked dry. It had been battered by every shape of disaster, natural and man-made. It had never had a chance to develop a sense of political pride or maturity.

Umberto explained that, until the 1950s, de facto control of the day-to-day destinies in southern Italy lay with largely absentee landlords and their estate managers, and the iniquitous system of *latifundia* – vast estates worked by landless peasantry. 'Then the Christian Democrat government appropriated much of the land owned by the latifundia landlords, and they did something very clever. They distributed their estates among the *contadini*. Each *contadino* got a few hectares to add to those they already had. There were two consequences of this policy. It gave the Christian Democrats an enduring majority among the grateful *contadini*. And it kept us poor because you can't build a successful agricultural system on a few hectares here and a few there owned by someone else.'

'Why do so many politicians come from the south, and do so little for it?' I asked.

Umberto shrugged his shoulders again.

'Do you expect things to change?' I asked him.

'No,' he said.

'Why not?'

'Because they are difficult to change here,' he said.

There might have been a moment when things could have been different, he went on, when Garibaldi liberated Calabria from the Bourbons. All his life Garibaldi had been dedicated to republican principles. But then he sacrificed his principles in the interests of Italian unity, and ceded his conquests to King Victor Emmanuel II, as he had always made it clear he would. It wasn't Garibaldi's exploits in the process of unification that southerners deplored but the betrayal of the republican ideal. The wrong man got the top job post-unification, and, as a consequence, southern Italy merely exchanged the tyranny of local *latifundia* for that of northern Italy, which perpetuates itself to this day through its banks and financial institutions. That was why some referred to Garibaldi as '*il traditore del sud*', betrayer of the south.

That was why there were no Garibaldi heritage trails.

I said goodbye to the Gaetanos at La Carolee with much emotion on both sides. They wouldn't let me pay, in spite of having fed me like a king and talked to me like an Italian for two days. I wondered what they made of me, a short, portly, balding Englishman, who badgered them remorselessly for details on food, history, people and politics and then vanished. They had drawn me into the life of their family for a few days, and now I had to move on. I had the sense of a half-developed friendship which I wished to continue, but could not. It troubled me. The truth was that, in spite of weather and lugubrious anticipation, I had fallen in love with Calabria, with the exuberance of its cooking, the generosity of its people and the magnificence of its inland landscape.

LE BRACIOLE DI CARNE E MELANZANE

Meat and Eggplant Fritters

Beef and pork? Once this would have been a dish for high days and holy days, although the addition of bread crumbs and cheese is a thrifty way of stretching the expensive ingredients. The recipe comes from the Gaetano family, as do those that follow. It is interesting just how hearty this food is. It is mouthwatering, stomach-filling stuff.

Serves 4

Peel the eggplants. Cut them lengthwise into strips about 3/4 inch thick and toss into boiling water. When cooked, drain and dry thoroughly.

Chop the eggplant slices, finely and mix with an equivalent amount of bread crumbs. Add the ground meats, eggs, pecorino, basil leaves, garlic and salt. Shape into short sausages about 2-3 inches long and 1-1½ inches thick. Fry 6 to 7 fritters at a time in extra virgin olive oil.

6 medium eggplants, sliced

Bread crumbs

6 oz ground beef

6 oz ground pork

4 eggs

1/2 cup pecorino, grated

2 basil leaves, chopped

1 clove garlic, crushed

Salt, to taste

Extra virgin olive oil, for frying

INVOLTINI DI MELANZANE

Eggplant Rolls

Serves 4

Coat the eggplant slices in flour and fry in extra virgin olive oil.

Cook the tagliatelle in salted boiling water. When half cooked, transfer to a frying pan with half of the tomato sauce, the garlic, basil and pecorino. Mix well and leave to cool.

Spoon the cooked pasta mixture over the fried eggplant slices and roll up tightly (securing with toothpicks if necessary). Cut off the tagliatelle sticking out at either end and use to stuff the next eggplant slice.

Place the rolls in an ovenproof dish, spoon more of the tomato sauce over the top, sprinkle with the Parmesan and bake for 30 minutes at 350°.

8 eggplant slices (1/2" thick)

All-purpose flour

Extra virgin olive oil

1 lb homemade tagliatelle

2 cups fresh tomato sauce

1 clove garlic, crushed

2 basil leaves, chopped

4 tablespoons grated pecorino

6 tablespoons grated Parmesan

CROCCHETTE DI PATATE

Potato croquettes

Serves 4

Wash and boil the potatoes. When cooked, drain, peel and mash well. Leave to cool. Mix with the eggs, Parmesan, pecorino, parsley and salt.

Shape into rolls 2-3 inches long and about 3/4 inches in diameter.

Fry 6 to 7 croquettes at a time in extra virgin olive oil.

2 lbs potatoes

5 eggs, beaten

1/2 cup of grated Parmesan or to taste

1 heaping tablespoon grated pecorino

Parsley, chopped, to taste

Salt, to taste

Extra virgin olive oil, for frying

LO SPEZZATINO DI CAPRETTO

Stewed kid (or lamb) offal

Why is it that the British have lost their taste for offal? I suppose it may be because, unlike most cuts of meat that bear no relation to the living animal from which they came, offal is the essence of animal. A brain looks like a brain, a heart like a heart, a testicle like a testicle. There's no sliding round the fact that these organs had functions, intimate functions at that. In confronting a brain, a heart or a testicle, we confront our own mortality, and doing so should make us appreciate our living state all the more. It would be charitable to think that the modern tendency in some countries to reject the gift of offal is some evidence of civilised refinement. In truth, it is a throwback to the sixteenth century when offal was thought to provoke "euyl humours."

Serves 8

Blanch the offal in water and wine vinegar for about 4 minutes. Drain, leave to cool, and chop finely.

Chop the kid or lamb into pieces. Grease a flameproof casserole with oil and sauté the kid or lamb meat in it with the garlic and bay leaf. After a few minutes, add the offal, tomatoes, a little tomato paste, a pinch of oregano, the fresh chilies and chili powder and salt to taste. Braise for about 20 minutes. Serve with plenty of freshly baked farmhouse bread.

3½ lbs kid or lamb (including the liver, lungs, kidneys, heart and spleen)

6 tablespoons wine vinegar

Extra virgin olive oil

1 clove garlic, chopped

1 bay leaf

3 tomatoes, skinned and seeded

Tomato paste

Oregano, to taste

Fresh chilies, to taste

Chili powder, to taste

Salt, to taste

LA PITTA PIENA
Stuffed focaccia alla nicocastro

When I first saw it, it lay in its baking tray, the colour of ripe wheat on top. Signora Gaetano briskly sliced it the length of its middle, and then in sections across. She lifted out a slice and passed it to me. The inside was pale and spongy, with a fat seam of soppressata, pecorino *and hard-boiled egg running through the middle. My teeth sank through. I relished the airy texture of the bread. The rich, spicy, weighty filling boomed through my mouth.*

Serves 10

Mix the focaccia dough in a bowl, knead until smooth and elastic, then leave in a warm place to rise.

Put the risen dough on the work surface, pull open in the middle and punch down. Add the softened pork fat. Knead until the dough is elastic and silky. Put back in the bowl and leave in a warm place to rise again.

Roll out half the dough to cover the bottom of a round baking pan greased with lard. Cover with the pork rind, sliced hard-boiled eggs, sausage and pecorino. Cover with the rest of the dough and seal with half the beaten egg. Prick the surface with a fork and brush with the remaining beaten egg. Bake at 350° for 30 minutes until golden brown.

2¼ lbs focaccia dough
    (made with 9 cups flour,
    1oz fresh or
    1 tablespoons dried
    yeast, 2¼ cups warm
    water, 1 teaspoon salt)

4 oz softened *strutto*
    (pork fat), plus extra for
    greasing

8 oz pork rind, blanched
    and diced

6 hard-boiled eggs, sliced

9 oz spicy sausage
    (preferably soppressata),
    cut into rounds

8 oz fresh pecorino, finely
    sliced

1 egg, beaten

3
GETTING STUFFED

PIANAPOLI
CASTROVILLARI
DIAMANTE – SCALEA
MARATEA –SAPRI – SALA
CONSILINA – NAPLES

Carne

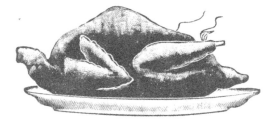

*Ah, but to taste, that was another matter. The chicken was redo-
lent of the farmyard, the lamb robust with free-ranging and the
pork subtle and unctuous as an undertaker.*

Federico guided me to the right road for Cosenza from Pianapoli and sped me on my way. Up and up Ginger and I climbed, heading north-east from Feroleto Antico, and passing by way of the straggling villages of Serrastretta, Soveria Mannelli and Rogliano towards the centre of the country. At some point I should have been able to see both the Ionian and Tyrrhenian Seas, but the cloud was low and thunderous, and I wasn't of a mind to hang around for another drenching.

The Sila Piccola, which I had now entered, wasn't as wild as the Aspromonte. The curves were gentler, the slopes not quite so fortress-like. The trees were much smaller, too, and only just coming into leaf. This area had been subjected to savage deforestation for several centuries, supplying wood for the shipping industries of many countries, including Britain. Now it was gradually returning in part to its former bosky glory under a process of planting begun under Mussolini, a little-sung legacy of Fascism. There were different wild flowers, too, yellow and red orchids, broom and gorse in flower, wild irises of a velvety, royal blue, rock rose, jonquils and campions. Jays and chaffinches looped along parallel to the road.

Then I felt as if I had suddenly come over the lip of a bowl and I swept down into new country of rolling, almost Alpine pastures, small squares of corn like mats and neat, *gemütlich* houses. I made good speed, and came within spitting distance of Cosenza, one of the provincial capitals of Calabria on the confluence of the Crati and Busento Rivers, by midday or so. Legend has it that Alaric the Visigoth was buried in the bed of the Busento, along with his treasure, but I hurried on, putting aside the urge for lunch in favour of the urge to make progress.

I surged on towards Castrovillari, up through the Albanian part of Calabria – old Albanian, not new, the Calabria of Spezzano Albanese and Santa Sofia d'Epiro. Albanians had been in these rolling hills since they fled Turkish persecution in the fifteenth century. In spite of five centuries of acclimatisation, they have kept their own customs, language and cooking. Albanians were now returning to Italy again, less welcomed than in previous centuries. European history has a habit of repeating itself.

I settled myself at a table at La Locanda de Alia in Castrovillari, and bit into a piece of bread. It was unusually good bread, rather chewy and full of bouncy, wheaty flavours.

While Italians don't subscribe to the division between haute cuisine and bourgeois or domestic cooking with the same enthusiasm as the French, they have developed a sophisticated range of places of public rest and recreation – *locanda, ristorante, trattoria, tavola calda, pizzeria,* bar, *caffè* – each with its own quite precise set of functions. A *locanda* is the equivalent to the English inn, by tradition anyway, a restaurant with rooms. It is not as formal as a hotel, nor as cosy as a guesthouse, but the Alia version was rather civilised, not to say cultured.

A couple wandered in with a very small child, all dressed in holiday gear that was as garish as it was scanty. The child proceeded to make the most tremendous din, howling as if he had been kicked. No one seemed to mind, or to take any notice, other than to raise his or her voice to be heard above the hullabaloo. Such social tolerance is as normal in restaurants of all classes in Italy as it is abnormal in Britain. It reflects the social democracy of public eating in Italy. Everyone feels quite at home in a restaurant in a way that we do not.

Then something odd happened. Hello, I thought, what's this? Carefully, and not wishing to attract too much attention, I eased what appeared to be a foreign body out into my hand. My eyes lit on half a tooth. The bloody baker had left a tooth in the bread, I thought. Disgusting. Then a second thought struck me. Gingerly I ran my tongue around my molars. I hadn't detected anything amiss. But, oh my God, there at the back on the right it was as if a great section of the cliffs at Dover had fallen into the sea.

Before I had time to digest this shattering piece of news, the antipasto arrived: *schiuma di zucchini con salsa di formaggi freschi.* Silently I thanked the kitchen for the gentle and dentally unchallenging mousse of zucchini with a sauce made of molten ricotta.

The second course, *panzerotti in salsa di semi di anice silano*, was altogether more potent. Aniseed is native to the Levant, and was used quite extensively by both the Greeks and the Romans. On the other hand, it was also used to flavour cakes and sweets in north Africa and northern Spain, both regions intimately involved with southern Italy, so who is to know how it really came to take its place in the Calabrian kitchen?

I was relieved that the process of chewing and swallowing did not seem to have been unduly affected. Here I was, a thousand miles or so from my dentist's surgery, in the middle of a trip which depended on the efficient functioning of my digestive processes, which begin with the teeth.

Carne 'ncatarata in salsa di miele e peperoncino followed, an idiosyncratic combination of honey and chili with pork, which was, according to the *maître d'*, Albanian in origin. Hmm. I wasn't convinced that chili figured prominently in Albanian cooking, so perhaps this was a Balkan dish with an Italian accent. Heat and sweetness make for ruminative eating, but I decided that it was really rather wonderful, not least because the pork was so tender that I could have sliced it up with a sheet of paper. It was a thoroughly modern dish in appearance, albeit one firmly locked into local ingredients and traditions.

Such blurring of cultural boundaries was unusual. Calabrian cooking had been defined by an awareness of absolute locality that made a coherent understanding of its essence difficult. It wasn't a potpourri, or a melting pot, because there was such a clear sense of identity tied up with each dish, product or ingredient. This fierce *campanilismo* was the result of the isolated nature of many communities, isolated by geography, politics and history. The homogeneity that rides on the back of integrated transport systems and the priorities of commerce that has affected so much of the rest of Europe has yet to make such headway in southern Italy.

I finished with the *ficchi secchi con salsa di cioccolato bianco*, dried figs with white chocolate sauce. It was difficult to know what to conclude from this weird confection. Decorated with a liberal dose of hundreds and thousands like tiny beads, it was as vulgar as some of the more lachrymose baroque Madonnas in roadside niches. To taste it was tooth-achingly succulent. All in all, the dish was a modern travesty of the classic *ficchi al cioccolato*, which unites the influences of Eastern spices, the Moors with their love of almonds and the Spanish, who financed the package tours to the Americas that led, in the final analysis, to Cadbury's Dairy Milk.

Of course, Britain can legitimately claim to be the world leader in puddings. No other country can match the wealth and variety of our pudding tradition, from fools to roly-polies, tarts to trifles, syllabubs to creams and custards. By comparison, the Italians are limited in their pudding horizons. True, zabaglione, the velvety combination of beaten eggs, sugar and Marsala, is a great pudding; panna cotta, happily adopted by contemporary British restaurants, passes muster in its finest form; and ice creams reach a degree of perfection in Italy that we can only dream of. But for the rest? That ludicrous confection, *tiramisu*? The trifle of an impoverished imagination. Crostade? Tarts as heavy as manhole covers. *Panettone*? Better turned into bread-and-butter pudding.

It was time to hit the road again. I knew it was time because it had just started to rain for a change.

'*Peperoncino* – chili – is most important to the cooking around Cosenza,' Silvia Cappello had told me in Reggio di Calabria. 'I know you find it everywhere now, but really, Cosenza is the capital of chili. We in Reggio' – her voice indicated that there was an unbridgeable gulf between Reggio and Cosenza – 'are more influenced by Sicilian cooking, and the Sicilians don't use chili so much.'

Enzo Monaco did not agree entirely with Silvia's authoritative statement. Enzo was the *Presidente dell' Accademia del Peperoncino*. He was a plausible, agreeable fellow, with thinning hair that crept like ground cover over the curve of his head, a long nose and, behind his glasses, sloping eyes that gave him a mournful look. He was a journalist and a fluent publicist for his cause. So fluent, indeed, that he had turned it into a minor industry, employing three or four people, organising festivals, colloquia, demonstrations, promotions and a newspaper from an office housed in a stump of low-rise flats in the dishevelled seaside town of Diamante.

Peperoncino, he said, fresh, dried, flaked or powdered, was the one essential of Calabrian cooking. It cropped up everywhere, in sauces, sausages and soups, in *antipasti, primi piatti* and *secondi piatti*. It lent light and shade to fish, meat and vegetables, to pastries, pasta and even puddings. Indeed, he assured me that there was *peperoncino* ice cream and *peperoncino* cake, and proudly showed me some *peperoncino* biscuits that were about to come on the market thanks to his efforts.

The chili, or *capsicum*, arrived in Europe from Mexico in 1492, along with potatoes, tomatoes, chocolate, tobacco, corn, turkey and sundry other delights. What on earth did the world eat before the treasure store of the Americas was opened up? The *capsicum* made its way to India and South East Asia by 1525, by way of Spanish and Portuguese merchant ships. The Italians gave chili (the name is a corruption of the Central American *nahuatl*) a warm welcome in 1526, a passion for its qualities taking particular root in southern Italy, which at that time was yoked to the Americas by the compass of the Spanish Empire.

According to Signor Monaco, the spice was taken up by the poor to start with, to put a spring into the step of their otherwise boring and monotonous fare of pulses and vegetables. Before *peperoncino* there had been other spices, principally vine pepper, but vine pepper had its limitations, notably price – it had been far too expensive for any but the better-off to afford.

Peperoncini, on the other hand, were easy to grow in the Calabrian climate, with plenty of sun and plenty of water. Not only did *peperoncino* make the local diet look lively; it also added a store cupboard of vitamins and minerals to the mix. In Enzo's masterwork, *Sua Maestà Il Peperoncino* (which translated, I think, means His Majesty the Peperoncino), he claims it's great for acne, dull hair, cellulite, heart problems, massage. Oh, and sex, naturally. No wonder *peperoncino* was known as *'la droga dei poveri'*, the poor man's drug.

But what, exactly, I longed to know, was this *peperoncino* or that? Was it habanero or jalapeñ̃o or Scotch bonnet, or one of the 2,000 other members of the pepper family? Was it better fresh or dried? Were certain dishes made with one or the other? Did you find one variety being used in one place and another elsewhere? And why did it come to have such a hold over the Calabrese kitchen (not to mention the kitchens of Basilicata, Campania and the Abruzzo)?

Signor Monaco was charming, he was voluble, he was a mine of arcane information about the history, the uses and the benefits of chilies, but when it came to identifying specific varieties and their uses, *'È peperoncino'* was about the best I could get.

Close study of his hagiography of the chili proved slightly more revealing. He identified six significant sorts of *Capsicum annuum: abbreviatum,* which is small – not exceeding 5 centimetres, and conical; *acuminatum, fasciculaatum, cerasferum, bicolor* and the distinctly non-Linnaeic 'Christmas Candle'. The smallest, hottest chilies are known as *diavolilli,* and are a speciality of the Abruzzo. Then there is a long fat chili, known as the *sigaretta;* a small, pointed chili that is dried and ground to make *pepe d'India* or *pepe di Caienna;* and *capsico,* a round chili shaped like a cherry. On the subject of which chili is used for which dish, it is impossible to provide a definitive answer because I rarely got the same answer from two different cooks.

I had other problems on my mind, too. Over lunch I told Enzo about my failure to find La Golosa, a pasta manufacturer where, I had been told, certain types of pasta were still made by hand. He smiled.

'La Golosa. No problem. I am working with them to develop some pasta with *peperoncino* in it. We'll go there now.'

It wasn't entirely surprising that I hadn't been able to find the factory. It was heavily disguised as a block of flats in Scalea, a Calabrian coastal Longridge or Basildon. In fact, it took up the whole of the substantial ground floor, deliveries being made on one side and the finished product being shipped out on the other. But there was no sign, name or indication of any kind that there was anything going on. As the lively and forceful Signora Golosa explained, what with the bureaucracy of a complexity and insanity that Kafka would have had trouble describing, complete with multiple sets of tax authorities, hygiene inspectors, planning offices, etc., they were not too keen on drawing attention to themselves. Hence, no signs outside.

Golosa was the family name, and the business involved husband, wife, son and the son's girlfriend, who shared the marketing, product development and administrative duties between them. There were four ladies doing the hands-on work, all properly dressed in white coats and regulation hats. Like many small-scale Italian producers, they managed to maintain a careful balance between preserving the essence of artisanal production while also making use of the most up-to-date technology. The production area comprised a couple of large, high-ceilinged rooms with white walls and marble-tiled flooring. It was well lit, with windows back and front, and cool, and so suitable for handling pasta. Odd bits of machinery; mixing machines for working the dough, rollers, cutters, vacuum-packing machines, drying frames – were scattered around the wide open spaces.

Not all the production was strictly artisanal, but the ladies were rolling a local pasta called *fusilli* (with the accent on the first 'i') round a short, metal spike called a *ferro*, or *firriettu* in dialect, literally by hand. These *fusilli* were not at all like the compressed corkscrews I was used to in England. More confusingly still, I had already come across them as *maccheroni* and *fileja*. Not that it was like what we think of *maccheroni*, either. And piling mystery on confusion, different parts of Calabria cut their *fusilli, fileji* or *maccheroni* to different lengths. Just to complicate the issue further, according to Signora Golosa, the metal spike was sometimes squared off, and the pasta called something else, and, that, naturally, needed an entirely different sauce. Sometimes I suspect Italians of inventing subtle variations in pasta, and insisting that each is better suited to this sauce or that, in much the same way that theologians squabble over minute differences in the interpretation of some text or other. Take that class of stuffed pasta known generally as ravioli, or *agnolotti* to the Piedmontese, which becomes *tordelli* to a Tuscan or *culingiones* to a Sardinian or *tortelli* to an Emiliani. That is before we get to *tortellini* and *tortelloni* and other subclasses. Each is favoured by a particular part of Italy, stuffed and sauced differently, and each claimed as superior by the natives of whatever particular region it comes from.

These *fusilli* were made by taking strips of pasta made of just *grano di semola* (ground durum wheat) and water about as long as a school ruler and as wide as a thumb, and with a light rolling motion of the hands, wrapping them round a long metal spike about the circumference of a knitting needle. The slightly irregular length of *fusilli* was then stripped off the spike and flipped on to a pile of those already finished.

There is always something of the thrill and bafflement of watching a magician in witnessing skilled people going about their business with effortless dexterity. The ladies took about five seconds to make each *fusillo* with easy nonchalance, hands moving with mesmerising assurance. Then came the hi-tech bit. The *fusilli* were spread out on fine-mesh drying racks with wooden frames, stacked on top of one another and then stacked on a trolley so that they could be popped into a special, state-of-the-art, computer-controlled drying chamber. Most were turned into *pastasciutta*, dry pasta of the kind you find in cellophane packets, and packed for sale. Some were kept undried for sale in Signora Golosa's shop in Scalea. She explained that many women still make *fusilli* or *maccheroni* at home for special occasions, but that this was the only hands-on production line, as it were, doing the artisanal business.

For once the sun shone, the birds sang and God was in his heaven. On such days voyaging by scooter was full of joy. The road unravelled pleasantly beneath Ginger's wheels. I could feel the warmth of the sun on my arms and back, and smelled the sweet freshness of spring leaf and flower. I revelled in the sense of freedom, and as I fancied taking this byway or that, why then, I did so, without the slightest concern. B roads, C roads and even, on occasion, tracks lured me down them. So I wove my way out of Calabria and into Basilicata.

Even for a part of the world where poverty is endemic, Basilicata, or Lucania as it was known until quite recently, is poor. Its glory days had passed with Magna Graecia, 3,000 years ago. Physical isolation, malaria, cholera and earthquakes kept the region in thrall until the 1960s. Its food – pork, lamb, kid, bread, pasta, pulses, salt cod – is specified by poverty, by the mountains that made up the greater part of the province, and by the seas that fringed it to the east and west. On the western side, up which I was travelling, the mountains end in gigantic natural flying buttresses, which drop vertically for a couple of hundred metres to the aquamarine sea. The road followed the line of the buttresses, apparently tacked on to them like a string of beads on the backside of an elephant.

Presently, at Marina di Maratea, I passed a scruffy side road with a battered handwritten sign that read *'Al Mare'*. Why not? I thought. It was a day to be beside the seaside. We turned off, Ginger and I, bounced down the track, passed a trattoria, and went over the coastal railway line to a small headland covered in umbrella pines and that characteristic Mediterranean green-grey scrub of broom, juniper and laurel. On either side of the headland were two small pebble-beached coves, apparently deserted.

Parking Ginger in the shade, I scrambled down to the further of the two coves. The sun winked and twinkled on the scarcely moving water. The harsh, ammoniac smell of rotting seaweed and flotsam mixed with fragrance of thyme and the spicy bush growing on and around the walls of the cove. The sea bed wobbled and rippled through the lapis lazuli water. I had been following the line of the Tyrrhenian Sea all these weeks and not so much as put a toe into it. It seemed silly not to have a little paddle.

I took off my boots and socks and rolled up my trousers. The water was pleasantly cool. The reflected sunlight shifted easily over the surface of the rocks. The winking light off the sea was mesmerising. Well, why not have a swim? Checking the high ground for potential voyeurs, I stripped to my underpants and slipped into the water. It was gently refreshing, and the sun was warm on my head. I paddled round and then eased myself out on to a rock and lay like a fat, white seal in the sun. And then the pagan spirit of the place took hold and I shed the last vestiges of civilisation and swam naked.

This is it, I thought. This is how I had imagined it would be.

That night, over an indifferent dinner at La Locanda delle Donne Monache – the Locanda of the Nuns – a suave hostelry made over with glossy, Provençal-style rusticity, in Maratea, I finally finished *Old Calabria* by Norman Douglas. Douglas's voice had kept me company, chattering away incessantly during solitary meals, mornings and that last half hour before lights out. And what an invariably diverting, amusing, learned, kindly voice it was.

It was instructive to contrast the vision of Old Calabria with that of another classic record of life in southern Italy, *Christ Stopped at Eboli* by Carlo Levi. Although Levi's record, based on his experiences as a political exile to two remote Calabrian villages between 1939 and 1942, post-dates Douglas's by twenty or so years, and the part of southern Italy about which he wrote was a little to the north of that which Douglas explored, the life they both describe cannot have differed very much in essence. Levi saw it as a northern Italian intellectual, a humanist and a doctor. For him, the closeness to nature was little different from that of beasts, and his doctor's training led him to record the physical and social effects of repression, exploitation and poverty with rather less gloss than Douglas, essentially a classicist, was wont to do. It seems probable that the reality lay closer to Levi's grim record than to Douglas's cheery travelogue.

The fact is that the life of the southern peasantry has always been viciously hard. Aside from social neglect, political corruption, the tradition of *latifundia* and criminal exploitation, much of the landscape is still guaranteed to immure those who live there in peasant poverty. There are only small areas of cultivatable land, and which are not productive on any scale that is meaningful in modern agroindustry. It was not until the agrarian reforms of the 1960s that many agricultural labourers had any rights at all, let alone the right to own land. And even then the land that became available was, on the whole, so poor as to be unable to support anything other than the basic family unit, and then only with incredible labour. It is small wonder that there was a massive migration from the south. Between 1946 and 1957, more than two million people emigrated to the Americas and northern Europe, and between 1951 and 1971 a further nine million were involved in inter-regional migration, taking with them the foods of their own localities.

While some aspects of rural life have changed since the 1960s, social and cultural attitudes have remained generally conservative. That conservatism, however, has been instrumental in producing food of unmatched flavour and quality. It is one of the abiding ironies of southern Italy that the beauty of the materials, the artisanal ricottas and pecorinos, *soppressate*, extra-virgin olive oils, particular wheats, wild salads, mountain lamb and goat, so appreciated by visitors passing though, so sought after by buyers for the chrome and plate-glass food emporia in London, New York and Tokyo, are sustained by a resolutely peasant underclass.

On the one hand, a vocal, gastronomically enfranchised élite decry the globalisation and homogenisation of food cultures. On the other, they – and we – fail to recognise the true cost of keeping traditional, indigenous cultures alive to the people who carry the burden of maintaining them. We endorse labour and indignity that we would not tolerate in our own lives. As a tourist, it is easy to escape from such things. It is in the nature of tourism to seek pleasure, not truth; to look for beauty, not mundanity.

I took to Sapri after the faux rusticity of Maratea. It was another coastal town, just over the border in Campania, on the Golfo di Policastro. It was a workaday kind of place, without pretension but with a proper human scale, agreeable, getting on with the business of life, with a small port, a decent market and at least one very good restaurant.

It seemed to be the rule in southern Italy that the showier the restaurant, the worse the food; the better the shop, or, by and large, the trattoria and even *ristorante*, the less the exterior display. Southern Italians seemed to reserve display for personal glory in the form of clothes or cars, but when it came to architecture, public design, shop fronts, advertising, window dressing – well, forget it. But walk past an unremarkable doorway, peer into the shaded interior beyond, and suddenly there was a huge space hanging with salamis, or a long, immaculately clean, neatly laid-out butcher's display, or boxes of fruit and vegetables stacked up, propped to present their wares to passing trade.

The Cantina Mustozza was one of these modest establishments. It had a slightly worn, warm, purposeful air. I knew that I was there to eat.

The restaurant was manned by an immensely conversational young man, and by his mother, who, after surveying the tables filling up, headed for the kitchen. When it came to my turn to order there was no menu and precious little choice.

'Antipastipastacarneopesce?' said the young man briskly.

'Eh?' I said.

'*Antipastipastacarneopesce*?' he repeated.

'Oh, *sì*,' I said.

'*Carne o pesce?*' he said with a touch of asperity.

'Oh, *carne*. Definitely *carne*,' I said.

'*Vino?*'

'*Sì, sì.*'

He whisked away.

Hardly had I had time to blink when plonk came the wine, plonk came the bread, plonk came the antipasti. Hey ho, I thought, and tucked in with a will: a couple of slices of mozzarella squeaking between the teeth; a thimble of ricotta like a breath of fresh herbs; a slice of cured ham, cut thick and tasty and sweet and salty; a coil or two of oily grilled peppers; a battered zucchini flower, fried and served cold and, to be honest, not terribly nice. And a substantial quantity of rough-hewn bread, all washed away with no-name, no-pack-drill wine.

The plate of ex-antipasti disappeared. Plonk, down came a plate of pasta.

'Er, what are these?'

'*Cavatelli.*'

'Oh, thanks.' They were short, fat cylinders, like gnocchi. I knew that, in theory, *cavatelli* was native to this corner of the Basilicata/Campania border. The trouble was, being something of an expert by now, I could have sworn they were *cecatelli.* The naming of dishes was becoming something of a problem. Just as I thought that I had got one safely identified, authenticated and located in one area, something remarkably like it to the untutored eye turned up somewhere else under a quite different name. For instance, Enzo Monaco had referred to a condiment of *neonati,* tiny fish pickled in chili and herbs, as *rosamarino,* when I knew it as *mustica* or *sardella.* There appeared to be as many authentic recipes in Campania as there were cooks and eaters, and whoever I spoke to on the subject would swear that this dish had nothing to do with the other dish at all, and they would name some ingredient or stage in the cooking process which made it altogether different, and markedly inferior, naturally.

Never mind, there and then, it was *cavatelli* with a heavy-duty tomato sauce made smoky with *provola affumicata* (a smoked cow's cheese) and with that ubiquitous condiment, of olive oil, garlic and chili served on the side.

'Thank you very much.'

Plonk. A second pasta dish arrived, a single *raviolo,* fat as a down pillow, stuffed with ricotta, lolling in a bright, fresh tomato sauce, brightened still further with clumps of fresh basil. Very nice it was, too.

There is a pleasure to eating on your own, allowing the wine to gently neutralise any natural inhibitions about watching your fellow diners too obviously, and so covertly observe dramas and relationships unfolding at other tables. There was a father entertaining a rather fussy grown-up daughter; a table of five men who looked like business colleagues; a brace of couples feeding and laughing. Everyone was eating with the minimum of fuss, without unnecessary reference or deference. Food was conveyed to the mouth with elegant economy, tasted, assessed, commented on. Eating, talking, socialising formed a single, seamless and indivisible continuum.

Plonk!

'What's this?'

'*Orecchiette con broccoli.*'

'Another pasta?'

'*Sì, signore.*'

I was beginning to sweat slightly. I wished that I hadn't gone at the bread with such vigour. Still, it was yet another potent dish. *Orechiette* are supposed to be the classic pasta of Puglia, next door to Basilicata, but what the hell. I had to take things as they came, and they seemed to be coming fast and hard just at that moment.

I was feeling rather smug about having managed that third pasta course when a fourth arrived, *tagliatelle con gamberi – tagliatelle* in a sauce of prawn stock and tomato. Even by the normal generous Italian standards, this was stretching things a bit. Although I was beginning to wonder if the walls of my stomach would stretch enough to accommodate it, my fellow lunchers didn't seem to notice anything unusual going on, and were motoring smoothly through the same dish.

I wondered where the standard four-course structure; antipasto/*primo piatto/secondo piatto/formaggio–frutta–dolce,* – had come from. Extensive research had turned up no clue. However, no one seemed to treat this model as inviolable. A meal was bent to the needs, mood or pleasure of the eater. A chap at another table had a bowl of soup followed by a salad followed by fried fish, while his daughter had the antipasto followed by grilled prawns. Not for them the pasta marathon.

Mum popped out of her kitchen to see how I was getting

on. I goggled at her, and remembered the meat still to come.

And meat it was, just meat; no sauce, no veg, no sprig of chervil, no dab of this or blob of that, simply a piece of chicken, a chunk of pork, a slab of veal, all grey and inert, and just about as unappetising as it is possible for meat to look. Ah, but to taste, that was another matter. The chicken was redolent of the farmyard, the lamb robust with free ranging and the pork subtle and unctuous as an undertaker. It was like being taken back to childhood and the novelty of flavours experienced then. No matter that getting each morsel down inside me was like stuffing the last presents into an overfilled Christmas stocking.

It was food that had its roots in the rural working class, not the educated middle class, as is the case with many dishes in France or Britain. In Italy there had once been a tradition of fancy cooking for the aristocratic houses – there is a memorable description of a dinner of immense elaboration and elaborate immensity in *The Leopard* by Giuseppe di Lampedusa – but that has largely disappeared. By some mysterious, radical process, the cooking of the *contadini* invaded the kitchens of their social superiors, perhaps riding on the coat tails of the ubiquitous *peperoncini*.

The final dish of early strawberries was unusually refreshing. They had been macerated in lemon juice and sugar for a few hours before serving. It caused the fruits to sweat a little of their juices, and sharpened the flavours.

I didn't exactly leap into the saddle after that. I took the first small back road that I could find, stopped and was asleep on the verge in an instant.

I turned away from the sea and hit the hill roads again, heading up through the Vallo di Diano, which, while it lacked the obvious drama of the Aspromonte or the Sila, had the charm of intimate grandeur – rushing streams, a lot of oak and chestnut, as well as pine, ilex and laurel, although, oddly, very few olive trees. There was the occasional open bit of country given over to mixed cultivation and extraordinary small fields of wheat. What were they for? They couldn't be economic or produce that much flour. And how were they harvested? Everything gave a little charge to the solitary brain, shut away inside the helmet.

I stopped to chat with a grizzled, recumbent shepherd, very Norman Douglas dozing away the afternoon on the verge while his goats shredded the greenery on the other side of the road; and for a second time to interrogate a lady picking *cicorie selvatiche* (wild salad leaves), *dente di leone* (dandelion), *portulaca* (purslane), and *valerianella* (valerian). The Italian taste for these pungent weeds with their varying degrees of bitterness is alien to sweeter-toothed northern Europeans.

The hills calmed down to a substantial, fertile, flat plain around the rather grubby small town of Sala Consilina. According to the guides, the Hotel La Pergola seemed to be the only reasonable hotel in the area, and, true, it was clean and perfectly respectable. But, gloomy, echoing and kitted out in cheap marble, it reminded me of the most melancholy kind of overnight stop for commercial travellers. It was run by a husband-and-wife team, and a skeleton crew of helpers, master-minded by the wife in a voice pitched permanently on penetrating. The husband seemed to be something of a dreamer, providing the waiting services at dinner in a crumpled white waiter's jacket with the top two buttons undone, forgetful of the bread, the water, the salad.

The dining room never had more than a sprinkling of other people. The giant television permanently on in the corner made thought, let alone speech, an impossibility. One dinner was accompanied by a programme about intimate aspects of women's bodies; another by one of the endless and mindless semi-quiz games that Italian television specialises in churning out. None of my fellow guests seemed much in the mood for merry banter.

The food was curious at best – a memorably vile pasta dish swimming in water with a revolting low-rent Bolognese sauce followed by a cheese dish of cold mozzarella and melted *cacio-cavallo* cheeses, *pizza casereccia*, bits of pizza base unadorned by anything, and salad, all at the same time, followed by a wretched fruit salad. Another night's feast was equally bizarre; *orecchiette* with a good tomato sauce pepped up with chili; a huge round of something unidentifiable, which reminded me of the watery, claggy scrambled egg we had had at school; bits of roast chicken; and then a plate of burnt peppers swimming for their lives in oil.

It was all the more memorable for being a rare experience. It was almost reassuring to discover that even Italians produce food quite as disgusting as anything in Britain. The difference was, of course, that in Britain such experiences are still the rule. So far in Italy they were the exception.

I left La Pergola with few misgivings, and crossed the floor of the valley, climbing the steep road to the pretty hill town of Teggiano in warm sunshine. I stripped down to my T-shirt and looked rather Marlon Brandoish, I thought. Well, perhaps later Brando in terms of girth, but certainly early Brando in terms of dash.

The road ran from Teggiano to Sacco and Piaggino, climbing between two ramparts of grey rock, surrounded by buttercups and daisies, orchids, carpets of wild thyme, and a host of other brilliantly coloured flowers whose names I didn't know. I stopped for a while. The only sounds were those of birds, including a most persistent cuckoo, bees and the clonking of cow bells from a small herd grazing serenely just below the bare rock line on the far side of the pass. I could not help thinking that those people who only experience the Italian coast, or the artlessly domesticated countryside of Tuscany and Umbria, have little idea of the astounding beauty of the hill and mountain areas which make up most of the south. With a sigh, I headed for Paestum, and Naples beyond.

Crossing the fertile, intensively cultivated flat plain between Paestum and Salerno was not too much of a challenge. Things got a bit tricky going into Salerno, and decidedly trickier getting out of it. All the obvious roads turned into autostradas on which scooters of Ginger's humble power were not allowed. More by luck than good judgement, I finally found myself on the road to Naples.

When I say that I found myself on the road to Naples, that doesn't quite describe the nature of my progress. I kept on thinking that I had got to Naples, when in fact I had only got as far as Pompei or Portici. I had lost the map somewhere in the back streets of Salerno. I'm not sure that it would have been much use, though. I am not much of a map-reader when it comes to close-combat stuff.

So I kept stopping to ask the way. *'Dov'è il centro di Napoli?'* This was always greeted by a strange look and the suggestion that I go back and take the *tangenziale*, the ring road. I would patiently explain that my scooter was only 50cc, whereupon my guide would look incredulous. A baffling set of instructions would follow, I would set out with new hope and continue for another couple of kilometres, and then the whole process would start all over again.

So, by the time I actually hit Naples, central Naples, a) it was getting dark; b) the city was in the grip of its daily evening traffic mayhem; and c) I was experiencing serious cobble fatigue. And so commenced the most hallucinatory and terrifying period of my life.

When a man has ridden a scooter in Naples, he does not need to boast. When others drawl on about wrestling with crocodiles, killing wild boar with their bare hands and bungee jumping from the top of the Niagara Falls, the man who has ridden a scooter in Naples has only to say, in a quiet voice, 'I have ridden a scooter in Naples', and, if they have any sense, those other thrill-seekers will fall silent and simply look at him with awe.

How can such an experience be described? There was something of the chariot race in *Ben Hur* about it, and something of the intergalactic battles in *Star Wars*, speeded up tenfold, and involving life, limb and the pursuit of happiness.

Vehicles came at me from all angles, all the time. There was a general suicidal recklessness. Cars stopped without warning, started without warning, pulled out without warning, reversed from hidden back alleys into my path without warning. Cars turned left without indicating, right without indicating, across in front of me without indicating. Traffic roared, leaped, hooted, tooted, peeled away, converged, moved in all directions at once with a terrible intensity.

Streets that were just wide enough for a single lane had two, those meant for two had three, those with three . . . and sometimes those meant for one had three, too. Streets were precipitous. Streets were sinuous. Streets converged, each delivering a stream of traffic into the path of the other, each stream determined to establish right of passage by *force majeure*.

Traffic lights? Of course there were traffic lights. The traffic lights were for decoration. Traffic lights signified that there might be a junction somewhere in view. Or not, as the case might be. Traffic lights were to be gone through, whatever their colour, pushed through, shimmied through, got through by guile or brute force.

And through all this mechanised chaos wove scooters, on this side of the road or that, now on this, now on that, now in the middle, at desperate speeds, one or two people perched on their backs, the riders chatting over one shoulder; half-squinting over the other shoulder at the same time; waving to a passing friend; stopping there, then for a few words; scooting off again, from nought to sixty in three metres.

Evidently this was normality. No one seemed to think this the least bit strange, but no one seemed to realise that there was something amiss in this brilliant, nervous, finely tuned, mechanised orchestra. They didn't know that there was someone who didn't know the rules, whose knuckles were white at the bone, whose tendons were taut as violin strings with throttle changes, who didn't dare to blink in case he missed the end of his life, who hadn't ever ridden a scooter over cobbles before.

Cobbles: the cobbles of Naples were an encyclopaedia of tests of technique and nerve in themselves. They came in an assortment of shapes and sizes. Some were large and squarish, never regular, never set at a consistent height. They delivered a sequence of bone-shuddering crashes through the suspension of the scooter to my body. Should I have had a puncture, which seemed inevitable as my front wheel crashed yet again against the edge of an unperceived irregularity, I would never have known.

Other cobbles were smaller, rounder, even more irregular, lying at odd angles to each other. The scooter leaped, bucked and skidded all in the same second. The handlebars twisted this way and that. At one point the back wheel slid away from beneath me. At the same moment, in the corner of my eye I noticed something streaking up on the inside, and registered a woman with a baby in a pushchair half on, half off the pavement, talking to someone on the other side the road. I noticed these things in spite of the fact that my head was nodding at such a speed in tune with my progress over the cobbles that any passer-by might think that I was the victim of an extreme nervous condition. Which, of course, I was.

Which way? This street or that? Decisions needed to be made in an instant. Decisions made in an instant have an uncanny way of being wrong. Of course, it would have helped to have known where I was going, and to have had a map, but the map had disappeared long ago. It was a matter of press on or U-turn? Turn right or left? Stop and ask?

In these instants – seconds, minutes, hours – I lived several lifetimes. I developed hair-trigger reactions where before there were a series of orderly, well-rehearsed mannerisms; a sense of self-preservation pitched to the finest level. I found resolution in the face of imminent disaster and a faith in fatalism; I achieved a kind of transcendental tranquillity that only the greatest masters of Buddhism achieve after decades of meditation; my mind and my soul were emptied of everything except here, now, this second – whoops-adaisy, squire, didn't see you coming. No offence.

No offence was taken. This was all part of the mayhem of rush hour in Naples. People were kindly. They didn't swear or rage. They didn't confront or abuse. No one was stationary long enough for such pointless pursuits. No one was going to waste energy on anger when all energy had to be concentrated on moving, forwards, sideways, backwards, whichever, just so long as it was moving.

When at last I reached a hotel that would give me a bed, I lay down on it fully clothed and passed out.

SPAGHETTI AGLIO, OLIO E PEPERONCINO

Spaghetti with garlic, olive oil and chili pepper

This simple masterpiece is one of the universal pasta dishes of southern Italy. Enzo Monaco lists four variants in his little booklet 'Il Peperoncino al Piatto'. This is what Enzo calls the basic recipe.

Serves 4

Slice the cloves of garlic thinly, put them into a frying pan with the olive oil and heat them over a low heat without letting the oil bubble. When the garlic begins to colour, take the frying pan off the heat.

Bring a saucepan full of salted water to the boil. Put the spaghetti into it. Just before it is cooked, put the frying pan back on the heat and add the chopped chilies. Drain the pasta and return it to the pan. Pour the sizzling oil with the chilies and garlic over the spaghetti. Garnish with leaves of parsley.

4 cloves garlic

Extra virgin olive oil

Salt

1 lb spaghetti

2 hot fresh or dried red chili peppers, finely chopped

Flat-leaf parsley

SARDE ALLA CETRARESE

Sardines in the style of Cetaro

Another charmer from Il Peperoncino al Piatto. *This is a speciality of Cetaro, a fishing port on the Tyrrhenian Sea.*

Serves as many as you like.

Wash, scale and fillet the sardines. Finely chop the onion. Splash some olive oil over the base of a baking dish. Cover the base of the baking dish with the sardines. Sprinkle them with salt, the chopped onion, oregano, chili powder and more oil. Continue doing this in layers until all the sardines are used up. Bake in a moderate oven (350°) for 30 minutes. Serve warm, with the lemon zest sprinkled on top.

2½ lbs fresh sardines

1 onion

Extra virgin olive oil

Salt

Oregano

Chili powder

Zest of 2 lemons

PANZEROTTI IN SALSA DI ANICE

Panzerotti in aniseed sauce

This and the following dish come from the repertoire of the inestimable Locanda di Alia. They represent sophisticated versions of local favourites.

Serves 4

To make the panzerotti, mix the flour with the eggs, salt and enough water to make a dough. Roll out and cut into 32 circles. Place a dollop of the cheese of your choice onto each circle, and fold over to form a crescent shape. Cook in salted boiling water for 4 minutes.

For the Panzerotti

2¾ cups durum flour

3 eggs

Salt to taste

1 cup ricotta or cream cheese

Melt the butter for the sauce in a frying pan, add the aniseed and salt to taste.

Mix in the drained panzerotti and serve piping hot.

For the Sauce

1/2 cup butter

1 tablespoon aniseed

Salt

CARNE 'NCANTARATA IN SALSA DI MIELE E PEPERONCINO

Marinated pork fillet in a sauce of honey and chili

Serves 4

Place the slices of pork fillet in a terra-cotta bowl, cover with sea salt and a cloth and place a weight on top. After a few hours, rinse under running water, dry and marinate in the orange juice and oil.

Bake for a few minutes at 350°.
Pour the baking juices into a frying pan and add the honey and chili powder. Reduce and pour on to dinner plates. Place the slices of pork on top and serve with mixed fresh greens.

8 slices of pork fillet

Sea salt

Juice of 1 orange

3/4 cup extra virgin olive oil

1/3 cup orange blossom honey

1 tablespoon chili powder

Fresh greens

Salt to taste

CAVATELLI CON PROVOLA AFFUMICATA

Cavatelli with smoked provola

To the inexperienced observer (i.e. me), cavatelli bear an uncanny resemblance to orecchiette (see the next recipe), but I wouldn't dare suggest that to the good people at Cantina i Mustazzo, who provided this and the following recipe. It may be worth noting that pasta does not get much more basic than this, it is made with just flour and water; the product of true poverty. Cavatelli comes from the word cavare, meaning to draw out or extract.

Serves 4

Make the cavatelli. Blend the two types of flour, gradually adding enough boiling water to make a dough. Knead well for about 10 minutes. Break into round pieces, pressing each with the fingertips to make a slightly convex shape like a tiny dome.

Toss the cavatelli into salted boiling water for about 10 minutes (the mixture of the two flours gives the pasta a higher density, so it takes longer to cook).

While the pasta cooks, put the tomato sauce and provola into a frying pan. When the cavatelli are cooked, drain and mix gently with the tomato and cheese over a low heat. Add the basil and, if desired, a pinch of chili. Serve immediately.

For the Cavatelli

1¾ cups semolina flour

1 cup whole wheat flour

For the Sauce

1 cup tomato sauce

1/3 cup *provola affumicata*

(smoked *provola*),

crumbled

10 basil leaves

Chili powder, optional

ORECCHIETTE CON BROCCOLI

Orecchiette with broccoli

The broccoli which served as a sauce with this pasta was not the tame, well-mannered chunky florets we are used to from our supermarket foraging, but wild, scrawny stuff with an unbridled flavour. Use cima di rape *if you can find it. In the likely event of your not being able to do so, you'll just have to fall back on our unexciting friend – but the dish loses much of its impact and point.*

Serves 4

Toss the orecchiette into boiling salted water. While they cook, heat the olive oil in a frying pan. Gently fry the garlic and, when it begins to brown, add the broccoli and cook, stirring occasionally. When the orecchiette are cooked, drain and transfer to the frying pan and gently mix with the broccoli. Serve with a pinch of chili powder and a sprinkling of ricotta salata.

1 cup orecchiette

Salt

3 tablespoons extra virgin
    olive oil

1 clove garlic, sliced

3½ cups broccoli, divided
    into small florets

Chili powder

Ricotta salata

THE SERVING OF STRAWBERRIES

Strawberries were very much in evidence during this section of the journey, and when things are in season that is what you get to eat, at every meal if necessary. Somehow, the strawberries of Calabria, Campania and Basilicata tasted more of strawberry than the ones I am used to at home. This may have something to do with variety – Britain has become a monoculture as far as strawberries are concerned and Elsanta are everywhere – but it may also have something to do with the Italian habit of macerating the strawberries at room temperature for at least an hour in lemon juice, or lemon juice with a little sugar, before they get eaten.

4
TURBULENCE, TRIPE AND TARALLI

NAPLES

Trippa napoletana

An oval plate appeared, piled high with ribbons of tripe and calf's head, glossy and reddish-gold with the sauce. The top had been dusted with Parmesan and a few basil leaves had been put on at the last moment. It had a gloriously rich, potent, ebullient look to it. This is food, it proclaimed. Indeed it was, but surprisingly delicate, the fruity tomato sauce, the discreet warmth of the chili and the vivid burst of colour from the basil all gently cloaking the soft tenderness of the meats.

There seemed to be only two constants about Naples; movement and noise.

Movement started with the smallest, most intimate details – the cocking of an eyebrow, the twitch of an earlobe, the flick of a finger. From there it spread to embrace the top half of the face, eyes and forehead, then the whole face, hands, up the arm, the shoulder, head, body, leg, foot, the whole being. From there it spread to the streets, to shoppers, beggars, pedestrians, to scooters, cars, motorbikes, motorini. The whole city was in movement, people and machines swirling like fish around a coral reef.

This movement made up part of the fabric of the noise – the whoosh and hiss of tyres on cobbles, the low-key murmur of engines, the higher-pitched whine of the scooters. This was the textured background into which were woven the chattering hoots of car horns and music – from an open car window, blasting from a kerb-side CD stall, full-throated, lachrymose ballads issuing from some unseen, unidentifiable source.

But these were all secondary to the sound of the human voice.

Neapolitans are champion talkers in a nation of champion talkers. They talked while they walked, while they stood, while they sat, while they shopped, while they drove or flashed by on motorbikes and scooters at dizzying speeds up, down, across the streets. Conversation bubbled, burbled, chattered, gushed, rattled, trundled, fizzed, gurgled, chuckled. All ages, all conditions, all Neapolitans talked all the time. Their talking gave the city a deeply humane tone. They talked even more than they ate, and they ate a lot.

According to Norman Lewis in *Naples '44*, his classic record of his days in the city as an intelligence officer with the British Army, 'Food, for Neapolitans, comes even before love, and its pursuit is equally insatiable and ingenious. They are almost as adaptable, too, as the Chinese in the matter of the foodstuffs they are prepared to consume.'

EATING UP ITALY

I had returned to Naples to start the second leg of my odyssey. It was mid-June, and the weather alternated between balmy sunshine and sudden, frenzied downpours. Again I was afflicted by heartsickness for the cheery regularity of family and home. I was not a born traveller, I decided. Solitude was not my natural state, silent contemplation not a condition to which I aspired.

Neapolitans didn't seem to take breakfast at home. Instead, their breakfast consisted of a pastry and a coffee, 'hot as hell, black as night, and sweet as a woman's kiss', as my brother James is prone to put it, quoting one of the lesser sayings of Talleyrand, which they took standing at the bar of any one of what seemed like several thousand coffee bars. It was not a leisurely, civilised ritual but a sharp, precise engagement, consistent with the sense of urgency that seemed to permeate not simply the Neapolitan working day but the whole of Neapolitan life.

Of the dozens of refinements available – espresso, *ristretto*, *macchiato*, cappuccino – I became addicted to *caffè con crema zuccherato*, black coffee with a liberal dose of cream beaten up with a lot of sugar. Actually, if the truth be told, it wasn't only the intense, cerebral depth charge of caffeine and soothing sweet foam to which I became addicted: it was the whole ceremony of coffee making.

Each cup was hand-drawn with nonchalant precision from a machine by means of pressure generated by a long lever. From the meanest slit in an alley of Spaccanapoli to Scatturchio in the Piazza San Domenico Maggiore, a temple to temptation in the form of pastry, ice cream and coffee, the artists of the espresso machine had no truck with push-button technology.

The cups were kept in a bath of hot water, which is no doubt excellent for hygiene but also meant the coffee kept warm between mouthfuls of *sfogliatelle* (a fat oyster of puff pastry stuffed with *crème pâtissière*), *cannoli, struffoli, babà cornetti* (little tarts filled with whipped cream and fruit) or another of the thousand and one pastries that glistened and gleamed beguilingly in the chilled display cabinets in bars and specialist shops.

From that moment in the morning on, it seemed, it was possible to eat something different every minute of every hour of every day of the year in Naples.

The use of *crème pâtissière* is a relic of Naples's historical ties with France. I did not come across those elaborations of the Franco-Neapolitan fusion food, such as *timballo di maccheroni* or *turbante di riso con gamberi*, which tend to be served only on high days and holidays. But there were one or two shops declaring themselves to be *boucherie* or *charcuterie*, and some of the pastries, such as the *babà*, the syrup-sodden pastry also known as *savarin*, a classic of French cooking, or the little tarts filled with whipped cream and fruit, could have come from any *pâtissier* in Burgundy or Provence.

On the other hand, the Tripperia Fiorenzano was utterly, distinctively Neapolitan. I was drawn in by a small display cabinet fronting the street, decorously hung with pale, languorous, blanched tripe, cows' feet, pigs' trotters and a bit of calf's head, all dripping with the water that continuously sprayed over them.

Beyond the cabinet was a tiny and immaculate dining room with five tables, each covered with a blue-check oilcloth, with big, battered fridges at the back, and a small kitchen down one side behind glass. Antonio Moglie, a small, feisty individual with receding hair, was a third-generation *trippaio* and ran the place with his son.

There was a steady trickle of customers, mostly women, buying to take home, as he cooked a dish for me. It was just oil, tomatoes, chili, salt and lots of pepper. That's the distinguishing spice in Neapolitan cookery, he told me, pepper. Why? He wasn't sure.

It was something of a mystery. The Romans had been inordinately fond of pepper, as they were of most spices and powerful, decisive flavours. But it could hardly be a remnant of imperial Rome. It could be that pepper was another culinary debt Naples owed to French former rulers. The French were keen on the spice before they were hoofed out of India after the battle of Plassey in 1756, but even this French connection is a bit too flimsy to justify more than a tentative theory. All the more puzzling was the Neapolitan predilection for white pepper, although I read somewhere that the reasons for this were purely aesthetic: Neapolitan cooks did not like the specks of black pepper showing up in a dish.

The ascendancy of the tomato was easier to assess. Tomatoes arrived in Europe from the Americas a little after chilis. The first reference to them appears to have been in the 1520s, and their first full-scale outing was in Pier Andrea Mattioli's commentary on the first-century herbal of Dioscorides. The southern Italians quickly took to the *pomodoro*, or golden apple, the Neapolitans in particular fixing on it with characteristic ferocious ingenuity to develop its variety and flavour. This resulted in the immensely savoury 'San Marzano', still the standard tomato for canning. The tomato migrated northwards with remarkable rapidity, cropping up in the herbals of Rembert Dodoens (1544) and Basilius Besler (1613), and reaching Britain some time in the sixteenth century, where it did not get a very good press from John Gerard, the barber/surgeon/ herbalist. Along the way, the tomato became a staple of the still life of such artists as Murillo, a process that reached its logical conclusion when it was immortalised in a can of soup by Andy Warhol.

Signor Moglie was not really interested in this speculation. His concerns were purely culinary. 'Up north they add carrots, celery, onion. This is not good – *troppi sapori*, too many flavours.' The Neapolitan version, he said, was simpler, the flavours purer. He was dismissive of all cooking north of the Abruzzo in general.

When the tomato sauce had reduced to the required intensity, he sliced up some tripe and added it to the *sugo*, along with some chopped calf's head *'per un consistenza differente* [a different texture] *e ricchezza* [richness]' and stewed everything for about twenty minutes.

As I ate it, with some springy bread with a thick, blackened crust from a shop round the corner, and a plastic cup of chilled red wine, Antonio treated me to a Neapolitan world view of tripe cooking and a missionary's sermon on the health-giving qualities of offal. Of course, he was right on both counts, but the sad thing is that nothing will bring people back to eating tripe again. He was a priest of a dying religion. 'Even in Naples people don't eat as much tripe as they used to,' he admitted sadly. 'It was a food of the poor, and people aren't so poor any more. The younger generation, it's difficult to persuade them to try it, and as for foreigners, they're hopeless. They just look and walk past. Some can't even bear to look.'

Before he sent me on my way, he insisted that I ate a helping of *friarielli*, a green-leafed vegetable, unique, he said, to Naples. It had that slightly bitter taste characteristic of vegetables of this kind in southern Italy, and had been cooked to an emollient sludge, oozy with oil and garlic. Then he pointed me in the direction of an excellent gelateria for a pudding, we shook hands warmly, and off I went.

It wasn't the singularity of the foods available that caused my head to spin, my stomach to palpitate and the juices to run in my mouth. It was the sheer diversity and number of opportunities to eat. The Via Tribunali is, I suppose, about one kilometre long. It runs between the Piazza Miraglia and the Castel Capuano. It is a little wider than most streets in Spaccanapoli, the old, labyrinthine part of the city, but not much. It is just wide enough for two cars to pass each other. In it were nine bars or cafés, one *rosticceria*, three wine shops, three fruit and veg shops (plus several more just round various corners, sixteen *salumerie* (grocers/delis), four fishmongers, five butchers, one cheese shop, a push cart selling lemon granita and soaked butter beans, three *pizzerie e friggitorie* (deep-fried pizza), one *tavola calda*, one trattoria and two *panifici e taralli* (bakers). And that was besides the hairdressers, electrical shops, tobacconists, typographers, shoe shops and clothes shops.

Each shop was quite small, and differed in character from the next. Each was an independent entity, a source of occupation and income for the family that ran it. It was as far removed from the homogeneity of the average British shopping experience as it was possible to imagine. In terms of life, social exchange, sense of community, competitiveness, service, abundance, variety and sheer energy, it made me realise what we have lost, what our spineless acquiescence to the culture of supermarkets and retail chains has cost us. No doubt there were proto-supermarkets attached like sucker fish to the edges of towns, but I had yet to see any meaningful version.

'These are all traditional breads and pastries,' said the handsome, raven-haired Signora Esposito, commandingly, ensconced beside the cash register of Panificio e Taralli Esposito.

Taralli are one of the defining foods of Naples. I found them all over the south, but they achieved their most perfect expression in Naples. Or that's what Neapolitans said. They are like slim, explosively crunchy bagels made from 'just flour, water, *strutto* – fat of the pig – yeast, salt, pepper, lots of pepper and almonds,' said Signora Esposito. 'The almonds come from Avellino. They are the best. But you can add anything you like, fennel seeds, chili, pistachios.' I had thought *taralli* were pretty boring initially, but I quickly became addicted to the combination of cracking crunch, the gloss of fat and the slow-burn heat of pepper.

'They have to be fresh, so we make them every morning, starting at four o'clock. We make the *taralli* and the bread here.' She waved a hand at the shelves behind the counter piled with golden loaves. 'We close at eight in the evening. And of course, we close between one and four, like all the shops.'

'Still, it's a long day,' I said.

'Well, those are the hours when we do business. It's no good being open when your customers are working or having lunch. Anyway, you get used to it. My father was a baker. I grew up in the trade.'

'And your children?'

'They all work here or at one of the other shops, along with my nephews and nieces. We have two other shops and we make sweet pastries at one of them.'

'Do you encourage them to work for the family business?' I asked.

'If any of them wanted to do something else, I wouldn't

stand in their way,' she said. 'But it's difficult here in Naples. There's a lot of unemployment, so if they have a job . . .' Her voiced trailed off.

'Then they grow up in the family business.'

'Exactly.'

'And that's how the traditions stay alive?'

'Oh, yes. We are very traditional, we Neapolitans.'

Before I went, she insisted that I take away a bag of *taralli 'per il viaggio'* – for the trip. I was only walking up the street.

In Naples nothing much seemed to have changed since Goethe described the city ecstatically in 1786. I had been reading his journal and letters which he wrote during his long trip to Italy. To begin with, I hadn't found him quite so congenial a companion as the endlessly gossipy Norman Douglas of *Old Calabria*. There was something studiously prosaic, an unimpeachable worthiness, about him. He was very literal. But just when I was beginning to tire of his high-minded reflections on art and nature and of his endless mineralogical analysis of rocks, landscapes and the like, he suddenly delighted with unexpected observations of people and scenes, and revealed a sense of humour and humanity that was as refreshing as a breeze.

And I could not but admire his boundless curiosity. I was sure that he was a more reliable witness than the old goat Douglas. He was certainly more generous in spirit. He wrote with an artless enthusiasm about everything he saw. He was very interested, and usually appalled, by the sanitary arrangements and the cleanliness or otherwise of the streets. More to my point, he was particularly observant about food.

He remarked on the *frittaruole*, who fried *calzoni* in barrels of hot oil beside the road, and on the pedlars selling lemonade from barrels – and here they still were, using refrigerated boxes fixed on to bicycles instead of barrels. He noted 'the abundance of fish and seafood . . . and the abundance and variety of fruits and vegetables at every season of the year'. He described how the fish were placed on a layer of green leaves, much as they are today. 'But nothing is more carefully planned than the display of meat, which, since their appetite is stimulated by a periodic fast, is particularly coveted by the common people.'

I don't know what had happened to the periodic fast but I couldn't help thinking that their eating habits must be truly prodigious to keep all these commercial interests in business. Given the range and multitude of food shops, street markets might seem superfluous, but that was not the case. Market stalls simply give Neapolitans yet another element of choice.

There were various markets about the city. I was told that the biggest was in Vomero, a district that looks down on the ant-heap maze of Spaccanapoli from its eminence on one of the hills above the city, but I never made it up there. I contented myself with another market in the working-class district of Poggioreale, which could have stood for dozens of others throughout the region.

There was stall after stall with lemons, peaches (three varieties), apricots (two varieties), cherries (three varieties), strawberries, lemons the size of rugby balls, loquats and, yes, apples and pears and oranges and bananas, tomatoes (six kinds), artichokes, purple *melanzane* and the rounder, paler violet ones, *fagiolini verdi*, cannellini beans, red and yellow peppers, lettuces (three varieties), and other green vegetables of mystifying provenance, all varying slightly in price, quality and state of preservation.

One stall sold snails, just snails, *Eobania vermiculata*, to be precise, also known as rigatella, their shells striped like toffee-cream whirls, their horned grey bodies protruding through the yellow netting of the sack in which they were kept. At another a little girl counted out eggs from a box on a table. There were a few loaves of bread beside it, and beyond some very dodgy looking wine, presumably home made, in plastic mineral-water bottles. The little girl took a piece of newspaper of about forty-five centimetres square and formed it into a cone, pushing up the bottom of the cone to strengthen it. Then she carefully counted the eggs into it, folded over the top of the cone, pressing down to seal in the eggs. She handed the package to her father, who passed it on to the woman waiting for it. Further along, an old lady, a *frittaruola*, fished a *calzone*, puffy and golden, with a long wrought-iron skewer from the surface of a tub of boiling oil in which it had been fried.

And round, behind, in front of each stall moved customers, intent in a way a supermarket shopper never seems to be. There was a sense of abundance and profusion, and engagement between seller and shopper, in a swirl and twirl of people, and those incessant Neapolitan voices.

But the market in Poggioreale was a placid affair compared with the seething Sunday fish market in the Via Diomede Marvasi and a number of streets off it. First I had to negotiate a *cordon sanitaire* of stalls devoted to shoes, handbags, dark glasses, skirts and knickers. It was only when I had fought my way through that scrimmage that I got to the heart of the market, where fish seller after fish seller sat cheek by jowl, sometimes cheek on jowl, displaying *cernia, spigola, cocci, orate, scorfani, saraghi, luveri, marmeri, pescatrice* and *pesce spada* – swordfish complete with magnificent head and bill.

Some fish I recognised. Some were strangers. All glistened as if freshly caught, some laid out on emerald seaweed in the same way that Goethe had noted some two hundred years before, the better to show off their glittering, silvery colours, others tied so that they formed a curve, for what reason I never found out. There were flat tubs full of live eels, too, and live lobsters, live octopuses, squid, cuttlefish. And great, round containers of six different kinds of clams, mussels and oysters, all sitting in water to keep them fresh. And around these swooped and circled the shoppers like gulls.

Taralli may be the most ubiquitous evidence of Naples's distinctive culinary culture, but, for many foreigners, food in Naples starts and ends with pizza. The Neapolitans give the impression that they invented the thing, although similar dishes crop up all over the Mediterranean – *pissaladière* in Provence, *pide* in Turkey and *lahma* in the Lebanon, for example. Even in Italy the Romans had something very similar, *laganum* and *pictae,* long before pizza became identified so closely with Naples in the nineteenth century. However, here it became so popular that King Ferdinand IV used the ovens at Capodimonte, more usually employed for firing porcelain, for cooking his pizzas – one of the rare occasions when a food of the poor became adopted by the aristocracy.

Now, I might have been deluded for years, or it could have been my fault in choosing badly, but for the life of me I couldn't find a pizza that measured up to my preconceptions. Pizza, it seems to me, is the food of poverty, an ingenious and delicious means of stretching a few, simple ingredients and converting them into a filling dish. Therefore, the base should be as thin and as crisp as a water biscuit. The topping should be frugal, but fired with flavour. Could I find this *bello ideale*? I could not.

I scoured the city, trying a neighbourhood pizzeria, Leonardo; a smarter one, Porto d'Alba; and the highly rated, much marbled Trianon. I wouldn't have gone as far as Augustus Hare, gossip and intrepid traveller, who in 1883 described pizza as 'a horrible condiment . . . made of dough baked with garlic, rancid bacon and strong cheese', but my pizza experiences left me with a heavy heart and a heavier stomach.

The most basic pizza of all is *pizza bianca,* which may be lubricated with olive oil and flavoured with garlic. Slightly more sophisticated and no less ancient, is *pizza marinara,* so called because sailors – *marinai* – could take the ingredients with them to sea. The ingredients for the topping were just tomato puree, garlic, olive oil and oregano. Had *pizzaioli* stuck to such inspired simplicity, all might have been fine, but they didn't. In 1889 Queen Margherita of Savoy paid a visit to the city, and the *pizza Margherita,* which combines tomato, mozzarella and basil leaves in imitation of the colours of the Italian flag, was invented in her honour and that has become the archetypal pizza, and the standard by which pizzas may be judged – and that is the problem.

There was no denying the impressive nature of the ritual that went into making the pizzas: the flattening out of the little balls of dough into the base, using rapid, gentle little pushes with the fingers; the practised dotting and dashing of the surface with the appropriate ingredients, followed by a dousing of vegetable oil; the way the floppy, uncooked pizza was eased on to a wooden paddle and given a final stretch; the placing of the pizzas, three at a time, on to the floor of a beehive-shaped oven, with the charcoal glowing around the edges; the rotation of the pizzas after about forty-five seconds with a rapid flick of the paddle; and, about one minute fifteen seconds after entering the inferno, the drawing out of the pizzas, the edges of the bases curled up and slightly burnt, the fillings molten and bubbling but not singed.

The economy of movement, the sweet precision of timing, the little elaborations – twirling the wooden paddle on withdrawing it after depositing the pizza in the oven, or the slight exaggeration in the flick of the wrist needed to turn the cooking pizza after a few seconds of baking – the rapidity of the whole operation, the absolute certainty of procedure, every movement, choreographed through long practice, mesmerised the waiting consumer, set the juices flowing, undermined the critical faculties. And yet – the result was invariably disconcertingly soggy and squidgy.

The coarsening of the pizza started with the base. This was thicker than I had expected, and therefore did not turn to the fine, crisp disc flecked with burnt blisters and bits of ash of my dreams. The consequences of this fundamental flaw were exaggerated by the excessive amount of oil – ordinary vegetable oil, not olive oil, because it has a higher burning point – sloshed on each pizza, and by the profligate use of mozzarella. This goes squidgy and soft when heated, and, in turn, turns the already wodgy base wodgier still. It was like eating clotted goo, rich and overfilling. Once, the mozzarella would have been added with a careful hand, as it was an expensive ingredient. But with the prosperity of recent years, conspicuous consumption of formerly luxury ingredients has become normal. What had started off as a tasty method of combining frugality and filling the stomach had turned into something very close to those deep-pie abominations, the product of the American obsession with gigantism.

Like the hamburger, which started off life as steak *hachis lyonnaise*, the frankfurter and numerous other foods, pizza subscribed to the American dream. It arrived, a staple of the poor, and, like them, was meagre and undernourished. It was taken to the bosom of its adopted country, was naturalised, and became rich and fat beyond the dreams of peasantdom.

But Naples had other joys. Twice I had lunch in a tiny trattoria, Da Titina e Gennaro in the Via Santa Chiara. The place was so ramshackle it looked as if it was about to fall down. It seemed to be made entirely out of plastic and decorated with a mass of pictures, mirrors and objects left over from a car-boot sale. The cheery sounds of eating were broken intermittently by the piercing chirruping of a budgie in a cage by the door. In Britain it would have sold eggs, beans, chips and sausages and tea all day. In Naples it offered everyday classics of the Neapolitan kitchen – *pasta e fagioli, spaghetti alle vongole, penne all' arrabbiata, orecchiette ai friarielli, pasta al forno, polpette fritte, provola ai ferri/al forno, polipo in cassuola.*

It is axiomatic in Italy that you only eat the dishes of a particular area when you are in it. The cosmopolitan gourmet, used to a daily choice of Chinese, Japanese, French, Spanish, Lebanese, Italian and Indian food and the cooking of a thousand other culinary cultures, might easily find this boring if he or she stayed too long in one place; but for the casual tourist, here this week, somewhere else the next, such considerations do not weigh heavily.

At one lunch I had antipasti of cold braised zucchini, *peperoncini, melanzane* and *broccoletti*, all sticky, rich, intense and singing with chili; *spaghetti alle vongole*, studded with sweet nuggets of clam; *alici fritte* (fried anchovies) that rustled like autumn leaves and tasted of the sea; at another, *pasta e fagioli*, a kind of exercise in variations on divine blandness, wonderfully comforting, full of soft, melting textures; and *polpette fritte*, crisp and crunchy shells holding sweet, moist minced pork. It may be called *cucina povera*, but poverty seemed to have stimulated a passion for clear, penetrating, mouth-filling flavours.

It was easy to see why Naples fascinated such a diversity of travellers throughout the centuries. The natural beauty of the bay that appealed to Goethe, Evelyn and Dickens may have been thoroughly traduced by modern development but, the well-advertised predilections of its citizens for sex aside (which, along with its celebrated criminality, completely escaped me), there was still a prodigious energy about the city. Its citizens engage with the business of life with unremitting energy and at every level. Hedonism and what Dickens called 'miserable depravity, degradation and wretchedness' vigorously co-existed within the coils of the city.

This duality captivates and repulses in equal measure. For some visitors, Dickens among them, repulsion outweighed captivation. For me, it was the other way round. Perhaps my judgement was undone by the sheer abundance of edibles, but as the antithesis to cultural homogeneity, globalisation and the despotism of Eurocracy, Naples seemed to be a wonderfully invigorating and attractive parallel universe.

Everyone goes to great pains to tell visitors how chaotic the city is. I believe this to be greatly exaggerated. It is a mythology assiduously promoted by Neapolitans to discourage over-nosy outsiders, principally other Italians. It gives them greater room for manœuvre. The truth is that, socially, Naples is probably the most highly geared city in Europe. What appears to be chaos, particularly to the orderly northern European mind, is, in fact, a carefully orchestrated pattern of cooperative behaviour evolved over centuries, in which each individual knows his or her place, and that of those around them. In effect, it is a vast collective, co-ordinated disorder that is governed by rules only comprehensible to those born and bred here. Neapolitans carefully maintain their reputation for anarchy, and, consequently, their liberty. The outsider hasn't a chance.

Throughout Italy you will find colossal doorways opening on to vast courtyards, which would remain unseen if the doors weren't open. Naples seemed to take this construction to a peculiar degree. I would look across a courtyard – there was one just off the Via Tribunali – at another vast doorway which opened on to another courtyard, and on the far side of that was yet another, and so on, repeating itself God knows how many times. It seemed impossible to get to the central courtyard of all. It seemed to me to be the same with Neapolitans and their city. There was always another area, another chamber to their minds. I never felt that I got to the heart of Naples. Perhaps it doesn't have a heart. Like Norman Lewis almost sixty years ago, I retreated, baffled, but in love.

EATING UP ITALY

Recipes

TARALLI

Taralli

Ubiquitous, addictive and explosively crunchy, this is the classic Neapolitan nibble, although all Campania claims it as their own. It is now found, so I am told, throughout Puglia, Calabria and even Sicily.

Makes about 30

Dissolve the yeast in 1/2 cup lukewarm water. Cut the *strutto* into small pieces and rub into the plain flour. Add the yeast and water, season with salt and plenty of white pepper, then add more water if necessary to make a workable dough. Work in the almonds. Break the dough into small pieces and roll each piece out to form a smooth sausage shape about 1 inch thick. Shape each sausage into a ring. Put in a warm place to rise for about 2 hours.

Bake at 300° for about 1 hour until crisp.

2 oz fresh yeast

4 oz *strutto* (pork fat)

4 1/2 cups all-purpose flour

Salt and white pepper, to taste

1 cup blanched almonds

PASTA E FAGIOLI

Pasta and beans

*There are versions of this all over Italy. It is the archetypal dish of poverty –
cheap, filling and sustaining. Some include pancetta, others use borlotti beans.
In the Abruzzo there's a version with pig's trotter and tail, in Verona they use
buckwheat bigoli, in the Veneto they might include a ham bone but no tomato.
This is the version of the keepers of the Neapolitan flame, Gennaro e Titina,
at whose tiny trattoria I lunched and dined with such satisfaction. The use of
cannellini beans is typically Neapolitan, as are the bits and bobs of pasta.*

Serves 6

If using dried cannellini beans, soak
them for 12 hours. Drain, cover
with fresh, unsalted water and cook
for 2 hours until tender. If you've
been lucky enough to find fresh
ones, simmer for 30–40 minutes in
unsalted water. In either case, strain
off about a quarter of the beans with
a little cooking liquid, and purée.
Drain the remaining beans and set
aside.

Finely chop the garlic, chili pepper,
celery stalks and leaves. Peel, seed
and chop the tomatoes. In a pan,
heat the olive oil, add the chopped
vegetables and fry for 3–4 minutes.
Add the water and season. Add the
bean purée and the whole beans.
Bring to a boil and add the pasta.
Simmer for 10 minutes or so, until
the pasta is cooked.

1 cup dried or 1 lb fresh
Cannellini beans

3 cloves garlic

1 small red chili pepper

2 celery stalks with leaves

2 large tomatoes

6 tablespoons extra virgin
    olive oil

4 cups water

Salt and pepper, to taste

1 1/2 cups mixed pasta bits

Fresh basil leaves

POLETTE FRITTE

Fried meatballs

Gennaro and Titina serve them naked on the plate, moist and succulent. For those who like something liquid with their polpette, *tomato sauce is recommended.*

Serves 6

Moisten the bread crumbs in the milk. Finely chop the garlic and parsley. Lightly beat the eggs. Chop up or grate the lard. Put all these ingredients into a bowl with the ground beef and Parmesan and knead until thoroughly mixed.

Take bits of the mixture and shape them into balls about the size of a large plum.

Heat some olive oil in a frying pan, and fry the meatballs until crisp and golden brown. Drain on kitchen paper.

1 cup soft bread crumbs

3-4 tablespoons milk

1 clove garlic

Bunch of parsley

2 eggs

1/4 cup shortening

2 1/4 lbs lean minced beef

1 1/2 cups grated Parmesan

Olive oil, for frying

POLIPO ALL'INSALATA

Octopus salad

This recipe assumes that the octopus has been cleaned and the hard central bone removed.

Serves 6

Bring 3½ quarts of water and 3 tablespoons salt to the boil. Dip octopus (or each one if using small ones) into the boiling water three times. This will cause the octopus to form a rose shape. Throw away the water, and bring a second 3½ quarts of water and 1 tablespoon of salt to the boil. Add the octopus and simmer for 20 minutes. Drain and cool. Splash olive oil and lemon juice over and sprinkle with chopped parsley.

3½ lbs octopus, whole
    (one large or 2 or three
    smaller)
3½ qts water x 2
4 tablespoons salt
Olive oil
Juice of 1 lemon
Parsley

TRIPPA NAPOLETANA

Neapolitan tripe

This is according to the gospel of Antonio Moglie, tripe master of Naples.

Serves 4–6

Dice the onions and garlic. Finely chop the chilies. Splash some olive oil into a large pan along with the onions, garlic and chilies. Heat until smoking, then add the canned tomatoes and simmer until you get an intensely flavoured sauce.

Slice the tripe and calf's head as thick or as thin as you like. Add to the tomato sauce and simmer for about 20 minutes. Season with salt and lots of black pepper.

Pile on plates, dust with plenty of grated Parmesan and garnish with basil leaves.

2 large onions

6 cloves garlic

2 dried red chili peppers

extra virgin olive oil

36 oz canned chopped
tomatoes

2¼ lb washed prepared
tripe

1/2 lb prepared blanched
calf's head

Salt and pepper, to taste

Grated Parmesan, to taste

Fresh basil leaves, to garnish

5
ONE FOR THE ROAD, AGAIN

NAPLES
PIEDIMONTE MATESE
Risciolli

The cherries were an almost translucent pinky-red, perfectly round and refreshingly tart. They were not unlike morellos, but less eye-poppingly acid.

I fetched my new Vespa from what looked like a motorcycle graveyard in a scene from *Mad Max* in a remote corner of Naples. This machine was state of the art, 125cc, a light cream, smooth as a Bentley Mulsanne. It made a sort of quiet, growly noise, quite unlike Ginger's high-pitched whine, and was rather easier on the ear.

Heading north for Piedimonte Matese on the northern edge of Campania, it took longer than I had hoped to escape the enveloping sprawl of the dusty towns that stand between Naples and Caserta, partly because I usually went round them twice in my search for the right road out. But the sun was on my back and the open road before me. 'And I can't wait to get on the road again', as the Willie Nelson had sung.

Between the dusty towns were dusty fields, the fine tilth of the earth the colour of milky coffee. This part of Campania forms a great plain that skirts the edge of the Monti del Matese to the north, which rise sharply but gracefully to provide a violently contrasting frame to the orderly profusion of the flat lands.

The artichoke season was finished, to judge by the sad, sagging, beheaded stalks, but tomatoes were beginning to ripen, the yolk-yellow trumpet flowers of zucchini flared against dark green leaves and there were lines of handsome plants with leaves as broad as shields that I took to be tobacco. At one point some cherry trees grew over the road, so I stopped to pick the fruit from my saddle. The cherries were an almost translucent pinky-red, perfectly round and refreshingly tart. They were not unlike morellos, but less eye-poppingly acid. I had no idea what they were called.

La Querceta was an *azienda agricola* at San Potito Sannitico, a village up the road from Piedimonte Matese, where I was staying. I was sitting alone in the dining room, working my way steadily through antipasto of *salame di pecora*, an interesting salami of lamb, exquisitely sweet prosciutto, ricotta made that morning, pecorino cheese, and fried and grilled zucchini, when in came a group of ten English people in their late fifties and sixties with mismatched holiday clothing and very drawly voices.

'You sit there. No, there. Now, Bill, you sit there. Christine sits there. Where's Christine?'

'She's gone to the loo.'

'Well, she can sit there when she gets back. No, Cyril, you can't sit there, or you will be next to your wife.'

'*Tutt' aposto*, darling.'

'So I can't sit next to him, but I can admire him opposite.'

'The Italians like to sit far apart. I can't think why. I like to be quite close together, myself.'

'*Mais, j'insiste.*'

It was all reminiscent of a scene from one of E. F. Benson's *Mapp and Lucia* novels.

I continued with *cavatelli con salsa* di castrato, a dense pasta with a sauce of distinctive, delicate gaminess. The local taste for *castrato* – castrated mutton – goes back to the nineteenth century, and is a pure peasant tradition. The rankness was once thought far too strong for the table in the big house, and it is yet another example of the remarkable migration of a food up the social hierarchy rather than down.

'The last time I saw Geoffrey he weighed twenty stone. I thought he was going to die.'

'I thought he had died.'

'He did.'

Then came airy ravioli stuffed with zucchini flowers and ricotta in a sauce of ricotta and zucchini.

'Wine for me.'

'Rosé, I think. I never drink rosé at home.'

'It's really extraordinary. The Germans have simply taken over the whole of Tuscany.'

After the ravioli had disappeared, there were some grilled lamb chops of rare quality, almost crisp on the outside, and very unfatty. Like the *castrato* sauce, they were very delicately flavoured.

'Now you must have the lamb chops.'

'Must we, Cissé? And why is that?'

'They come from this farm. The sheep are called Laticaudia, and they are very rare.'

'Should we be eating them, then?'

'Don't be silly, Bill. They are bred here. We are trying to save them. They were much favoured by the Bourboni, but they originally came from North Africa.'

'Then we *must* have them.'

'But I never eat lamb.'

I finished with a *semi-freddo* ice with a sauce of alchermes, a kind of liqueur. As I left, the party was beginning to pick up speed.

'A toast to Cissé.'

'Prosit.'

'Prosit.'

'Prosit.'

'Santé.'

I went back to La Querceta the next morning. Aside from the Laticaudia sheep, it was a centre for breeding the even rarer *maiale di Teano* or Teanese pigs, great black beasts, not far removed from wild boars. They had provided the sweet, silky prosciutto the night before. The breeding programmes for each of these rare breeds was supervised by the University of Naples, as part of a policy of what, in Britain, I suppose might be called alternative land use. However, I passed on the attractions of the pigs in favour of watching Filomena and Leonora making pecorino and ricotta, which they did from the same batch of milk in a pleasingly integrated process.

The dairy was situated in one of the many outhouses on the *azienda*, which is, as seems to be increasingly the fashion, tutto *biologico*. *Tutto biologico* it might be, but picturesquely rustic it wasn't. The dairy was small, but very EU regulation – stainless-steel work surfaces and equipment, white-tiled walls and non-slip flooring.

Leonora was the younger, chattier of the two, and quite flirtatious. She was in charge of the farm shop where all the produce from the *azienda* is sold – honey, jams, zucchini, *melanzane* and *funghi porcini* (mushrooms) bottled in olive oil, bread, biscuits, salami, prosciutto, sausages. Filomena had a sad, stern face, and an odd way of talking so that her eyes were never on my face but somewhere on the wall behind me.

'I don't really come from here. I come from another village a few kilometres away,' she said to the wall behind me. 'But I live here now to make the cheese. Yes, I like making it.' She broke up the clotted white curds with her hands. 'It's not really a passion of mine. But my father was a cheesemaker and his father before him. I've just made cheese all my life.' She began packing the dripping curds, like loose balls of snow, into plastic moulds standing on a long, sloping, stainless-steel table. Whey, grainy with odd clots of curd, dripped from the moulds and then flowed down the table, through a hole at the end and into a bucket below.

They made about twenty kilograms a day of three cheeses here, Leonora explained: pecorino, which came in two sizes, the smaller of which was aged for a month, the larger for five or six months, and ricotta, both made of sheep or goat's milk; and *caciocavallo*, a mild, tangy cows' milk cheese. None of the cheeses was specific to the area, as Parmesan is further north, or Lancashire is in England. I had come across them every step of the way since I had left Melito di Porto Salvo. Nevertheless, each cheese was local in the sense that its character and quality varied widely, depending on the forage and the skill of the cheesemaker.

Having made the day's batch of pecorino and *caciocavallo*, they used the whey residue to make ricotta. They poured the whey and curds from the bucket into a large pot, which stood over a gas ring, and heated it to 80°C, which made it clot all over again. They spooned this carefully into small plastic moulds, ready to be eaten right away. I thought of a shepherd I had seen in the market at Pizzo who sold ricottas from the back of his motorino, his large grainy hands turning out his little rush thimbles of ricotta. His cheeses were ethereal with a delicate, fresh, herbal tang. This cheese was soft, evanescent, slightly eggy, like the breath of a baby who's just been fed, and very easy to digest – one of the qualities of the milk from the Laticaudia sheep, Leonora said. Anything left over, mostly whey, was given to the fat black pigs.

'The *azienda* is important here,' she said, as she introduced me to the lady baker who was carefully placing loaves in a large, wood-fired, brick oven the shape of a beehive. 'So many kids go off to the towns to work, but here there are twenty people of all ages with jobs.'

Before I went, she pressed on me a loaf of wonderfully elastic bread with a crust like a shell of a tortoise, some fresh ricotta and a slice of pecorino. As we stood chatting, I saw some of the cherries that I had enjoyed the day before, growing around the courtyard.

'They're called *risciolli*,' she said. 'They're a kind of wild cherry. We use them for jam.'

Undeterred, I picked some and ate them after the bread and cheese, for lunch. The pecorino had a pronounced, clean flavour, with a touch of sharpness.

The stubble on Manfredo Fossa's chin matched that on his head. He was a rather reserved chap in his early thirties, I guessed.

He needed wheedling out of himself, but once up and running, he exhibited a lambent passion for the culture, culinary and otherwise, of the northern Campania and the Monti del Matese.

One of the many aspects of the area that I might never have come across if it had not been for his guidance was *elicicoltura*, or snail farming. Snails do not form such a central part of the Italian culinary repertoire that I automatically think of them when I see a menu, and yet they are produced and eaten, in volume, all over Italy, from Val d'Aosta to Sicily, in *gnocchi di ricotta con ragu di lumache* and *frittata di lumache e cipolle, bigne di lumache* and *stufato di lumache con polenta*, to name a few of the dishes they inspire. There is even the Associazione Nazionale

Elicicoltore at Cherasco near Cuneo, which, unsurprisingly, declares itself 'Città delle Lumache' – City of Snails. There is clearly money in snail farming. Mauro Caruso, a rather unlikely snail farmer, drove a brand-new, dark blue Audi. He was a very engaging fellow, young, with a smooth, plump face. He was dressed in a minor-key Hawaiian-style shirt, jeans, trainers and some rather sexy dark glasses pushed up on his wavy hair. His face was very mobile, with eyes alert and twinkly, his manner energetic and lively, and he had plenty more to say on the subject of snails, only part of which I ever managed to understand, such was the flow of words from his mouth.

There are several varieties of snail that you can eat, he explained, from *Helix pomata*, the classic snail for *escargot de Bourgogne*, to *Helix asperta*, the common garden snail, the stone-grey bane of every British gardener's life, by way of *Helix lucorum* and *Eobania vermiculata*. Even more confusingly, in Italy snails appear to be known as *la chiocciola* while they have a shell, but *lumaca* without one, usually when they are ready for cooking. Signor Caruso concentrated on the *Helix asperta*.

'We Italians have been eating snails since the Romans,' he said. 'Apicius gives several recipes for them. Every region has its own way with them. For example, around here we eat them with *sugo*, but further south they like them very hot, with lots of chili.'

The sex life of the snail has a certain charm to it. Snails are hermaphroditic, being able to both conceive and fertilise. When they feel in the mood, they crawl alongside one another, and, like two ships-of-the-line, fire love darts at each other, before going off to extrude the fertilised eggs. After that, the life of the snail may not be very long or very exciting, but on Signor Caruso's property they lived in considerable luxury, about seven thousand of them to a pen about fifty metres long and ten metres wide, which was planted with a seed catalogue of greenery – spinach, chard, chicory, poppies, lettuces, sunflowers – all growing with great vigour. And here the snails munched away, growing plump and tasty.

After five to six months of easy living, they were gathered in, and put into cages in what appeared to be a large garage, which they shared with some rabbits and a young calf. Here they purged for a few days, being fed nothing before being packed into sacks and sent off to meet their eaters. It seemed a pretty tranquil business to me, but even the slow-moving business of heliculture, it seemed, was not without its seamy side.

'We can't produce enough snails in Italy to satisfy demand,' said Signor Caruso. 'So a lot of snails are imported, from Croatia, from Greece, and North Africa, Algeria and Tunisia especially. In those countries snails are much cheaper. Certain unscrupulous people take the snails and ship them to Sardinia, which is Italian territory, and from Sardinia they go to Corsica, which is French territory, and from Corsica they go to France, where they are labelled as French snails and sold at twice the price.'

We peered into the snail pens, looking for signs of life. Nothing stirred. There were no slime trails, no mottled grey shells like turbans on the move, no extended horns sifting the portents. Snails are not sun worshippers, and so they were hidden away in the shady recesses of the pens, protected from insect predators by a brigade of brown chickens, which were allowed in from time to time to clear out any dangerous pests. But in the heat of the noonday sun, the snail minders were slumped in the dust in the shade, looking rather fed up with life.

Clattering through the countryside around Piedimonte Matese in Manfredo's beaten-up Fiat gave me a clearer idea of the riches of this obscure region. Few Italians know the area, let alone foreign tourists who march through the rest of the country. It had an idyllic, pre-Lapsarian quality to it.

What livens the fields, at the prompting of what star
The earth should be turned and vines be joined to elms,
The breeding of sheep and cattle, the care of the herd,
And how to profit by the sweet reserves of bees,
These are my themes, Maecenas.

So wrote Virgil at the beginning of the *Georgics,* a work that blighted my youth. He might have been writing about this area; although he grew up in the Po valley near Mantua, he spent much of his life in southern Italy. Everything grew here with ease and in immense profusion – olives, grapes, walnuts, tomatoes, zucchini, artichokes, peas, broad beans, borlotti beans, cannellini beans, *fagiolini verdi.* There were orchards of cherries, peaches, apricots, nectarines, loquats, figs, apples and pears. There were very fine honeys, cheeses, hams and sausages, and snails, of course. It would be difficult to starve here.

Over lunch in the Ristorante da Lorenzo, a little trattoria in San Gregorio Matese, slapped on the side of the mountains above Piedimonte Matese, Manfredo developed a theory to explain the four-course structure of the Italian meal that was so satisfying that I was sure that he was right. It went like this:

Antipasto (in our case pecorino, a slice or two of local prosciutto, and a very dark, delicate and mild salami made with pork, pig's liver and a little blood; zucchini and dried tomatoes preserved in oil, wonderful olives and a little round pepper stuffed with chopped olives): 'This is usually made up of prepared items that can be quickly assembled. This will pacify the immediate frenzy of the eaters, and keep them quiet while the *primo piatto,* pasta or whatever, which has to be freshly cooked, is being made.'

Primo piatto (*garganelli* with finely sliced zucchini and *funghi porcini*): 'Pasta or risotto, or whatever, is to fill people up. When a man has been outside at work all day, he is starving. So pasta is there to stop him feeling hungry and fill him up. Pasta is also cheap.'

Secondo piatto (a salad of cold *fagiolini verdi* or green beans in oil and a slice of *pollo ripieno* which looked like a mosaic tile of pearly, coarsely chopped chicken and pink *prosciutto crudo* with seams of yellow Parmesan and eggs and green parsley running through it; each ingredient was sharply defined and the chicken meat had the baritone note of a true free-range bird): 'Meat or fish. These are the most expensive ingredients, and so people can't afford to fill up on them. They also have the most complex flavours. But the hungry eater is no longer hungry because he has eaten the pasta, so he can smell the cooked meat or fish, eat it slowly, and savour its flavours.'

Formaggio–frutta–dolce (a single, perfect peach): 'Cheese and fruit or pudding. This is just to finish things off, clear the palate, fill in the odd corners and provide a sense of completion.'

Of course, not all Molisani, or even all Italians, eat on this scale at every meal, or feel themselves bound slavishly to four courses. Even I thought that the amounts were daunting, although I found it difficult to discipline my greed and curiosity.

What was so appealing about food of this kind was its absolute naturalness, its lack of preciosity. Here it was cooked by a very lively middle-aged woman, with twinkly eyes. It was made, she said, from stuff specific to the place and the season. The *garganelli* are particular to Campania. The salami would have been another clue to the region for a palate better informed than my own. The *funghi porcini* were early that year, and still quite scarce, so they were put together with the zucchini, which had just started to become plentiful. The ham was made by a neighbour's son.

'I know his mother, and she tells me it's good,' continued *la signora*. 'Giorgio makes the salami. His family have always made this salami. I know it's the best around here. The peppers and vegetables, well, they all come in a rush, so what can we do with them so that we don't have to throw them away? The chicken? I get the chickens from my cousin, who lets them have the run of his place. The cheese? Grated pecorino from a really old cheese. It's better than Parmesan for some dishes.'

That day ended back in San Gregorio Matese with an impromptu cheese tasting in the front room of Agostino Frasca, a relation of Manfredo by marriage. Agostino, Manfredo told me, was a Communist, 'not one of the new Communists – one of the old-fashioned kind'. Communist or not, he clearly had a finely honed entrepreneurial instinct. Everything in the room was dark brown and shiny and new – the suite of furniture, the marble floor, the table at which we sat, even the television, which, as usual, was roaring away.

Agostino was, I suppose, what would once have been called a higgler in rural England of the late nineteenth and early twentieth centuries, who acted as a kind of commercial go-between between remote farms and the nearest markets of towns, bartering farm produce for essentials. A. E. Coppard wrote one of the most poignant short stories in English about such a man. Agostino's tale, clearly, was anything but tragic. He had the complexion of someone who lived outdoors most of the time, ruddy and a bit lined. His wavy hair was grey. The shadows of his younger self seemed to haunt his face, but he exuded a kind of decisive confidence.

It seemed odd at this stage of the twenty-first century, but according to Agostino, the way of life in the Monti del Matese seemed hardly to have been touched by the nineteenth or even the eighteenth centuries, let alone the twentieth. He spoke about it not with any sense of nostalgia, but with down-to-earth immediacy and practicality.

The shepherds, he said, lived much as they had always done, driving their flocks from grazing to grazing throughout the spring and summer, coming down to their farms intermittently, until the autumn. There were about 200,000 sheep on the Matese, Spagnola and Bergamasca, and 100,000 Podolica cows. The farmers paid a tax, *fida pascotto*, for the privilege of grazing their animals, which seemed to me a pretty medieval notion.

Agostino collected cheeses from the farms, where they were made by hand with unpasteurised milk by the farmers' wives. In exchange, he brought them what they needed, flour, salt, pepper, washing powder or any other of the necessities of life.

The cheeses were stored out the back in a large, cool room in defiance of every EU and Italian hygiene law. They were neatly laid out on tables, arranged according to age, chunky and round, ranging in colour from the pale straw yellow of the most recent arrivals a few weeks old, to grey mould-encrusted cheeses like stones. A number of *caciocavallo* cheeses hung by strings from a pipe at the back. Around the walls were shelves laden with tomatoes, artichokes, zucchini, *melanzane*, peppers and mushrooms in oil, and a large deep freeze packed with bags of snails, wild asparagus and *funghi porcini*, all of which he had picked from the woods around.

We sipped a lethal dose of walnut liqueur as we tasted some very old and pungent pecorino, like essence of cheese, all crumbly and smelly, usually used just for grating, and a mild, fresh *caciocavallo* with a slight, sour, lactic tang; and we chatted about cheese, fishing and football – football most of all.

Between dismissive comments about the form of the current Italian football team, a subject that seemed to occupy the mind of every male I met, Agostino seemed quite buoyant about the state of cheese producers in the area.

'There are about fifty or so that I know about. True, that's fewer than a few years back. There used to be a hundred or so in the Matese. But still a good many survive. They make cheeses as they always have, to bring a bit of spending money.'

'So what would happen if they had to stick to EU or Italian hygiene regulations?' I wondered.

'They'd stop making cheese,' said Agostino. 'All that bureaucracy, and investment, it wouldn't be worth their while.'

It made me wonder how much longer the agricultural economy of the Monti del Matese would remain untouched by the wider world. Would he be the last of a long line of higglers? It was difficult to believe that the next generation, schooled in the disciplines of the modern state with matching economic expectations, would find it possible to share his empathy, his fierce independence, his sense of freedom, his disregard of authority and his inherent modesty. And who would be prepared to bear the harshness of the mountain life?

I had hardly left Piedimonte Matese and started through the mountains on my way to Sulmona, when I saw a woman selling cheeses, the ubiquitous ricotta, pecorino and caciocavallo, from a stall beside the road. I bought a small pecorino from her, and she chucked in a hefty slice of caciocavallo with chili in it for good measure. Was there anywhere where I could buy some bread and water to go with her cheese to make up a picnic lunch? I asked. She pointed to a bar at the crossroads a few metres behind me.

The place fell silent as I went in. In my best Italian, I asked if they had any bread.

'Certainly,' said the big-bosomed, motherly woman behind the counter in English in the flat, nasal accent of Coventry. 'Would you like bread or *panini* – rolls?'

Startled, I settled on bread, and she sold me some slices of home-roasted pork as well.

'I knew you were English as soon as you walked in,' she said. 'We don't get many foreigners around here.'

I asked her how she came to be here.

'Oh,' she said, as she wrapped my purchases, 'I met my husband in Scotland, where he had gone to find work, and we married and lived there for twelve years. Then I had my son, and we decided to move back here, where he came from originally. I didn't know a word of Italian in those days, and there I was with this little baby boy. I thought, "What have I done?" Every day I thought about running away, back to England. Not now, though. I wouldn't run anywhere.'

I rode up the giddy, tree-shaded mountains, in the golden morning, into sunshine, into shade, back into sunshine, back into shade, shadows rippling and dappling the road, which curved this way and that, twisted back on itself, up and up, the verges brilliant with ox-eye daisies, buttercups, poppies and vetch, and laced with eglantine.

If ever there was a forgotten corner, it was the Matese. Was it in Campania or Molise? Did it matter? It seemed to exist in a kind geographical and temporal limbo. It had a disarming innocence, unchanged and unspoiled. It was as it had always been. People went about their business, herding flop-eared sheep from pasture to pasture, following the clonking bells around the necks of the cattle, as they had always done. There was hardly a sign of any accommodation to the culture of tourism – no hotels, no tat centres, no stalls selling ersatz craft products; just sheep, cattle, woods, pastures and the occasional cluster of buildings.

Riding a scooter, or, I suppose, a motorcycle, is a curious business. You are locked inside your helmet for several hours, left to the devices and limitations of your own thoughts. In my case these were circular, revolving around food, family, what I had seen or heard and the irritating limitations of my Italian. There had been times when I had been so confused by being caught between two languages that all the words I knew formed into a tangled ball from which I found it impossible to extract one in any language.

I began to wonder about the effect that long periods in the saddle of a Vespa might have on the regularity of the bowels – it was curious how such concerns suddenly grew in the mind of the solitary rider. One thought led inexorably to another. I thought of other people who spent long hours in the saddle, the cowboys of the American West. Did they suffer from constipation? Were piles an occupational hazard? History, as usual when it comes to the really important topics, remains silent.

The new Vespa was a big improvement on Ginger, who, for all his stalwart character, lacked the gravitas that 125cc gave me. Its steady murmur spoke of dependability and strength of character, and when I had to open the throttle on a particularly steep bit of road, the murmur became an appreciable roar. The name Bud took root in my mind.

I stopped beside a stream in the high Matese to eat my lunch. The stream was fringed with willow and alder, which provided welcome shade. There was me, a grey wagtail, a dipper, a wren, innumerable butterflies and a donkey on the other side of the stream. The bread was fresh and springy. The chilies gave a slightly smoky heat to the cheese and the pork tasted of rosemary, garlic and roasted oil. Afterwards, I lay down on the bank of the stream and fell asleep with a large orchid at my feet.

My reverie was shattered when the donkey started braying, signalling the arrival of two families with children. I moved off again, up and over, and then up again, through a valley of almost Swiss neatness and Alpine fecundity. The grass in the fields was lush, waist high, splashed with the white, red and yellow brilliance of flowers. Some of the fields had been cut, the grass lying in long snaking lines, ready to be bound into bales. The roofs of the houses had a distinctive steep pitch, designed to send snow sliding off. Balconies ran the width of the front of the houses, which in many cases were built to provide shelter for animals underneath.

The road wound into the hills again, covered in part with a thick pelt of oak and beech, in part by short grass and, where that didn't grow, by scree and rock. I crossed and recrossed the Volturno, the longest river in southern Italy, which got smaller and smaller at each crossing. I passed a small lake beside Gallo and another at Barrea. The charming bosky heights of the Matese gave way to the imperious crags of the Abruzzo. As they did so, there was a perceptible change not so much in the nature of the landscape as in its tone, style and sophistication.

The Parco d'Abruzzo, for all its natural majesty of sweeping grassy bowls stretched like vast green sheets between vaulting craggy mountains, bears civilising – corrupting, if you like – marks: smart, modern hotels, souvenir shops, bars at convenient places, parking bays at panoramic spots. It was difficult to think of Agostino Frasca operating in the Abruzzo in the same unfettered way that he did in the Matese.

Eventually I came down from the mountains to Sulmona, with a sense of approaching one of the Cities of the Plain.

EATING UP ITALY

Recipes

GNOCCHI DI RICOTTA CON RAGOUT DI LUMACHE

Ricotta gnocchi with snail ragù

A tribute to the vibrant, but largely unsung, contribution snails make to the Italian diet. To start with, two recipes from a collection produced by their indefatigable champion, Signor Caruso. 'Ragout' is not a misspelling – that is how Signor Caruso spells it.

Serves 6

Prepare the snails. Wash them in fresh water with salt, swirling them round from time to time and changing the water every so often to get rid of the slime. Fill a pan with water and put over the heat. When the water is lukewarm, tip in the snails and bring to the boil. Cook for a few minutes. Drain in a colander. Extract the snail meat from the shells with a pin.

Prepare the court-bouillon. Add the snails and cook for 3 to 4 hours, depending on their size. Drain the snails and keep the broth.

Make the gnocchi. Beat the ricotta, flour, Parmesan and egg together, season and shape into small gnocchi. Cook in a pan of boiling salted water (they are ready when they float). Scoop out and drain.

Make the ragout. Heat the olive oil in a pan and add the chopped garlic and rosemary. Roughly chop the snails and add them. Season with salt and pepper and finely chopped sage if wanted. Add a

1 1/2 - 2 lbs snails
Salt

For the Court-Bouillon

1 stick celery, grated or finely diced
1 carrot, grated or finely diced
1 onion, grated or finely diced
2 bay leaves
1 clove garlic
1 teaspoon salt
1 quart water

For the gnocchi

3 cups ricotta (preferably sheep's)
1/2 cup durum flour
1 cup grated Parmesan
1 egg
Salt and pepper, to taste

For the ragout

3 tablespoons olive oil
1 teaspoon garlic, very finely chopped

spoonful or so of the snail broth. Just before serving, sprinkle a little grappa over the ragout and set fire to it. Pour over the gnocchi.

A little rosemary, finely chopped
A little sage, finely chopped
A splash of grappa

PEPERONI RIPIENE CON OLIVE VERDE

Peppers stuffed with green olives

Ah, but which peppers? Good question. At the trattoria in question, the name of which seems to have slipped from my notebook, they were red, small (about the size of a small plum), round, sweet and warm rather than hot. I suspect that they were Capsicum annuum, the tomato chili, one of the first to come to Europe. Olives are green when they are unripe or partially ripened.

Serves 12

Pit the olives and chop finely. Peel and finely chop the garlic. Mix the olives, garlic and bread crumbs. Cut the tops off the tomato chilies and scoop out the seeds. Fill each chili about half to two-thirds full with the olive mixture, place in a baking dish and pop into a moderately hot oven (375°) for 20–30 minutes. The chilis should be soft. Take out and allow to cool. Serve warm or cold. If there are any left over, pop them into a glass jar and cover with olive oil.

1 lb green olives
4 cloves garlic
1/2 cup bread crumbs
24 tomato chilis

AGNELLO DEL MATESE ALLA BRACE

Grilled Matese lamb chops

It may seem the counsul of perfection to keep emphasising the origin of the raw materials, but their quality and character lies at the heart of all the dishes that make Italy such a wonderful country in which to eat. Perhaps we might learn to distinguish, and value, the qualities of the varieties of sheep we have in Britain in the same way. The sheep of the Monti del Matese are espagnola or bergamasca. They have long bodies and floppy ears, and their chops are thin, delicate things compared to the sturdy, fleshy chops we tend to favour in Britain. For all their thinness, they have a pronounced sweetness and grassy flavour. This thinness also lends itself to high-temperature treatment, which leaves them cooked all the way through but tender. In Campania/Molise, they will be served completely naked, i.e. just the chops on the plate, with half a lemon to squeeze over them.

Serves 6

Trim all the fat off the chops, leaving only the nut of meat at the end of the bone. Mix 4 tablespoons olive oil with the lemon juice and oregano and pour over the chops. Marinate for at least an hour, preferably 3 or 4 hours.

Take the chops out of the marinade and pat dry. Place on a hot barbecue or under a hot broiler or on a very hot griddle pan in which you have heated a little olive oil until it is smoking. Leave the chops for 5 minutes, without turning. Turn and cook for an additional 5 minutes. Allow to rest for 5 minutes. Sprinkle with salt and pepper. Serve with lemon halves, for squeezing.

18 thin lamb chops
4 tablespoons olive oil
Juice of 1/2 lemon
Oregano (known as arecetto in the mountains)
Salt and pepper, to taste
3 lemons, halved

GARGANELLI CON ZUCCHINI E FUNGHI PORCINI

Garganelli with zucchini and porcini mushrooms

Is this really a recipe? It was just a way of using two ingredients that had come into high season. It illustrates the natural thrift and seasonality of Campanian cooking, but, aside from that, I am not sure it is profoundly regional. Indeed, garganelli *are supposed to be typical of Emilia-Romagna. There you go, and there I went.*

Serves 4

Wash and finely slice the zucchini. Clean the porcini, but do not wash them. Slice finely. Heat some olive oil in a frying pan with the clove of garlic. When the garlic is brown and sizzling, take it out and discard. Tip the zucchini into the hot oil and fry until just brown. Take them out and drain on kitchen towel. Tip the porcini into the oil and fry until soft. Cook the garganelli in the normal way. Drain and anoint with a little fresh olive oil. Divide the pasta between the plates, heaping the porcini and zucchini on top.

1/2 lb zucchini
1/2 lb fresh porcini
Extra virgin olive oil
1 clove garlic
1 1/2 cup garganelli

POLLO IMBOTTITO CON FORMAGGIO, PROSCIUTTO E VERDURE

Chicken stuffed with cheese, prosciutto and greens

Serves 4–6

Skin the chicken, keeping the skin in as complete a piece as possible. Cut all the meat off the carcass and chop coarsely. Set aside.

Blanch the orabe/spinach/parsley in boiling water, drain and squeeze out as much water as possible. Chop finely. Chop the prosciutto finely. Mix the eggs, chicken, prosciutto, cheese and greens in a bowl and season.

Lay out the chicken skin on a piece of muslin larger than the skin. Place as much of the chicken mixture on the skin as possible, bearing in mind you want to be able to wrap the skin around it, and shape it into a loaf or fat sausage. Wrap the muslin around it to hold it together and tie securely. Place the package in a casserole and cover with cold water. Slowly bring to simmering point, then simmer very gently for 90 minutes. Unwrap, slice and serve.

2¼ lbs chicken

1/4 lb orabe (a local spinach variant, possibly orach, picked in the fields), or

Spinach or parsley

4 oz prosciutto crudo

2 eggs

6 tablespoon grated pecorino

Salt and pepper, to taste

6
SWEET CHARMS

PIEDIMONTE MATESE
SULMONA
FARA SAN MARTINO
GUARDIAGRELE
Confetti di Sulmona

I found them as addictive as the taralli *had been, not too sweet, the white sugar coating releasing a slight taste of vanilla if I sucked it; or a wonderful soft crunch of sugar and, when I couldn't resist chewing them, the escaping flavour of almond.*

Nescioqua natale solum dulcidine cunctos
Ducit et immemores non sinit esse sui

By what sweet charm I know not the native land draws all men nor allows them to forget her,' wrote the Latin bard of Sulmona, Ovidius Naso, better known as Ovid, who was born there in 43 BC and continued to celebrate its charms for the rest of his life.

Sulmona was a handsome, amiable, prosperous town. Its sweet charms now included Max Mara and Mariella and many gelaterias, and it wore an air of restrained sophistication. It was the first town in which I had been aware that the exuberant, tortured curves of the southern baroque had given way to the linear, classical order of Renaissance northern Italy, with handsome pediments and porticos, symmetry, finely detailed stonework and scrolled balconies, in familiar golden stone. The streets were smoothly cobbled (not like the rattling ones of Naples), and ended in raking vistas of the surrounding mountains.

In the Roman section of his journals, Goethe recounts how, during the annual carnival in Rome, women were permitted to throw *confetti* at any man they fancied. Originally the *confetti* were almonds covered in white sugar, although, because their expense was prohibitive, paste ones were usually substituted. So vigorously did the women of Rome pursue this particular dating method that, according to Goethe, battles would break out between women over a particular man, which ended up with them pelting each other with armfuls of *confetti* supplied by wandering *confetti* sellers. Sulmona was the town where the original *confetti*, the sugared almonds, were made. They still are.

The outside of Confetti Rapone – *'antichissima fabbrica artigianale di confetti. Premiata con "Medaglie d'oro e Diplomi di Gran Premio". Iscritta nel "Libro d'Oro d'Italia"* ', as its promotional literature had it – on the edge of the Piazza XX Settembre, was faded and old-fashioned. Inside, it had that warm, comforting smell of sugar and nostalgia. Small, glass-fronted cabinets glittered with white, green, scarlet, azure and pink *confetti*, with centres, or *anime,* of pistachio, cinnamon, chocolate, cannellini beans and fruit jellies, as well as almonds.

The present Signor Rapone sat by the door, his leg encased in plaster, a metal contraption bracing it. He was a small, uncompromising man, and gravely suspicious of my intentions.

'Where are the *confetti* made?' I asked him.

'In the premises next door,' he said, eyeing me.

'Can I see them being made?'

'No.'

'Why not?'

'Because there are certain processes . . .'

'Ah, trade secrets!'

'Exactly.'

'Can I just have a look?'

'No.'

'All right, then, how did the making of *confetti* come about in Sulmona? Can you tell me that?'

'Why certainly. The sweets were originally started by the nuns of the Monastery of Santa Chiara here in Sulmona, but they used honey, not sugar. In those days the almond trees grew all around here. And then about two hundred years ago people started using sugar. My family started making *confetti* in the eighteenth century. We were the first. You must write that down. Rapone is the oldest company making *confetti* here in Sulmona. Then the almond trees disappeared from around here. Our almond groves were where the industrial zone is now.'

'Why?'

'Because they drained the Lago Fucino.' He said this with considerable bitterness, as if this had happened quite recently. In fact, the draining of the lake near Avezzano, which had once been the third largest in Italy, started in 88 AD, and was finally completed in 1878. 'This caused a change in the microclimate. There was much more snow and frost. The almond trees used to blossom very early, in January, but with the frosts, the blossoms never turned into fruit. So now we get the almonds from Avola in Sicily. They are flatter than normal almonds, and have less oil in them.'

He showed me an old photograph of *confetti* being made at the turn of the century. In the foreground women in traditional dress were making the fancy flowers and decorations that must have always been a part of the industry. At the back were a couple of moustachioed individuals standing by what looked like huge copper basins set over fires. It seemed that the almonds were peeled and chucked into these basins, which were full of syrup. The moustachioed *signori* slowly rotated the basins for several hours. The almonds were taken out, dried overnight and then treated the same way the next day, and so on for about a week until they were coated in several hardened layers of sugar. He explained that the colours weren't accidental. People gave different colours for different birthdays – pink for one, red for five, yellow for ten, beige for fifteen, silver for twenty-five, aquamarine for thirty, dark blue for thirty-five, green for forty, red for forty-five, gold for fifty, ivory for fifty-five and white for sixty. He pointed to some particularly hideous confection of elasticated material in the shape of a bloom with sugared almonds woven into it: 'That was my idea. You must write that down. Now they're all doing it.' Signor Rapone tried to persuade me that things hadn't changed that much in the *laboratorio* Rapone. As it turned out, he might have been exaggerating, but only slightly.

I left armed with a bag of Signor Rapone's finest straight almond *confetti*, and wandered out into the sunlight, munching as I went. I found them as addictive as the *taralli* had been, not too sweet, the white sugar coating releasing a slight taste of vanilla if I sucked it; or a wonderful soft crunch of sugar and, when I couldn't resist chewing them, the escaping flavour of almond. My fingers closed on the last sugared almond long before I reached the Piazza Risorgimento and the House of Pelino.

The House of Pelino was at the other end of the scale of *confetti* production from the House of Rapone, as sophisticated in its marketing and packaging as Rapone was antique and artless. It also had a museum devoted to the history of *confetti*, and an intelligent young woman who explained things more explicitly than Signor Rapone. The museum was of limited appeal, I would say, but my guide's exposition of the development of the industry in Sulmona was admirably crisp and lucid. As usual, there were more mundane explanations for the tides of fortune in the *confetti* industry.

The nuns had, indeed, started the tradition of sweet making in Sulmona using almonds and honey, although that particular taste goes back to the Romans. Then, in the fifteenth century, a local Venetian import/export merchant started bringing cane sugar from the Indies, and that clearly made more attractive *confetti* than the sticky honey. But the real explosion among *confetti* makers didn't happen until the nineteenth century, when Karl Franz Archard in Germany, using the discovery of his mentor, Magraaf, set up the first factory to make sugar from sugar beet. It wasn't long before sharp Italian sugar producers cottoned on to the new process and made use of the beet which was grown around Avezzano and Teramo, respectively west and north of Sulmona.

And today's manufacture actually didn't differ that much from yesteryear's. The copper basins were deeper and had narrower mouths, and they were rotated by electricity now, rather than by hand, but the principle was exactly the same. I watched a line of about twenty *bassine* rolling round and round quite vigorously, attended by a number of women in white coats and white hats who, from time to time, would take a ladle of some liquid from battered aluminium cooking pots on stands and plop the contents into the rotating *bassine*. At the end of the day the almonds would be dried, and the process was repeated each day until they were ready.

Now that I had cracked the code of the *confetti* makers, I was ready to investigate another of Sulmona's culinary mysteries, the *salsiccie al fegato* – a pork liver sausage, which comes in both fresh and dried forms. Its distinguishing feature is the inclusion of pig's liver in the mix and, according to a gentleman at the Taverna dei Caldora, a very smart restaurant in nearby

Pacentro that specialised in the traditional cooking of the Abruzzo, a little blood.

'Not so,' said Butcher One, a large congenial man with a limp. 'No blood. Blood would make it spoil. I should know. I make my own. It's one third belly to one third shoulder meat, to one third liver, black liver. Salt. Pepper. Garlic if you like, just a touch. Chili, if you like. That's it. Here, try some.'

'Blood?' said Butcher Two. 'I should say not. Anyway, it isn't made at this time of year. It's too hot. Here, try some.'

Butcher Three agreed with Butcher Two.

Butcher Four said he didn't make it at all, ever.

Butcher Five, however, had a different take on it altogether. 'Yes, we make it. Once a week,' he said, a smiling, cheerful sort with a ruddy complexion. 'It's hot, but we can make it in the cold room. You have to eat it soon because it goes off quite quickly when the weather's like this. We use a third belly to a third of shoulder or cheek – cheek is better – and a third of liver, and we add just a little heart, too. Salt and pepper, very little pepper, and a touch of chili. Now at Pratola [about eight kilometres away], they add lungs, which makes a richer, heavier sausage. Very good, in its way, but different from ours. Blood? Oh, yes, they used to, in the old days, for colour, but not now.'

If five butchers in the same town couldn't agree on what constitutes the correct ingredients for a basic local sausage, what chance had even the most conscientious of researchers? And I wasn't even one of those. I thought with envy of the clarity and certitude in those cookery books and compendia of Italian food that I had read before setting out. They gave to Italian food a settled quality that it didn't seem to possess *in situ*. Each time I formulated a point of view or came to a conclusion, I would come across something that caused the ground to slide out from under my feet. I realised that the kind of authority that I had hoped would be mine by the journey's end was going to be very hard to come by. On second thoughts, it was going to be impossible.

The sun shone, and the road wound up into the mountains, away from the heat of the Sulmona valley, into shadow and out, past hillsides of scree and fields sanguine with poppies or purple with vetch, through small scatterings of houses with fat cattle grazing in fields, stomach-deep in pasture.

Heading north-west, I passed the length of a plateau, La Piana delle Cinquemiglia, slung like a colossal hammock between the surrounding peaks, undulating gently along its length, rippling with waist-high grass set with poppies, daisies and vetch, broken here and there by patches of tilled earth, like the first squares of a quilt. Such an open vista was liberating after the closed-in world of gorges, narrow valleys and steep-sided mountains. My eyes filled with light and sky.

It was over these natural pastures that, for centuries, the shepherds of the Molise and the Abruzzo had driven their sheep, in flocks tens of thousand strong, in an annual trek called *la transumanza*, heading for Lecce in Puglia. '*E vanno pel tratturo antico al piano, quasi per un erbal fiume silente,*' wrote Gabriele D'Annunzio of *transumanza*. 'And they go along the ancient drove-path to the plain, as if by a grassy, silent river.' The shepherds did not own the sheep they drove, and they were forbidden to kill any for food *en route*. Strict account of the numbers was kept by overseers on horseback, but some, inevitably, died along the way. The culinary legacy of sheep and goat recipes marks the routes – *calzoncini abruzzese, scrippelle m'busse, gnocchi col ragù di pecora, conchiglie al ragù con la ricotta, agnello brodettato, agnello in crosta di pane, coscio d'agnello, agnello all' abruzzese, strengozze*. The regular migration had ended about forty years ago, but hillsides covered with derelict shelters, large beehives built of stone, bore mute witness to the scale of the traffic. But I came across no sheep. If they were still grazed on these mountains, they must have been on yet higher levels.

Presently I came to a second plateau like the first, Il Valico della Forchetta, colonised here and there by clusters of beehives, painted in colours as brilliant as the wild flowers. Around the edge of it curved a single-track, narrow-gauge railway, along which chugged a two-coach flyer, driven by Signor

Ferdinando Fantini, who, I had been told, collected the honey from the hives.

The plateau was intimidatingly remote, and must have been desolate and lonely in winter. Yet the buildings that I saw showed no sign of neglect, nor of being abandoned. There didn't seem to have been the wholesale desertion of remote landscapes here that took place in France and Spain. Somehow the Abruzzesi had made it possible and, more importantly, desirable, for people to maintain their traditional lives, at least in the south.

Fara San Martino was perched high in the Abruzzo, in the heart of the Parco della Maiella. It was a small town, on the edge of which was a gigantic modern factory, a monolithic block of silos in brilliant white with a heavy band of topaz-blue running around the top. Colossal, gleaming, bright, inhuman. It looked completely at odds with its surroundings. It was as if I had come across an outpost of some intergalactic visitor. The factory bore the logo of De Cecco, a well-known brand of pasta.

Just as puddings are Britain's pre-eminent contribution to world culinary culture, so pasta is Italy's. Other countries – China, Japan, Malaysia, India – have their own noodles, but none has developed them with the same passion and variety as the Italians. There are endless monographs about the origins of pasta. It is pretty much accepted now that the history of pasta in Italy goes back at least until the Etruscans, but I can't think that it matters very much who first made a strand of spaghetti. It is not so much its historicity as the immense ingenuity the Italians have invested in it that is truly interesting.

There is a theory that pasta is the great unifying food of Italy, and it is true that, in an uncountable variety of forms, it is universal. But, far from unifying, pastas, their ingredients, shape and saucing, help define Italians' sense of regional identity: *orecchiette* of Puglia, *ditalini* of Campania, *garganelli* of Emilia-Romagna, *spaghetti alla chitarra* of the Abruzzo, *tajarin* of

Piedmont. Even more microcosmic than regional specialities are zonal or even city specialities – *tortelli di zucca mantovani, strangozzi di Spoleto, fettuccine alla trasteverina, spaghetti allo viareggina.*

Nothing illustrates the fact that pasta is the repository of regional difference more clearly than the critical dichotomy between *pasta asciutta* and *pasta fresca. Pasta asciutta* – dried pasta – is sometimes known as *pasta alimentari.* There are subclasses of pasta, such as *pasta di semola grano duro secca* – dried durum wheat semolina pasta – and *pasta all'uova secca* – pasta made with eggs, which is only produced commercially. The pasta of the south has always been *pasta asciutta*, made from just hard durum wheat with, possibly, semolina, and water. It is a fundamental food, the food of poverty, that would fill a stomach quickly and cheaply, that would keep indefinitely in a society where there was little refrigeration. The most desirable dried pasta still comes from Calabria and Campania, Puglia and the Abruzzo.

Of course, dried pasta is made in the north, too. In fact, more dried pasta is now made in the north than in the south. Mussolini was responsible for switching pasta production from the south to the north – he himself came from Emilia-Romagna – in order to feed the Italian army. The largest producer of all, Barilla, is based in Parma. But the true pasta of the north is *pasta fresca* – fresh pasta. This is usually *pasta all'uovo*, made with softer flour and eggs, luxuries that, once, were not readily available in the impoverished south, although just to confuse matters still further, *pasta di semola fresca*, such as *orecchiette*, are found in the south. Now, of course, Italian pasta has achieved world domination, and this shiny, new De Cecco hyperplant was a statement of that domination.

De Cecco had been making pasta in Fara San Martino since 1887, taking advantage of the area's plentiful supply of water and easy access to the hard wheat of the Abruzzo. These days, wheat was coming from far beyond the borders of the province, to judge by the articulated lorries queuing up to make their deliveries – an observation that was borne out by an

Italian television programme investigating the origin of the wheat that goes into Italian pasta which I saw a few days later. Apparently most Italians believe that the durum wheat for their pasta is grown in Italy. It is a given part of the food culture. However, it turned out that this was not the case at all. A significant proportion – 20 per cent – comes from inside the EU, and a further 10 per cent from North America. There was a most amusing moment when the formerly smooth spokesman for Barilla could be seen wriggling like a worm on a hook when confronted with this information. 'I am sure the Italian consumer is intelligent enough . . . no one could seriously believe . . . have never claimed . . .'

It turns out, too, that the artisanal producers are in much the same boat. With a few local exceptions, they are supplied by flour merchants who buy their wheat on the open market, bag it up and send it off. The quality of the end pasta product may not be compromised, but I couldn't help wondering whether *territorio* – the ground in which the wheat was grown – differing microclimates and different varieties of wheat didn't produce rather different flavours. Further, if the wheat is a standardised product and industrial production techniques are fully understood and standardised, why bother to make the stuff in Italy at all, except for the purposes of marketing and branding?

I stopped to see if I could look around, but the security was so tight – lots of men with stubble chins, dark glasses and stomachs bulging over their cinched-in belts – that you would have thought the site was a military complex, and, while they were happy to hand over a forest's worth of promotional literature, they wouldn't let me on to the premises. It was all a far cry from the cosy world of the ladies of La Golosa.

Oddly, I passed yet another *pastificio* in Fara San Martino, Cocco, a minnow by comparison, but producing a small range of fine pastas that I had come across in England. Unfortunately, a thin, suspicious young man was as successful in keeping me out as the muscled might of De Cecco. I suppose that he had every right to be suspicious. I must have looked very odd. Rather crestfallen, I pressed on.

Presently I came to a fork in the road. 'Does this road lead anywhere?' I asked an old crone in black carrying a switch of broom, who was standing at the unsigned junction.

'Yes,' she said. 'To —,' though I couldn't decipher the name. Reassured, I headed on in the direction in which she had gestured. It wasn't long before the road became a track, and it wasn't much longer before the track became very bumpy. It wound down and down, curving round the edge of the mountain. It made for interesting riding but I wasn't too concerned. Sweet chestnut and oak grew thickly on either side. There were clumps of golden broom, and butterflies like flying flowers. Every now and then there was a car parked to one side of the track. Mushroom hunters, I thought. Well, they've come from somewhere.

No, they hadn't. I had just negotiated a particularly testing and bumpy stretch when I met a car coming in the opposite direction.

'Where does this road come out?' I asked.

'It doesn't,' said the man driving. 'It just stops.' I looked shocked.

'Are you German?' said the passenger.

'No, English,' I said.

'Aaah, English,' he said, nodding sagely, as if everything had suddenly become clear, and they drove on. I turned round and made my way back in the direction from which I had come.

Some time later I passed the old crone in black again. She was sitting on a bench just where the dirt track turned back into a tarmacked road again at the edge of the village that I had left half an hour before. She grinned at me as I went past. I wanted to kick her.

Finally, I left the high majesty of the central Abruzzo, and came down to the hills above the Adriatic coast. The topography was still pretty vertically challenging, but suddenly it was more intensively inhabited, cultured and cultivated. The fields had the appearance of being divided into strips. The result was a panorama of longitudinal contrasts – gold wheat beside brown earth beside brilliant green *erba medica* (clover for forage) beside grey olives. There were views that took in several lines of hills, orchards, neat smallholdings with rows of tomatoes, zucchini, beans, chicories and lettuces, and a man turning cut grass with a pitchfork.

Guardiagrele was a small, trim, tidy town on a sharpish slope with a quite extraordinary number of butchers. I counted ten, including one *macelleria di cavallo* that dealt in horsemeat. It was the first time that I had registered one of these, although a good deal of horsemeat is consumed in the south around Taranto in Puglia.

Vegetarianism seemed to be barely recognised in Italy. Indeed, whenever I had suggested the possibility that people should voluntarily not eat meat, I was greeted with incredulity. Of course, Italy has a richer store of purely vegetable dishes than any other European country, but the memory of widespread agrarian poverty, and the consequent rarity of meat as a regular part of the menu, is too recent for people not to indulge now that modern productivity and prosperity have made it available to almost every family on a daily basis. Still less would they be able to deny themselves the panoply of porky creations which, just as much as pasta, are the product and definition of local identity.

Not far from Guardiagrele, Antonio Santoleri grew *farro*, a kind of spelt or emmer wheat, a cereal that was a key grain for the Romans, and the Macedonians before them. Then it rather fell out of favour, being replaced by easier-to-grow, more productive wheat, the history of commerce in a husk. Actually *farro* never went away completely; I remember having a delicious simple soup of it in Rome, where appreciation of it as the grain of the poor has never wavered.

Signor Santoleri was a handsome man, whose luxuriant, greying and drooping moustache and despondent, mournful manner made him look older than he probably was. Between taking and making phone calls in his somewhat jumbled office in the old farm *casina*, he told me that recently *farro* had been enjoying something of a revival among discerning gourmets and health obsessives, who warmed to its easy digestibility, highly nutritious qualities and the fact that it wasn't wheat. Some of it was used for making pasta, which had the colour of toasted hazelnuts and a slight chestnut flavour. Or it was added to soups in *semiperlato* form, made by slightly pearling the grain without the husk, which takes twenty-five to thirty minutes to cook; or *farricello*, which is the broken grain without the husk.

He said that he had two crops per growing season, spring and autumn, although there was another variety that could be harvested in winter. The *farro* of the Marche was different, he explained, from the *farro* of the Garfagna in Tuscany and the Val del Nera and Monteleone di Spoleto in Umbria, which was larger and softer, good for soups. *Farro d'Abruzzo* was smaller and harder, better for grinding into flour or for kibbling into a *farro semolina*, to be used as a legume. He started to give me chapter and verse on every aspect of *farro* history and culture, but to be truthful, he rather lost me along the way. He lost himself as well, because what he really wanted to talk about was green politics.

'I take a very pessimistic view of food in this country,' he said. 'The Italians have a very narrow view of their food culture. They simply don't see what's going on around them. They don't know that so much of their milk, eggs, meat are imported. They don't know that companies like Bertolli, Monini and Sasso are owned by multinational companies. Unilever is Italy's largest producer of olive oil. And ice cream.

There is a complete division between the north and the south. In the south, the *contadini* have their small farms, producing what they have always produced, and that's all they care about. They can't see the threat to their way of producing things. And up in the north, agriculture is completely industrialised. Businessmen and politicians get together to protect the interests of the agri-industry. And then there are the multinationals who want to genetically modify foods so that they can control the complete food supply. Already they control most of the world's seed production. And the Italians, what do they care? They don't even see it.'

Such is the spirit of a man who, after fifteen years and in the face of his own rampant pessimism, still grows 25–35 hectares of *farro*, as well as wheat, along strictly organic lines on a 135-hectare farm. As in Britain, the organic sector was not free of controversy. There were the usual bitter disagreements between authorising agencies over conversion periods, policing of organic production, the role of the state, the role of supermarkets. He told me that Italy has the largest number of hectares under organic production in the EU. I wondered if this was true.

Gloomily, he took me outside to show me the fields of organic wheat that grew around the *casina*. It was much taller than the wheat I was used to seeing in England. That was because, he said, the modern strains of wheat were grown on short stems that made them less prone to wind or rain damage, and the height was convenient for the combines. Unfortunately, shorter stems meant that more sunlight penetrated to the earth between the rows of wheat, and that encouraged weed growth, which could only be controlled by use of herbicides. The great advantage of *farro* and the older strains of wheat was that they grew tall, kept the light off the earth and so created their own weed-control protocol.

Then we inspected the antiquated machinery, in a handsome wooden casing like an enormous siege cannon, used to thresh the ears of *farro*. He ran his hands over the casing. It was old, he admitted, but it still worked perfectly well, and he preferred it for processing the *farro* because it was kinder to the grain.

'Are you really riding around Italy on a scooter?' he asked as we said goodbye under the acacias outside the *casina*. His face lit up in a smile. 'What a great idea,' he said.

The road from the *casina* Santoleri ran up and down the patchwork hills, between plantations of olive trees, their trunks and branches as twisted as arthritic hands, their leafy masses as fluffy as shaving brushes. They erupted from ground that appeared to be a mass of stones. Between the plantations of olives were odd clusters of apple and pear trees, and fields in which serpentine swathes of cut animal forage waited to be taken away. The sun was very warm. A vertiginous track turned off the road. I took it and freewheeled down it until I lurched to a halt under a mulberry tree outside the *azienda agricola* Tommaso Mascantonio. I was in time for lunch with Tommaso and his brother Giovanni, who grew, pressed and bottled their own organic olive oil in Caprafico, as their family had for several hundred years.

I had come across their olive oil already in the hotel where I was staying. It was luscious, sweetly grassy and smoothly viscous, with very little of the aggressive pepperiness I associated with Tuscan oil. It was made, I knew from the promotional material that seemed to accompany everything comsumable, from Gentile di Chieti, Intosso and Leccino olives, picked quite early in the ripening cycle to catch the freshness and fruit.

Tommaso, as the eldest, sat at the head of the table in the kitchen, with his brother on one side of him and myself on the other. Their respective wives, who had prepared the lunch, sat opposite one another, while an old man, full of wartime memories that he was ready to share on an inconsequential basis with anyone who would listen, took a seat towards the end of the table. A very large television occupied pride of place on a dresser opposite Tommaso. It also provided most of the conversation, as the news was on throughout lunch, which was perhaps just as well as Tommaso and Giovanni weren't natural conversationalists.

During the *maccheroni alla chitarra* there was a brief sally over the performance of the Italian football team and the comment '*L'arbitro era —*', together with a great deal of eye rolling and rubbing together of forefinger and thumb to indicate that the official had been bribed. *Maccheroni alla chitarra* is a classic of Abruzzese cooking, square-cut pasta made by pressing it through the strings of a *chitarra* device which was held to bear a resemblance to a rudimentary guitar. We helped ourselves to red and white wine, made on the estate.

A commercial on the television prompted a careful exchange about Mussolini, while we ate chunks of roast chicken, zucchini fried in batter and salad, all from the farm. Mussolini was a man of his time, we agreed, and left it that, but I was quite relieved to learn that in 1944 the British who had been billeted in a house that we could see set among the olive trees had behaved impeccably.

As the honoured guest, I had been helped first to the pasta and to the prime pieces of chicken. Every part of the lunch tasted of its provenance and had flavours that were like memories. The only part that had been bought was the bread. The women cleared away and did the washing up.

Over peaches and apricots from trees on the estate, the brothers reflected on the difficulties of the olive oil business. Times were hard, they agreed, and the young didn't want to work the hours or live the way of life it required. Giovanni had a son studying agriculture at university. 'I don't know – he wants to join us, but I'm not sure it's worth his while,' he concluded dejectedly. Keeping things organic was labour-intensive. They were proud of the rock roses, broom, wild thyme and juniper that flowered among their 3,000 trees, but being organic meant that their oil was expensive by comparison with other brands, and considered too expensive for the home market.

Most of their oil went overseas, to Germany in particular, and Switzerland, both countries that appreciated organic production and were prepared to pay for it. 'Italians use the cheapest, worst oil. All the best goes to other countries.'

I left the brothers packing up an order for a German customer. Their massive bronzed hands, battered by labour, handled the handsome square-cut bottles, with their elegantly designed labels and cloudy, gold-green liquid, with a care that almost amounted to tenderness.

EATING UP ITALY

Recipes

SALSICCIA DI FEGATO

Liver sausage

It doesn't sound so enticing in English as it does in Italian. As my experiences in Sulmona showed, there are many variations. This is the basic recipe based on that in the invaluable Salumi d'Italia *published by Slow Food. It is a soft sausage.*

Put the liver, heart and lungs through a fine grinder twice. Add salt, pepper, garlic, orange zest and bay leaves all cut very small, and chili powder if you like. The casing of pig's intestine should be thoroughly washed in vinegar and salt, then rinsed and dried. Stuff the casing, making links by twisting the casing every 4 inches. Hang the links suspended from a pole in a chimney and leave them there for 4–5 days. Then keep the sausage for a month in a fresh, damp room before eating it. If you want to keep it longer, cover it in olive oil or pork fat.

FAGIOLINI BORLOTTI CON FUNGHI PORCINI

Borlotti beans with porcini mushrooms

Up in the mountains just outside Sulmona is the village of Pacentro, and in the village of Pacentro is the Taverna dei Caldora, which manages to be both a restaurant of impeccable smartness and a repository of the most superlative versions of traditional cooking. This is the first of two of the sixteen dishes that I enjoyed at one memorable dinner. You must use fresh borlotti beans for this dish.

Serves 6

Clean and slice the porcini. Boil the borlotti beans in unsalted water until soft – about 20 minutes. Heat some olive oil with the garlic clove in a frying pan. When the garlic starts to go brown, take it out. Add the porcini slices and fry until soft. Add to the drained beans. Finely chop the parsley, mix into the stew, season and serve just warm.

1 lb fresh porcini mushrooms

1 lb fresh borlotti beans

Olive oil

1 clove garlic

1 bunch parsley

Salt and pepper, to taste

CAPRETTO CACIO E UOVA

Kid with cheese and egg sauce

A relic of the transumanza, *the great annual herding pilgrimage that once brought sheep and goats from the high plateaux of the Abruzzo to the markets of Puglia. The recipe is for kid, but lamb would do just as well. Cheese and egg may seem odd ingredients to put with meat, but the result is very persuasive. For rustic authenticity, cook in an earthenware casserole.*

Serves 8

Dice the kid into large squares. Chop the onion. Heat some olive oil in an earthenware casserole and fry the onion until soft. Add the kid and brown lightly on all sides. Pour in the wine and boil until it has evaporated. Cover and cook gently until the meat is tender, about 1 hour. Add a little stock or water if it gets too dry.

Beat the eggs and grated cheese together. Add a pinch of salt and a grind or two of pepper. Pour this over the meat and leave for 5 minutes. The residual heat should cook the mixture through. If not, heat very gently – very gently indeed. You don't want to curdle the sauce.

3 1/2 lbs kid

1 onion

Olive oil

1 cup dry white wine

2/3 cup water or lamb stock

4 eggs

2/3 cup grated pecorino

Salt and pepper, to taste

SFARRATA

Farro soup

One of the ways to use the delicious, digestible organic farro of Antonio Santoleri . A winter warmer, I think, and if you can get hold of Signor Santoleri's olive oil or that of the Mascantonio brothers, so much the better.

Serves 4

Cook the *farro*, chickpeas, lentils and pearl barley in unsalted water, taking note of the different cooking times. Discard the water. Chop the onions and carrots quite finely. Fry in olive oil until the onion is translucent. Add the legumes and enough water or stock to make it as thick or as thin as you like. Season. Just before serving, chop the parsley and add that and a splash of olive oil to each plate.

1/2 cup faro (or spelt grains)

1/2 cup chickpeas, lentils and Pearl barley

2 onions

2 carrots

Extra virgin olive oil

Salt and pepper, to taste

Bunch of parsley

PANE DI FARRO

Farro bread

You can substitute spelt flour if you can't get farro *flour.*

Makes 1 loaf

Dissolve the yeast in a little warm water. Mix the flour with the olive oil, sugar and salt. Add the yeast and enough water to make a firm dough. Leave the dough in a warm place to rise for 1 hour.

Shape the dough into whatever bread shape you fancy. Leave to rise again for 1 hour. Bake for 30–40 minutes at 425°.

2 oz (2 cakes) fresh yeast

4 1/2 cups farro or spelt flour

2 tablespoons olive oil

1 tablespoons superfine sugar

1 teaspoon salt

MACCHERONI ALLA CHITARRA

Maccheroni made with a 'guitar'

This is typical of the Abruzzo. The name refers to the shape of the strands of pasta, which are cut square by pressing the rolled-out pasta through the steel wires of a chitarra, a box with vague similarities to the base of a guitar. It is rarely made in the traditional way these days. It is easy to get the square-cut effect by cutting the pasta with a knife. Also, very fine semolina is used in place of the usual flour. I usually came across it served with a simple tomato sauce, with, on occasion, a touch of chili and some grated pecorino.

Serves 6

Pour the semolina with a pinch of salt on to a work surface and make a well in the centre. Beat the eggs and pour into the well. Mix the semolina, eggs and salt together using a fork, pulling the semolina into the egg from the sides. When it is well mixed, start kneading. The secret of success is in the kneading. Work at it for at least 20 minutes, until the dough is very springy, silky and elastic. Now let it stand for 15 minutes.

5½ cups very fine semolina

Salt

8 eggs

Break the dough into pieces and roll out each piece until it is about 1 inch thick. If you have a *chitarra*, press each rectangle of pasta dough through the wires with a rolling pin. Assuming you don't have one, dust the surface with more fine semolina, and roll it up like a carpet. Then cutting across the roll, slice it into fine strands perhaps 1 inch. Boil in salted water as you would do any fresh pasta, and serve with *sugo*, *ragù or salsa di castrato* .

SALSA DI CASTRATO

Sauce of castrated ram

Use the shoulder, neck or breast of lamb if castrated lamb is not ready to hand.

Serves 12

Finely chop the garlic and parsley. Bone out the meat, keeping the bone. Open out the meat and sprinkle with the garlic and parsley. Season, roll up and tie with string. Finely chop the onion, but leave the carrot and celery whole.

Heat the olive oil in an earthenware casserole, add the onion, carrot, celery and meat, and brown the meat all over. Add the wine and let it evaporate over high heat. Add the tomato sauce and the tomatoes. Cook over a gentle heat for 2 hours, stirring from time to time. Remove the carrot and celery with the meat and the bone. Use the sauce with *maccheroni alla chittara* and grated pecorino. Eat the meat separately.

4 garlic cloves

1 bunch parsley

2 1/2 lb lean castrated ram meat, in a piece on the bone

1 onion

1 carrot

1 stick celery

2/3 cup extra virgin olive oil

1 1/2 glasses (approximate 3/4-1 cup) of Montepulciano d'Abruzzo

1 quart tomato sauce

2 tomatoes, chopped

1 1/4 cups grated pecorino

7
OLIVE BRANCHES
AND POTATO
PASSIONS

GUARDIAGRELE – PENNE
ASCOLI PICENO

Olive all' ascolana

Even the inhabitants of Ascoli Piceno described it as 'barocco'. Indeed it was. The dainty involved splitting a large green local olive, the ascolana, *taking out the stone, stuffing it with a mixture of very finely minced pork, beef and chicken or turkey, rolling each one in very fine breadcrumbs and deep-frying them.*

It was time to move on again. I followed a road that ran north along the foothills of the Apennines, parallel to the sea, but some twenty kilometres from it.

Rolling through the sunshine in T-shirt and shorts, I came to the conclusion that the upright nature of the scooter suited the figure of the middle-aged British male rather better than the more crouched position of the motorcycle. Better still, alfresco transport came complete with a built-in air-conditioning system, which was a boon with the temperatures in the nineties day after day. I experimented to find exactly the right angle at which to stick out my elbows to allow a stream of fresh air to gush up my shirt sleeves. I was open, too, to the passing perfumes of lime trees, sweet chestnut and onions, and to the reek of cattle or sheep. The only drawback to scooter travel was being pebble-dashed with the bodies of flattened insects, although at the speed at which I travelled, this was less of a hazard than it might have been.

Although I was still in the Abruzzo, there was a distinct change as I moved north of the old Roman Via Tiburtina Valeria, which ran from Rome to Pescara. Quite suddenly, the haphazard smallholdings of Molise, the southern Abruzzo and further south, with their higgledy-piggledy olive groves and apple orchards ('Golden Delicious', if you please) underplanted with vegetables, vanished.

It was farewell to the south south, the south of smallholdings, traditional patterns of society and agriculture, of small communities, of deep conservatism and suspicion of the outside world, of herds of sheep moving freely between pastures, of tomatoes and onions and cheeses and bread, of pure, direct flavours, of simple dishes that rely on the virtues of the primary ingredients for their luminous beauty.

The terrain began to roll more, and took on the appearance of countryside familiar from Renaissance painting and modern film – hill after hill after hill in hazy silhouette. Each hilltop seemed to be crowned with a cluster of ancient towers and steeples. Between were handsome, square-shouldered villas and farmhouses, each with a dusty white track marked by cypresses shaped like watercolour paintbrushes leading to it, and vineyards, olive groves and sunflower fields.

The landscape was even more fully cultivated than further south. The holdings were bigger, the strip plantings of wheat, corn, vines and sunflowers wider, more orderly and more purposeful. The planted lines were longer and straighter, the crops less varied. The density of human occupation was greater, too, with more houses linking small villages – Cupoli, Roccafinadamo, Arsita, Bisenti, Villa Vomano. And the dreaded word supermarket suddenly appeared, albeit stuck on the outside of what in Britain would be considered small corner shops. Perhaps because supermarkets are the very antithesis of local identity and daily shopping, the vast, vacuous temples of commerce with which we are familiar had yet to make much of an impact in the part of Italy through which I had passed.

My next major goal was Ascoli Piceno, just over the border of Abruzzo in Le Marche, but I had decided to stop overnight on the way, on the urgent recommendation of my sister-in-law in Rome, so that I could try the food of La Bandiera, which, it seemed, came garlanded with every kind of glowing report.

With some difficulty I found it at the end of a long, rough and twisty track near Civitella Casanova, not far from Penne, where I had elected to stay. It was as improbable as it was sophisticated. It had something of the triple-Michelin-starred provincial French restaurant about it, with large, comfortable rooms full of furniture, pictures and curtains of well-bred and expensive pedigree.

The place was run by Marcello Spadone and Bruna Sablone, a husband-and-wife team. I suspected that she did the real cooking because he spent most of the evening fussing about the dining room in his chef's whites, taking orders and chatting up the customers, and he didn't know the answer when, later, I asked him what one of the ingredients was. Whoever was responsible for the cooking, the result was a stupendous dinner, with antipasti coming in battalions: a plate of ricotta with a little salad of rocket arugula with sliced raw *funghi porcini*, black truffle and slivers of Parmesan; a bit of grilled onion in *saba* (boiled must); a pizzetta, with a little selection of *salumi* on it; a frittata of herbs and black truffle, a kind of divine scrambled egg; and a plate on which there were a couple of slices of cow's milk cheese inside a very fine shell of tempura batter, with a little warm salad of potatoes and French beans.

There was a short reprieve before the arrival of *zuppa di virtù*, a broth with chickpeas, borlotti beans, pasta bits and vegetables, the fresh beauty of which belied its name – 'Know then this truth, enough for man to know, "Virtue alone is happiness below", ' as Alexander Pope put it. He was spot on, although I rather doubt that he had soup in mind when he wrote the lines.

After that came *maccheroni alla chitarra*, sauced this time with salt cod, broad beans and olives; and then roast lamb with a single large roast potato. Finally, all thoughts of hunger for at least a decade were put to one side by a light custard flavoured with Aurum, an orange liqueur from Pescara.

There was nothing really here that you might not have found on the menu of a dozen other restaurants, but each dish was made with such panache, the primary ingredients were, without exception, of astounding quality, and they were handled with a luminous intelligence. The refinement in the cooking came in the selection and the restrained use of highly skilled techniques to prepare them. The presentation, too, was different from the unconsidered plate arrangements of the average Italian restaurant. It wasn't artful, but it was considered, more French-influenced, with an eye for colour combinations.

But still, in essence, it was traditional cooking, albeit of a pretty polished kind. The dishes arose quite naturally out of agricultural convention, seasonal constraints and domestic thrift. Even the salt cod would once have been a dish of red-letter days, an ingredient for a community that rarely had access to fresh fish but had links to trade ports.

The French elevated the concept of haute cuisine as the pinnacle for cooks to strive towards, and then sold the idea to the rest of the world. Haute cuisine is, by definition, élitist and expensive, even if the tradition of French social democracy means that every Frenchman, *de haut en bas*, sees it as their natural right to eat at the finest tables. The Italians, by contrast, elevated the cooking of the agricultural classes to the position of honour, and this is now sought after in its purest forms, *dal basso in alto*. This was the natural consequence of emigration from country to town, which happened in its most concentrated form in the 1960s, a generation and a half ago.

Food, as well as language, carries the culture and history of a people, and, given the Italians' loyalty to locality, perhaps it is not surprising that that even thoroughly urbanised Italians retain a passion for the cooking of their place of birth.

There are, I know, restaurants in Italy where haute cuisine and *la cucina nuova*, the creative genius of the chef, find expression, but they are few and far between compared with the host of excellent and well-patronised restaurants that do not stir very far from strict orthodoxy. In this they are being no more than pragmatic, faithfully reflecting the expectations of their clientele. Even those who do have ambitions to evolve Italian cooking tend to run parallel menus, one listing the traditional dishes of an area, the other the chef's own creations.

In keeping with the absence of pretence in Italian food is an equal absence of formality, ritual or ponciness in the manner of the customers. Of course, there are restaurants of absurd formality, but they are rare. Generally speaking, whether at a classy establishment such as La Bandiera, or some more humble place, customers show a democratic independence in matters of dress code, even smart rich ones. Personal ease, it seemed to me, was the guiding principle for public eating in Italy. Eating well, treating yourself, your family, your friends, was as much a part of life as working or playing or sleeping.

Heady with pleasure, I mounted again, and steered back down the track. The air was full of the scents of summer, and the way was lit by fireflies.

According to André Gide, Ascoli Piceno is the most beautiful town in Italy. I wouldn't have gone that far, but it certainly had great charm and a quiet sense of past wealth. Quite a long way in the past, in fact. Ascoli grew rich under the Romans because it controlled the Via Flaminia Salaria, the old salt road between the coast and Rome, and the street grid has hardly changed since. Most of the handsomest buildings are the product of the thirteenth century, the city's most glorious period. After centuries of unbiddable independence, decline set in with the coming of papal rule in the fifteenth century.

Now, however, Ascoli seemed to be in the ascendant again, partly because of the agricultural richness of the hinterland, and partly because of the centralisation of local industry along the River Tronto. Walking round Ascoli, I came across bits of Roman, bits of Longobard, bits of every century between the thirteenth and the twentieth, if you counted the industrial belt. The sight of a youth shooting up in the reconstructed Roman guardhouse on the bridge over the Torrente Castellano by the Castello Malatesta seemed to telescope past and present. Even in Sulmona, the sense of history was relatively one--, or possibly two--, dimensional by comparison.

Italian towns appear to have a happy knack of accommodating the demands of the twenty-first century without wholesale destruction of what went before. Tourists are carefully corralled into designated areas, as if they are animals of rather uncertain temperament, to be kept docile by culture, large quantities of ice cream and the civilising qualities of the cafés.

The Caffè Meletti in the Piazza del Popolo could have been the model for the Café Momus in Puccini's *La Bohème*. This was the palace that liquorice built. Aniseed grows plentifully in the area, and found its way into local consumption through a liqueur incorporating it. Indeed, the legend that runs across the pink front of the building reads 'Anisetti Meletti'. The café's recent history had been chequered, and it had to be rescued from genteel decay by a local bank, but, restored, revived and revitalised, it would stand out in Rome, Paris, Milan, Turin, New York, London, anywhere. It was suave, but not chic. It was scenic, but did not pose. It had a tremendous confidence, but it didn't swagger. It took up one quarter of one side of the Piazza del Popolo, a side which it shared with the magnificent Palazzo dei Capitani, but was not diminished by it.

The floor was well-polished wood. The ceiling high above was decorated in a fairly loose Art Deco pattern in green on a mottled yellow background. At one end was a colossal mirror, at the other a bar displaying panini and other things to eat. There was a second bar surmounted by bottles running down part of the wall opposite the entrance, which was situated right in the centre of the long front. Half the floor space was empty, and the other half full of tables with gracefully curving bentwood chairs.

The waiters had that casual professionalism that distinguishes Italian service. It hovered on the brink of laconic dismissal, but dropped into engaged charm at the slightest encouragement. Over a Campari, I watched these exemplars at their trade. Italians make the best maîtres d'hôtels in the world. It's all in the walk, the leisurely, relaxed but purposeful glide, the quick flick of the foot straightening the trouser at the end of each stride, in preserving immaculate poise and allowing plenty of time for the head to swivel and the eye to catch any small happening. Men practise this from birth in piazzas and streets all over Italy; and in restaurants from Manhattan to Melbourne, where it is exported along with emigrants searching for work.

From there it was a casual wander to the Ristorante Vittoria. I inspected two trattorie recommended by the tourist office, but didn't like the look of either of them. Much too modern for my taste, and I could never trust a restaurant that offers *bistecca alla fiorentina* outside Tuscany, risotto outside Lombardy, *bollito misto* outside Piedmont or *pasta asciutta* north of the Abruzzo.

The Ristorante Vittoria had none of that nonsense. It was a prime example of the kind of watering hole of which, once, you would have found two or three in every Italian town – cool and airy, with white or near white walls, much-laundered tablecloths and a single waiter, a worn man in his fifties who knew the regulars and their habits, and who ran the dining room with a kind of weary excellence. The menu in such places changed no more than he did over the years, so here it was an antipasto of cold veg, and *spaghetti all ascolana* (tomato, minced tuna and green olives), *fritto misto ascolana* (fried stuffed olives, fried battered zucchini, oddly sweet and fruity squares of custard) and a thin, breadcrumbed lamb chop.

Had I known what lay in store for me at dinner at the Villa Cicchi, I might have passed on lunch altogether.

The Villa Cicchi was another *azienda agriturismo* of great charm. I don't suppose it had ever been more than the well-to-do establishment of a gentleman farmer. The house was rambling and extensive, with a vast and splendid cellar that ran the full length of the building. The house was probably made up of several small buildings knocked together some time around 1740, that's when the estate's chapel was built. It had obviously fallen into disrepair: the owners were still restoring some rooms in considerable late eighteenth- early nineteenth-century style. It seemed that this was a labour of love for the late Signor Cicchi, who had died suddenly the previous year, leaving Signora Cicchi, a handsome, careworn lady, and two grown-up daughters, Elena and Beatrice, to run the place, along with the help of their husbands and a changing rota of ladies.

I got the feeling that the late Signor Cicchi had been a generous man of considerable kindness and appetite for life. He was a great supporter of classical music in the area; there were a number of cats, known as *'gli abbandonati'*, which he had insisted on feeding and which still frequented the villa's gardens; and his two daughters were very independent, freethinking types. The villa also housed almost as many old women as there were cats. They moved like shadows among the private rooms.

Apart from the house and the considerable terraced gardens, the main part of the estate was below the house, separated from it by a road, where there were vines, olives trees, vegetables, and the rabbits, chickens and pheasants that found their way to the table. The area wasn't large, a few hectares, but it produced enough wine, oil and food for the house and its guests. There would have been something of distressed gentle-folk about the Cicchi family, but for the fact that they tackled the *agriturismo* business together, and with such vigour. And that night, Saturday, was the night of the big blow-out. Behind the scenes, in kitchen and in larder, the chaotic ballet of food preparation was in full swing.

In the main kitchen, Nonna, Signora Cicchi's mother, was gently stirring a sauce of goose and tomato to go with *maccheroni alla chitarra*. A second pot, filled with sliced *funghi porcini* speckled with chopped parsley to sauce some *tagliatelle*, rested quietly to one side.

'Is there a choice of pasta tonight?' I asked innocently.

Nonna looked surprised. 'No,' she said. 'Everyone will expect all three.'

'Three?' I was alarmed.

'Yes,' she said. 'There's a lovely ravioli filled with ricotta and herbs as well. You will eat very well tonight.'

Oh, God, I thought.

I lifted the top off a casserole. 'What's this?'

'Braised pheasant, to go with roast potatoes.'

Give me strength, I thought.

Beside the cooker was a plate piled with *olive ascolane*, ready to be fried. Even the inhabitants of Ascoli Piceno described it as '*barocco*'. Indeed it was. The dainty involved splitting a large green local olive, the *ascolana*, taking out the stone, stuffing it with a mixture of very finely minced pork, beef and chicken or turkey, rolling each one in very fine breadcrumbs and deep-frying them. Most people had delegated the production of them to local factories, but having eaten the real thing, made by hand at the Villa Cicchi, I could say that there was no comparison. The mass-produced version was less stuffed, less plump and tended to dryness, while the custom-built version was the size of a pheasant's egg, moist and weighty. No one seemed to really know how this masterpiece of the olive turner's art came about. It suddenly appeared on dinner plates 200 years ago. One theory held that it represented the union between the daughter of an olive grower and the son of a butcher, but who knows? From the oven wafted the rich, complex odours of *coniglio 'ncip 'nciap*, roasting stuffed rabbit.

At the sink, Signora Cicchi stoically washed dishes. Beatrice was slicing zucchini, later to be dipped in batter and fried. Beside her were several tarts: crostata di limone and crostata di marmellata di fichi. They didn't look exactly light-weight, either.

Elena, six months pregnant, was piling slices of bread with a mixture of pork, herbs, capers and vinegar as *crostini*. In the corner her grandmother was cutting more bread for the table.

In the larder Coco, the family's old cook, was making ravioli, as she had been doing for an unguessable number of years. She had a face like a cheerful frog, and a short muscular body.

'It's just flour and eggs, just flour and eggs and lots of work, lots of work,' she said. She grinned. Her dialect was hard to understand. The dough was yellow from the colour of the yolks. It had a satiny plasticity. She had worked it for twenty minutes, she said, maybe more, and then let it rest.

She cut a hunk off a large loaf of dough, and flattened it slightly before feeding it into a little hand-operated pasta roller. It went through easily enough, at the thickness of a silk tie. She dusted it lightly with flour, folded it up and fed it through again.

Beatrice came in. 'What are the numbers tonight, Mamma?'

Her mother lifted her eyebrows and pressed the back of her hand against her forehead. 'There's one table of six, an eight, a four and two twos. And another four.'

Coco altered the setting to make the next rolling thinner. Through it came again, draped over the back of her hand as she led it from the roller and laid it down on the wooden board that ran down from the roller like a scarf, with the elegant minimalism of long practice. It was now the thickness of a heavy cotton shirt. She altered the setting a third time, cut the scarf into two, dusted it again, and fed it through for the last time. It came out like tissue.

'That's how it should look,' she said. 'Smooth.'

Deftly she plopped scoops of the ricotta and herb mixture

down the middle at regular intervals.

Sandro, Elena's husband, came in with several bottles of wine. 'This should be enough,' he said.

Coco folded the scarf of pasta over on itself, trapping the ricotta and herbs in the fold. Then she pressed down on the pasta between each rounded mound with the side of her hand. She took the pasta cutter and worked swift semicircles round each mound. She stripped off the superfluous dough and there were eight ravioli, not quite regular, but plump and neat.

Elena came, picked them up and placed them quickly on a tray covered in a clean drying-up cloth. She went back to her business of making the *crostini*.

Several hours later, I retired to bed, defeated. I fell at the hurdle presented by crostata di marmellata di fichi. I had eaten too many *olive ascolane* earlier.

The SS16 ran parallel to the coast through Porto d'Ascoli, San Benedetto del Tronto and Grottamare, to name a few of the coastal resorts, quite as seedy and ramshackle as those on our own south coast. Even among the urban slurry of car dealerships, mobile phone agencies, Blockbuster shops, Sport bars and Twinky nightclubs on either side of it, there was the occasional gem. The Osteria Caserma Guelfa was one of them.

The eighteenth-century building in which the restaurant was housed was particularly handsome, a former customs post near where the old Roman Via Salaria met the coastal road. It was made of narrow bricks, the exterior battered by the fumes of passing traffic, but the inside was airy, with high arched rooms. It was a fish restaurant run with bustling brio by Federico Palestrino, once a fisherman who had given up the unequal struggle with the elements and declining catches in favour of shore life.

It was 9:15 p.m. I sat waiting for Francesco's friend, Sandro, who was going to take me down to the port at Ascoli to watch the fishing boats come in. Francesco and one other waiter brought a succession of plates to other tables – marinated little rock red mullet and anchovies; octopus salad; *carpaccio* of smoked tuna; oysters; poached mantis shrimp; deep-fried soft-shell crabs. 'Simple food,' Francesco told me. 'Just the kind of stuff the fishermen eat themselves.' I ate a plate of grilled fish – a tiny sole, a single *langoustine*, a roll of squid, a small monkfish tail. The fierce, brief carbonisation had brought out a caramel sweetness in the very fresh fish. Bread, salad and half a carafe of the house's white wine completed my dinner.

'He is on his way,' said Francesco, mopping his brow and the back of his neck. It was 9:45 p.m.

Sandro appeared at 10 p.m. He was a short, amiable young man, with fine black hair standing up like a long crew cut and at least one day's stubble on his very sunburnt cheeks. He seemed quite relaxed about the lateness of his arrival.

'It's not a problem,' he said. 'The boats I am interested in won't be in until eleven, eleven fifteen.'

We changed from a large estate car into a little Fiat van near the shop he co-owns with Francesco.

'This is the one I take to the port,' he said mysteriously.

I guessed he didn't want to flaunt his respectability and prosperity in front of his ex-colleagues, or give them reason to charge him higher prices for their fish. He, too, had been a fisherman, like his father and grandfather before. 'My family used to have three boats, but when my uncle died, well, that was the end. Anyway, now I have children. I don't want to be away all the time. It's too hard.'

The port was a single, medium-sized basin, separated from the open sea by a long sea wall. It was very dark, and thick cloud covered the stars and moon. The light from a lighthouse a couple of kilometres away travelled relentlessly round and round, its reflection oscillating over the corrugated surface of the sea.

Along one part of the quay were half-a-dozen or so fishing boats, dark and still on the shiny, black, plastic surface of the harbour water. The long outer wall glimmered softly beyond them.

'These have been decommissioned,' said Sandro. 'EU restrictions.'

Just along from them, the day boats were moored, three

abreast. They were small, purposeful craft with nothing pretty or fanciful about them. They went out at daybreak to fish the inshore waters for scampi, prawns, rock red mullet, small octopus and the myriad tiny fish that are used in a *fritto misto*, the ubiquitous dish of fish fried in a light batter. Their day was finished by the afternoon. Beyond them, like a whale among dolphins, was a *tonnara*, a tuna boat, dark and rocking.

A large fishing boat quietly sidled up to an empty mooring, its decks a sulphurous yellow under sodium lighting.

'Ho, Giovà.'

'Ho, Matté. Loré. Riccà.' The rest was lost in a blast of dialect.

The unloading began within a few minutes of docking, a human chain bringing up box after box of scampi, scabbard fish, bream, octopus and anchovies from below deck. Each box was full of neatly packed fish beneath a film of transparent plastic and a layer of mushed ice. Some of the boxes went straight into the back of a refrigerated truck; some were stacked up on a trolley, on one of the long shafts of which sat a carbuncular old man with a commanding presence.

Sandro went up to him and whispered earnestly in his ear.

'Eh, Matté.' He gestured me over. 'This is the *capo*,' he said. 'He used to be a captain. Not any more.'

'I have three sons who are captains,' said the old man. 'And two daughters who keep the books. They are good at those things. They have a head for detail, women.'

The light from the deck of the boat lit up the faces and arms of the men working and the hangers about, as in a painting by Luca Giordano. The air smelt of diesel, sea and fish.

Sandro waited his turn. He needed to buy specific boxes, not the big-number fish, but the select, high-price fish – the best scampi, monkfish, red mullet, John Dory, gurnard. He took the boxes containing them and piled them up on the quay. He went back and whispered in the *capo's* ear. A short bout of haggling took place. The *capo* scribbled on a piece of paper and handed it to Sandro.

'Now we have to go to another boat,' he said. He explained he only bought the fish from two boats. Each buyer had a special relationship with particular boats. The port itself, the landings, were run by two or three families. '*Sono tutti bravi ragazzi,*' said Sandro. 'They're all good blokes.'

The main fish auction would begin later over in a huge building like an amphitheatre. The fish would be shipped off to the markets in Rome, Milan, Naples, Turin and Ancona. By that time, Sandro would be long gone. Even so, his wife would not be happy. 'I get back at 2 a.m., 3 a.m. She is cross about that. But we get used to it. It is better than being at sea.'

The polystyrene boxes were already flowing from the other boat. We waited patiently, half in darkness, half in light. Sandro watched each of the boxes. They squeaked as they were piled on top of each other.

I said that I thought the fish looked pretty small. Sandro said that was the way with the fish in the Adriatic. The big fish were out in the Mediterranean.

The red mullet and monkfish he needed were among the last to be offloaded. When they came, he rejected the mullet. They were too big, he said. One of the fishermen shrugged and slid the box of red mullet on to a trolley.

We went back to the old *capo* for another bout of haggling. At last the terms were settled. Sandro loaded the boxes into the back of the van.

'The sea has changed since I used to go out,' the old capo said, resting on a fish trolley. 'I used to go all over the Mediterranean. We used to catch the prawns off Tunisia, quite close in. They were this big.' He extended one forefinger and marked the length off with the other. It was about ten centimetres. 'Then the currents changed and they became small,' he marked about two centimetres, 'and not very good, so we had to go out further and fish deeper to catch the big ones.'

A fishing boat backed off its mooring, and slid off into the night. Another one quietly took its place. More refrigerated vans gathered around it, like gulls. The unloading began again.

The night before I left the Villa Cicchi, I dined with the family and with Don Pepe, the priest, who was to officiate at the christening of Beatrice's daughter. He bore an uncanny resemblance to the *capo* in John Huston's film *Prizzi's Honor*, even down to the hoarse, harsh, breathy voice.

The first thing that Don Pepe did upon sitting down was to announce that he had to eat right away. 'I am finished by nine o'clock,' he said. 'I just go to sleep. I don't eat much.'

He proceeded to help himself to a great mound of crushed potato, yellow from the oil it contained, mellow with garlic and parsley. 'This is very fine potato,' he announced, shovelling down several forkfuls. 'Simply wonderful potato. Where did these potatoes come from?'

And that was it. Away they went, chatting about potatoes, all thoughts of the christening banished.

'They're Sicilian,' said Signora Cicchi.

'They've got just the right texture,' said Don Pepe.

'They're the best. I always think that Sicilian potatoes are the best for mash. Last year we tried some local ones, and they weren't so good.'

'Three years ago in Puglia we had some very good ones.'

'But were they as good as these?'

'Maybe not quite so good.'

'Sergio and I ate wonderful potatoes in Amandola, didn't we, Sergio? Do you remember?'

'Those were different. Those were roasted.'

'On the other hand, these wouldn't do for gnocchi. For gnocchi Coco insists on—' I didn't quite catch the name of the variety.

For forty minutes they discussed potatoes. The Italians bring the same matter-of-fact passion to food that the English do to the weather. They report on what they ate at the last meal, comment on what they are currently eating and speculate on what they might eat on the morrow. It wasn't hard to be beguiled by such lucid enthusiasm.

EATING UP ITALY

Recipes

OLIVE ASCOLANE

Olives Ascoli style

This recipe and all but one of the others in this chapter come from the generous, joyous Cicchi family. The complexity of this antipasto makes clear the difference between the cooking of the south and that of central and northern Italy. It is an incredible amount of work for a nibble that will probably last no more than a second, but it is a true labour of love – or a labour of true love. You really need the mild giant green Ascolano olives that grow in the area.

Makes 60 stuffed olives

Heat some olive oil in a pan. Add the ground meats and the lemon zest, a dusting of nutmeg and salt and pepper and fry for 3 minutes. Stir in the white wine and cook gently for 30–40 minutes. Cool.

Add the Parmesan, parsley and 2 of the 5 eggs. Stir thoroughly. Give it a quick whizz in a food processor if you think the mixture is too coarse. Stone the olives any way you can, but you must leave the flesh in one piece. Stuff each olive with a squidge of filling, pushing them back into an olive shape. Beat the remaining eggs. Dust the olives in flour, dip them in the beaten eggs, roll them in breadcrumbs and deep fry in olive oil until golden brown. Drain on kitchen towel.

Olive oil

4 oz finely ground pork

4 oz finely ground beef

4 oz finely ground chicken
or turkey

Grated zest of 1 lemon

Nutmeg

Salt and pepper, to taste

1 glass (1/2- 2/3 cup) of dry
white wine

1/2 cup grated Parmesan

3 tablespoons parsley,
chopped

5 eggs

60 very large green olives

Flour

Bread crumbs

RAVIOLI CON RICOTTA ED ERBE

Ravioli with ricotta and herbs

Serves 4

Make the filling. Boil the chard in as little unsalted water as possible for 5 to 7 minutes. When cooked, rinse in cold water, drain and squeeze out as much water as possible. Chop finely. Chop the herbs finely. Mix with the ricotta, Parmesan and the egg yolk, and chill for 30 minutes or so.

Make pasta dough in the normal way, and roll out into flat sheets. Beat the whole egg. Plonk a small dollop of mixture at regular intervals on the pasta sheets. Paint around them with the beaten egg. Lay a second sheet on top. Press down around the little mounds of filling to seal them in. Cut out with a pasta cutter. Cook in the usual way, and serve with a fresh tomato sauce or on their own.

1 1/2 cups pasta

1 egg

For Filling

4 oz chard

1 bunch of mixed parsley, basil and marjoram, finely chopped

2/3 cup fresh sheep's milk ricotta

1/3 (generous) cup grated Parmesan

1 egg yolk

CROSTATA DI MARMELLATA DI FICHI

Fig preserve tart

Serves 6

Mix the flour, confectioner's sugar, butter and lard in a bowl. Add the whole eggs and the lemon juice. Work the mixture as lightly as possible, adding a little cold milk if too dry. Wrap the pastry in plastic wrap, and put in the fridge to rest for an hour.

Wash and dry the figs, and chop them finely. Put them into a nonreactive bowl – glass, porcelain or earthenware – with the sugar. Leave to macerate for at least 2 hours.

Remove to a saucepan (or leave in earthenware). Bring to the boil and cook until setting point is reached. Remove from the heat and stir in the lemon juice.

Heat the oven to 350°. Grease a pie plate with butter. Roll out the pastry and line the dish with it. Spread the fig marmellata over the pastry, as thick or as thin as you like. Trim off any surplus pastry, press together and roll out again, then cut into strips and lay across the top of the *marmellata*. Beat the egg yolk and glaze the pastry strips. Bake for 30–45 minutes until the pastry is golden.

For the pastry

3 cups plain flour

1½ cups confectioner's sugar

3/4 cup softened butter

1/4 cup lard

2 whole eggs

Juice of 1 lemon

A little cold milk, if needed

For the marmellata

2½ lbs. very ripe figs

3½ cups sugar

Juice of 1 lemon

Assembly and Baking

1 egg yolk

BRODETTO SANBENEDETTESE

Fish stew from San Benedetto del Tronto

On the north and central Adriatic coast, zuppa di pesce *is called* brodetto. *Different but closely related to* caciucco *and* buridde *from the Tyrrhenian coast, this dish has spawned legends, and there are fiercely defended local claims as to its invention, authenticity and unique qualities. The true origin is that it was made on board the fishing boats as a way to use up the rejected fish, and there are as many recipes as there are fishing ports. This recipe is one interpretation, from the restaurateur/fisherman Federico Palestini. It is characterised by its heightened acidity (green tomatoes and vinegar), a legacy of the days when it was necessary to take unripe vegetables on the fishing boats so they would keep longer, and when the fishermen did not drink wine but a mixture of water and vinegar known as masa. I have identified the fish as best I can, but local dialect will defeat even so great an authority as Alan Davidson, whose Mediterranean Seafood is still the standard text in these matters. Basically, use a mix of fish and shellfish.*

The brodetto *takes 2 hours to prepare, plus an extra 4 or 5 hours to stand.*

Serves 10

Clean all the fish carefully and with patience. As well as taking out the insides, remove the backbones, gills, any scales and odd bones. Wash and dry the fish and cut the larger fish into chunks.

In a saucepan large enough to hold all the fish, gently fry the finely chopped onion in olive oil. Add the cuttlefish and octopus, and toss them in the oil until they begin to colour. Moisten with the white wine

1 white onion, finely chopped

2/3 cup extra virgin olive oil

1 glass (1/2 – 2/3 cup)
    of dry white wine

2 glasses (1-1 1/3 cup)
    of white wine vinegar

3 peppers – 1 each yellow,
    red and green

3 underripe tomatoes

1 slice of slightly stale bread

1 teaspoon of salt

and cook gently for 15 minutes.

Pour the vinegar over the mixture in the pan and cook until it has evaporated. Add the peppers and tomatoes cut into pieces and a ladleful of water. Allow to cook for a further 10 minutes.

Now put all the remaining fish into the pan in layers. Cover everything with water and cook for a further 10–15 minutes without touching or stirring the fish, but just giving the pan a good shake every now and then.

Transfer the contents of the pan to a large terra-cotta dish and leave it to rest for several hours, preferably half a day, before reheating and serving on lightly toasted slices of bread placed in the bottom of soup plates.

6¾ lb fish or shellfish of the following sorts: cuttlefish, octopus, tracina (weaver fish), scorfano (scorpion fish), bocca in capo (star-gazer), mazzolina, mackerel, sauro, angler fish, dogfish, mullet, skate, murmure (only in summer)

8
PULSES FROM THE OLD YEAR
ASCOLI PICENO
SERRA DE' CONTI
PORTONOVO – ANCONA

Cicerchia

The cicerchia, a peculiar and particularly primitive pulse [legume], a kind of proto-chickpea that looked like gravel, had a mild, mushroomy flavour and a mealy texture.

In the morning I left the kindly Cicchi family. They were working themselves up into a frenzy for the christening.

As I was about to ride off, Signora Cicchi came bustling up carrying a basket of peaches and plums. 'But you can't go until I've packed you some of our peaches for your travels. They really are very special,' she said. 'Completely untouched by any chemical, and no one seems to know what variety there are.' They were quite small and dark, almost black. 'And Sergio has sent over some of his family's plums, too.'

I ate them both later, beside the road that runs through the high passes between Ascoli Piceno and Treia, just beyond Macerata, in the dappled shade of a walnut tree. The plums were blue and very sweet, and the peaches had a sublime, perfumed delicacy.

Le Marche occupies a curious position in Italian cultural geography. For southern Italians, the country is divided between the south and the north. For northern Italians it is the same. Inhabitants of both lament the shortcomings of the other. Northern Italians see the southern Italians as bone idle, and the south – everywhere below Tuscany and Emilia-Romagna – as a sink of corruption, a drain on the country's resources and a drag on the prosperity and progress of the north. The southerners, conversely, see the northerners as crude colonisers and exploiters little different from the tyrants who had enslaved the south for centuries. For southerners, the north begins at the border of Campania. So Italy is a country with no middle.

While the Abruzzesi and Molesani would qualify as honorary southerners by virtue of their relative poverty and fundamentally agricultural societies, the Marchigiani would be horrified to be classified as such, as, I expect, would be the Laziali on the other side of the country. They see themselves as quite as hard working as their northern neighbours. Their cooking, too, has something of the complexity and voluptuousness of the north, although their agricultural production still seems to be linked spiritually to that further south.

When I reached the Marche, coming up from the south, a change suddenly came over the cooking. The direct simplicity that characterised dishes as far as the Abruzzo was gone. Pasta was no longer pasta asciutta, but *pasta Fresca*, fresh pasta made with eggs. Cheese was paired with meat. There were dishes such as *olive all'ascolana* and *vincisgrassi*, the fabulous layered pasta of meat and cheese, which was as rich as its name sounded. For the first time, there began to be layers of flavour to match the layers of history.

I turned off the main road at Monte Vidon Combatte, a small village on top of a hill overlooking the flat, fertile Aso valley, with its patchwork of apple orchards and groves of nectarines and peaches, its fields of sunflowers, toasted wheat and sugar beet, its sense of order and industry. I was drawn not by the promise of fruit and veg but by the lure of porky perfection, *salumi* in the form of *ciauscolo, salame lardellato* and prosciutto.

The Salumeria Passamonti occupied the ground floor of a large eighteenth-century building, part of which used to be a convent on the edge of the village. It was lunchtime, and the whole family – father Girolamo, mother Linda, daughter Clotilde, son Candido, Candido's wife, and two family retainers who worked in the family's vineyards and olive groves were eating lunch in the informal eating room next to the kitchen, with its shiny marblised floor and shiny dark cupboards and dressers. The television was not on, for once. Instead, everyone was playing up to the antics of Candido's four-year-old son Matteo.

Lunch was not elaborate – a tasting plate of the Passamonti *salumi* and ham; *penne al sugo*; slices of cold *porchetta* with rosemary and wild fennel packed into its crannies and crevices; steamed *courgettes* sliced lengthways, doused in oil; wilted green spinach or chard; nectarines, peaches and apricots, which the Marchigiani, like the Abruzzesi, seem to prefer semi-ripe and crunchy. The wine came from the estate, like the olive oil, and the porchetta came from downstairs.

The talk was about pigs, pork, hams and salamis, because that's what the Passamontis do, cure hams, make *ciauscolo, salame lardellato, salame magro, salamella* and *lonzino*; they are famous for them and have been famous for them for decades and decades. These are the pinnacle of porky products, gold medallists, award winners, the standard by which others are judged. Girolamo – Giro to all and sundry – had retired, although he manned the shop downstairs and charmed the customers. Candido ran the establishment, cured the hams, made the salamis and did the talking. He, not his father, sat at the end of the table, his round, smooth tanned face with a hint of high colour around his cheeks, his eyes watchful behind his rimless spectacles and bright with the nature of his obsession.

'We only make the *salumi* between 1 September and 31 March,' he said, as he showed me round the work areas, clean, tidy and quiet. 'That is when the weather is cold and dry enough. If it is too wet, that is not good for the hams and salamis. And we have to be very careful because we don't use preservatives of any kind, just salt and pepper, and the juice of garlic and whatever flavourings are particular to each sausage or product.

'The pigs are Middle Whites, because they have a good layer of fat in them, and they all come from local farms within fifteen kilometres from here, so we know how they've been kept and what they've been fed on. That is very important in the quality. You have to be quite certain about every stage. A lot of the pork used in the commercial salami comes from Germany and Eastern Europe, and you have no idea how it has been treated.' Each observation was energised by an uncalculating passion.

The Passamontis made only 600 hams a year, and each ham took two years to ripen slowly in the hanging chambers above the shop. But before being hung up to mature, they were salted for four weeks, and then hung in a room where a fire in an open fireplace helped to dry and lightly smoke the meat for forty-eight hours for the smaller *salamis*, three or four months for the prosciutti. Then they were transferred to racks in a second cold room to hang like giant fruit in the tranquil gloom, gradually darkening as they aged, developing their sweetness and power.

'Then we test them to see if they are ready, with a *spinto*,' said Candido. A *spinto* was a probe made of a horse's tibia, whittled to a sharp point. It was thrust into the ham at specific spots, withdrawn and smelt. The smell indicated whether or not the ham was ready to be sliced. 'There are three places to test, but actually you can tell just from the smell of the fat.' He held it to my nose. The smell was clean and rich and sweet.

'In Parma, they use smaller hams, and they are cured for only maybe a year, maybe less. The hams we use are much larger, and so they take longer to mature. But the flavour is better.' There was no doubt in his voice, and he was right. When the prosciutto was sliced into thin, silky folds, each fold was the colour of pink coral, edged by a wide ruff of snowy fat. The flavour of the ham crept around the corners of my mouth, sweet as cream, salty, fruity, minerally, subtle, teasing and potent. The flavours lingered long after the last shred had disappeared.

In another cool, dark room hung the *salame lardellato*, with a thick square of fat running down it; *salame magro*, with its finer mix of fat and meat; *lonzino*, cured fillet; *lonzino steso*, rolled up, elongated and thin, made deliberately dense and chewy so that the action of the teeth on the meat released the flavourings; and the most traditional of local salamis, the semi-soft *ciauscolo*, in its natural casing, like the other salamis, and flavoured with grated fennel, garlic and *vino cotto*, or *misto fegato*, which contained 20 per cent liver, grated orange peel, nutmeg and *vino cotto* – wine which is reduced to a nerve-tingling intensity by boiling it down (and which by law can only be produced in and around Ascoli Piceno). Each salame or product was differentiated as much by the cut of pork that went into it as by the added flavourings, but this worked to the advantage of the salumeria.

'*Non viene sprecato niente*,' said Candido. 'Nothing is wasted. The bits we don't use for this, we can use for that.' He gave a *salame lardellato* an affectionate squeeze, and closed the door of the maturing room.

⁓

It was blowy and cool when I left Treia, where I had been staying. There was a touch of rain in the wind. After days of languid sunshine, I had forgotten what cooler weather was like. It was back to long trousers, socks, motorcycle jacket and gloves, and even then I didn't feel too warm.

I stopped at the Saturday market at San Severino Marche, held in the Piazza Mercato below the old town. It didn't have the bustle of Naples or the social cheer of Ascoli Piceno, but it was busy enough. There was a constant flow of cars dropping off shoppers and picking them up. The stalls all seemed to me to be run by professional market traders. They were large and well stocked – melons from Romagna, apples from Trentino, local peaches. There were vast speckled watermelons, too, cut open to show their shimmering pinky-red flesh, and rounded pale purple aubergines and cannellini beans still in their white pods slashed with red. There were, I suppose, fifteen stalls, all but three of them devoted to fruit and veg. The other three sold *porchetta*, salami, cheese, salted anchovies in large tins, salt cod and *stocca-fisso* (wind-dried cod or haddock), and tiny cuttlefish and octopus deep-fried in batter. One of the stallholders gave me some to taste. They were crunchy and rather good.

He was a large, burly man, jowls darkly stubbled, a standard-issue rimless white catering hat straining around his head. He told me that he used to drive trucks delivering plastic goods to 'Corby, Birmingham, Manchester, Nottingham. *Molto bella*, Nottingham. *Molto bella.*' He didn't drive any more. Now all this *'è mio'* – he gestured to the long-sided wagon with its built-in oven and frying equipment.

It wasn't a bad life, he said, not too hard at all, a different market every day, except Sunday, all around Macerata

– Castelraimondo, Cingoli, Fiuminata, Petriolo. The markets were good, he said, in good shape, did good business.

For how much longer? I wondered. Certainly there were enough markets, one every day of the week in a different town or village. But they started at seven or eight in the morning and closed at one, the hours when most modern couples were powering their way to, or at, work. In reality the customer base must have been declining. Only retired couples or the rare non-working parent had the time to visit them. Shops, on the other hand, ran their hours of business to suit the lives of their customers. As I had found in Naples. They opened early, closed between 1 p.m. and 4 or 5 p.m., opened again, and then closed finally at 7 or 8 p.m., as did supermarkets. Of course, in Britain most food shops operate to suit the shopkeeper, not the client. They open all the hours that their customers are at work, and close promptly when they are returning home. No wonder supermarkets have such an easy time of it in the UK.

The measured hubbub was suddenly broken by the raucous din of a tinny Tannoy strapped to the roof of a car announcing the joys of a festival of erotica in Macerata. The Saturday shoppers didn't seem that interested.

I bought a bag of early figs. They didn't have that glorious musky sweetness of the ripe fruit in full season, but they were a pleasant reminder of the inherent seasonality of Italian eating.

> The proper way to eat a fig, [wrote D. H. Lawrence]
> Is to split it into four, holding it by the stump,
> And open it, so that it is a glittering, rosy, moist,
>   honied, heavy petalled flower.
> Then you throw away the skin
> Which is just like a four-sepalled calyx,
> After you have taken off the blossom with your lips.
>
> But the vulgar way
> Is just to put your mouth to the crack, and take
>   out the flesh in one bite.

Vulgar is better, but first I like to gently squeeze the top half of the fig, so that the crack at the bottom widens, and pearly fig juice begins to gather in it, and then to suck flesh, pearls of juice and all into my mouth.

I was doing this when a man stopped to chat about my scooter.

Was it expensive? he asked. It was, I said. But it's a good machine, he said. Very good, I said. The best, he said, staring at it. After a while he bid me good day. *'Belle cose,'* he wished me; beautiful things.

The beautiful things took a little while to materialise. The weather turned cool and showery. The shaded trails of the mountains had been a blessed relief when the weather was sun-blastingly hot, but in chill damp their attractions were substantially reduced. Cold had a nasty way of finding a way through the cracks and along the hidden pathways of clothing to the inner body. The road was slippery, and led upwards most of the time, requiring constant concentration, and, with my visor down against the rain, my horizons dropped from the panoramic to the immediate until I reached Serra de' Conti in the Colli del Verdicchio just beyond Jesi, and the courteous comforts of the Hotel de' Conti.

Gianfranco Mancini, the proprietor of the Hotel de' Conti, said, 'I am not interested in giving people food just because they want to eat. Every food is a part of local culture. There is a story attached to every dish. As far as I am concerned, the *cicerchia* [a chickpea-like pulse] is as important a cultural monument as the Colosseum. It tells us something about our culture.'

He looked more like a computer technician than the keeper of the flame of tradition and local lore. He was a small, neat man, with neatly trimmed hair, a wide mouth and keen eyes behind large round rimless glasses. He was always immaculate in crisply ironed shirt and tie. He reminded me irresistibly of Fisher, the librarian in a television play of many years ago called *Robin Redbreast,* who turned out to be the leader of a local pagan sect which fattened up unwary individuals for ritual sacrifice in the interests of a good harvest.

'But,' he added, 'the locals don't order these dishes. Other Italians and tourists do.'

He talked lovingly about *lonzino di fichi* – dried figs and chopped almonds formed into a cylinder and wrapped in fig leaves, which is sliced like a salami. He showed me one sealed in a vacuum bag. When I commented that modern technology had come to the aid of a traditional food, he said not a bit of it. The Romans used to make *lonzino di fichi*, and kept them sealed inside the cleaned gut of certain fish so that they didn't dry out too much. But it was the *cicerchia* that caused his eyes to glow behind his steel-rimmed spectacles. The *cicerchia*, a peculiar and particularly primitive pulse, a kind of proto-chickpea that looked like gravel, had a mild, mushroomy flavour and a mealy texture.

'I remember my grandmother used to sow *cicerchia* in spring, along with her beans and chickpeas. She sowed them between rows of maize, to make best use of the space. We used to pull up the plants in August and hang the plants with their fat pods over a wall in the sun to dry. After a few days we would thresh them with a large flail. Then we would sit and sort the *cicerchia* peas by hand, sitting in the shade of a giant elm. But when my grandmother left us, the *cicerchia* also went out of our lives.

'Then, thirty years later, I heard that someone was growing them in a corner of the Verdicchio hills. They were the fine and tasty *cicerchia* of my childhood, and I decided to take up the tradition once more.'

So, as well as serving *cicerchia* and *farro* soup or *farro* spaghetti with *cicerchia* and a salad of vegetables in the restaurant in his hotel, once a year he organised *'una festa della cicerchia'*, to celebrate the humble pulse.

He sent me off to see Dino Salustro, who supplied some of the *cicerchia*. Dino's primary business was wine, and he was one of the stars of the revival of the reputation of Verdicchio wines, but among the hectares of vines and olive trees of the *azienda* Casalfarneto, he also devoted a small patch to the *cicerchia*.

'It is a hobby, not a business. You have to keep these things going or they will disappear, and once they have disappeared, they will never come back,' he said. While they were grown using modern techniques, the actual selection of the pulses was carried out, as it always had been, by women sitting around a table, carefully picking out each *cicerchia* by hand. The women were old now, and the youngsters didn't have the knowledge.

'The *contadini* used to grow the *cicerchie* on odd corners and slopes of the land,' he said. 'They were very much the food of the poor and important during the war and just after, because they were easy to grow, and grew where other pulses and vegetables would not. Those were hard years for people around here. Now they don't eat *cicerchia* because they don't want to be reminded of the hard times or their poverty.'

Everything about Italian food seemed to reach back into the past in one way or another, and some Marchigiani still had an instinctive respect for their culinary heritage. In that pragmatic fashion that seems to characterise all Italians, they also saw the clear connection between the maintenance of regional food cultures and tourism. People like Gianfanco Mancini and Dino Salustro managed to combine missionary zeal for the one with commercial canniness for the other. But there were other important forces at work – a sense of thrift and a passion for domestic cultivation.

We British think of ourselves as keen gardeners, but in truth we are neophytes compared with the Italians. In Italy there is scarcely a patch of land, on the edge of a field of wheat, between two lines of vines or along the kerb of a road, even on a corner outside a block of flats, that does not carry its complement of tomatoes, zucchini, lettuces, chicory, beans, basil and parsley.

The keepers of these kitchen gardens are, for the most part, retired men and women. 'What else have they got to do?' someone said to me. It keeps them active and out of trouble, and everyone gets to eat good vegetables. And the food culture hangs on.

Perhaps it is simply a manifestation of the respective geniuses of the two nations that the British grow things to look at while the Italians grow things to eat. Even when we grow vegetables, often it is for visual effect, not culinary delight, and giganticism is the defining criteria. An Italian would only grow a giant leek if it tasted nice.

The whole region around Serra de' Conti seemed to be in a ferment celebrating food and wine. There was the Sagra delle Tagliatellé in Passo Ripe, La Cucina è Memoria in Cingoli and Verdicchio in Festa at Montecarrotto. Even the Communist Party was getting in on the act, with food stalls at its celebrations at Moie.

Determined to play my part in the universal celebration, and to investigate the more cerebral side of the appetites, I rose bright and early to hurry off to Cingoli, *'il balcone delle Marche'*, about twenty-five kilometres away from Serra de' Conti, where there was a *convegno*, or conference, on the subject of *'La cucina specchio di vita e civiltà'* which I took to mean 'cooking as a mirror of life and civility', or something like that. I wondered how a convention with a title like that would go down in Kirby Lonsdale or Bury St Edmunds.

Halfway through the ride, I began to regret bitterly that I had set off. Rain speckled the visor of my helmet. I was chilled to the marrow. I could feel a damp patch spreading up my thighs. The sky was a uniform lowering grey that drained all colour from the landscape. The occasional distant flash of lightning did little to brighten my mood.

I just managed to make it to the slickly appointed conference room in the Palazzo Comunale in Cingoli before the rain really began to sluice down. I spared a brief thought for the hardy souls I had seen setting up stalls of local specialities in a square near by.

There were about thirty or so people at the start of proceedings, although this rose steadily throughout to about double that number, many of whom were seeking refuge from the downpour outside, I presumed. They were a sharply dressed crowd for the most part, wearing plenty of linen and smart shoes, mostly well-to-do, urban, I would guess.

The reason for all this activity became clear. The first three speakers represented various aspects of the tourist industry, and treated us to exhortations to the effect that food was the key to increasing tourism, and that the Marche had wine and food products second to none, etc.

I have always admired the fluency with which all Italians, irrespective of class, sex or age, seem to be able at the drop of a hat to hold forth at interminable length, without pause or even hesitation, and without notes. Words seem to flow from Italians in an effortless, baffling stream. It isn't so much a gush as a steady, musical abundance. Words are an interest-free currency, a limitless resource. Italians use language in the same way that Shakespeare used images, pouring out a sequence of dazzling phrases to describe or elaborate on a single idea.

It was difficult to know whether this fluency is inborn or a cultural inheritance. The Greeks had schools for public speaking, and the Romans rated oratory pretty highly – think of the reverence accorded Cato, Cicero and Tacitus; and Jacob Burkhardt demonstrates the importance of the humanist and religious preachers of the fifteenth and sixteenth centuries in *The Civilisation of Renaissance Italy*, where he devotes a chapter to them. So there has always been a tradition of logorrhoea, and the tradition is perpetuated by the Italian educational system, which calls for exams to be verbal. Consequently students are inculcated with the skills needed to express themselves fluently and coherently.

The men from the tourist boards were relatively restrained in comparison with the lady from the University of Rome, who rattled on about the medieval diet for half an hour in a relentless monotone. I slipped into a comfortable doze. Even the intent audience began to get restless, the volume of private conversations rising perceptibly towards the end. I am afraid that was enough for me. I could see that, what with the rain and the line of speakers still to come, luncheon was going to be delayed to an unacceptable hour, and the thought of trudging round the soggy stands had little appeal. So I opted for a return to base camp.

I was only about a quarter of the way home when I thought that I could get no colder or wetter. I was wrong. The rain came straight down out of the heavens. The road became a river. I could feel the water running down my legs inside my trousers into my shoes. My biker's jacket stuck to my shirt, which enveloped my chest and stomach in a chilled, clammy embrace. More water ran up my sleeves. Then I began to feel cold wetness spreading up my crutch as the speed of travel forced a tide of rain up the saddle and into my trousers. What could I do but laugh?

When I reached the hotel, I was appalled to see that the car park was full and a line of smartly dressed people were queuing up under umbrellas to go through the front door. For a moment I wondered what kind of figure I was going to cut among the celebrating gentry of Serra de' Conti, but not for long. I could bear my discomfort no longer. I squelched across the reception area, leaving a trail of puddles on the marble floor and a few very dubious faces behind me, and made for my room, safety, warmth and dry clothing.

But I was still hungry, so I made my way back downstairs to enquire about lunch.

'Food? Certainly,' said the unflappable Signor Mancini. 'We are having a banquet today, but, please, come and join in.'

'Banquet?' I said. 'Are you sure?'

'Of course,' he said. 'They will be happy if you join them.'

He led me downstairs to a vast hall where there were two lines of tables running parallel about half the length of the room, at which were sitting about a hundred people.

'These are all the seventy-year-olds of Serra de' Conti and the country around,' he said, 'and their families, of course, some of them, anyway. Please, please. Sit down.'

So, rather bemused, I did.

My lunchtime companions were as puzzled as I was, but they were a jolly lot, soon chatting away, cracking jokes and quizzing me about my travels, mostly in heavy dialect, which usually required several attempts at explanation before I got the gist of what they were saying. I suppose that it would be much the same if an Italian had to grapple with the refinements of Geordie or Glasgow accents.

Age did not seem to have withered their appetites for either food or drink. They had already had two pasta courses, cannelloni in a cheesy bechamel, and handmade tagliatelle with a sauce of tomato and pork. Then there were roasted potatoes in the shape of large chips with grilled meats, rabbit and guinea fowl as well as lamb, and salad.

'Another bottle, please, Anna,' commanded Livio opposite, waving an empty bottle of Verdicchio, which registered at a formidable 13.5 per cent.

'Some more rabbit, please,' said Maria, his wife. She had already demolished several chicken wings that her husband had abandoned, as well as her own helping. She drank both red and white wine with no apparent discrimination.

'Do you always eat like this?' I asked.

'Not two *primi piatti*, usually,' said Tonino, who must have been at least seventy-five. 'And no antipasto. A little salami or cheese occasionally. Then the pasta.'

'Or soup. Sometimes soup,' said Maria.

'Pasta or soup. Then meat, and them some fruit. *Basta*. Enough.' God knows how they managed it, because they all looked remarkably trim, fit and vigorous. Obesity didn't seem to be the problem it is Britain and America.

'And do you make the pasta by hand at home?' I asked Maria.

'Oh, yes,' she said. 'By hand. Like my mother.'

'And your children, will they make pasta by hand as well?'

'Ah, the children,' said Livio. 'They don't have time for cooking.'

There was a pudding of cake, custard and cream in layers to round things off, speeches and photographs and more speeches, more drinking, talk and laughter. Three hours later I crept away, exhausted by the septuagenarian energy still pulsating round the tables. The rain had stopped. The sun shone out over the fields of wheat, sunflowers and vines. The air was very clear and still. I could hear voices drifting up from the fields, and a pigeon woo-wooing and a dog barking. The landscape looked as if it had never changed; but that was a lie. It had changed, was changing still. Even the strands of social life that had been woven through it for centuries were changing little by little.

The next day, in bright sunshine, I rode down from the hills to Portonovo on the coast, just south of Ancona. It was mid-July. Portonovo marked the end of the second leg of my odyssey. In a day or two, I would leave Bud in nearby Ancona to await my return in September for the final run to Turin.

I had come to Portonovo for the first time in the summer of 1968. It must have been just about the same time of year. I had been touring Italy with my cousins, Sarah and Mary, in Sarah's Austin Mini Countryman. The car did not excite as much attention as the two girls. It was, in my memory, an idyllic two weeks, a period of unbroken good spirits and hilarity. Mary passed the time trying not to resist the advances of every unsuitable male we encountered. Sarah passed the time remonstrating with her sister for not trying harder to resist the advances of every unsuitable male we encountered. And I, well, I just tagged along, enjoying it all.

I can't remember now why we came to Portonovo, one of the very few dramatically beautiful parts of Italy's Adriatic coast back then, or who tipped us off about it. There had been a campsite, occupied for the most part by bouncing, pink and blond Germans, and two restaurants, and that was it by way of civilization. Nothing else spoiled the elegiac curve of the bay and the brush-covered cliffs above, and the fuzz of Ajaccio pines that ran along the rim.

Even the Italians hadn't really discovered Portonovo then, and those who had tended to congregate up one end of the three-kilometre-long pebble beach, giving us the run of the rest. So we passed the days, the girls burnishing under a sheen of oil, while I, pink as a boiled shrimp, paddled around in the clear, azure water, hobbling painfully over the cobbled beach. In the evenings we ate baked mussels and grilled fish in one of the two restaurants, with the water lapping over the pebbles just below where we sat, and watched the sun disappear behind the Monte Conero, and waited for the moon to fill the bay with white light.

In some ways Portonovo hadn't changed that much. The campsite was still there, and the great curve of the bay, the scrub, the Ajaccio pines, the clear, azure water and even the same two restaurants. But the old frontier freedom had gone. There were many more Italians now, even if most of them still congregated on the first third of the beach, looking and sounding like a nesting colony of exceptionally exotic sea birds. There were umbrellas, too, candy-striped and ranged in rows, each accompanied by something like a camp bed, on which to take the pain out of tanning. There was the odd *pedalò* and the two restaurants had been joined by several more.

I dined alone in the Ristorante Emilia, on the site of the one we patronised thirty-four years ago. It had grown a bit in the intervening years, both in size and panache. It had a proper, printed menu, and the waiters came in white aprons and black trousers. The tables had cloths and the ceiling was a rather fancy sail-cloth awning.

Naturally I ordered *cozze gratinate* and *pesce fritto dell' Adriatico*. They were not as good as memory insisted. The mussels were small and shrivelled beneath a dry thatch of weary breadcrumbs. The plate of fried anchovies, little rock red mullet, scampi, a prawn, three little soles and a mound of calamari was too casual for nostalgia.

At the next table a baby howled, while the little boy of the same family was roundly abused for trying to throw stones from the beach up on to the sail-cloth awning. Some of the stones missed their mark and clattered down among the startled diners. His father gave him a dressing down, with no effect that I could see. Perhaps this wasn't surprising, as the man had a voice like a duck. It was all more Monsieur Hulot than romantic memory.

But then the family quietened down and the dining area filled up. Dusk fell, gradually veiling the dark green of the bush on the sloped, grey-cream cliff face, muting the colour of the sea, dissolving the boundaries between sea, sky and land. The sound of the small waves came through the gathering night, the little rushing surges, and the rattle of the pebbles. There was no moon. Slowly the bay filled with blue, which grew steadily darker and darker, until all I could see was the glimmering line between the sea and the shore.

EATING UP ITALY

Recipes

CIAUSCOLO

Ciauscolo

Aka ciavuscolo, ciabuscolo. *You might find it difficult to make most of the Passamonti masterpieces, but you might try this, the ubiquitous soft spreading sausage of the Marche. You come across variations all the way from Ascoli Piceno to Ancona.*

It is made from pork belly, shoulder and leg, finely ground and mixed with between 30 and 50 per cent fat, seasoned with salt, pepper, orange zest, fennel, garlic and vino cotto. *Everything is then ground even finer to a kind of paste before being packed inside a casing of pig's intestine. The sausage should be hung in a cool, airy room for 3 to 4 weeks, after which it is ready to be eaten. Some people age it for up to 2 months, which gives it a firmer consistency. It is supposed to be soft.*

ZUPPA DI CICERCHIA

Cicerchia soup

A forgotten classic from the Marche, rediscovered thanks to Gianfranco Mancini. Today, few locals eat this primitive chickpea, as it reminds them so clearly of their days of poverty.

Serves 6

Soak the cannellini and borlotti beans and chickpeas overnight. Soak the *cicerchia* in lukewarm water for 6 hours, changing the water 2 or 3 times. Take off the outer skin, which is easily removed after soaking. Dice the vegetables. Put the beans and chickpeas in a saucepan, cover with unsalted water and boil gently for 2 hours. Boil the pre-soaked *cicerchia* for 40 minutes and leave in the cooking liquid.

Purée the beans in a blender with enough cooking liquid to form a thin cream. Pour olive oil into a saucepan, but do not heat it until you have added the diced vegetables. Stew for a few minutes. Drain the *cichercia* and add to the vegetables, followed by the bean and chickpea purée and the vegetable stock. Continue cooking for 10 minutes.

Prepare 6 bowls by rubbing the cloves of garlic round the inside. Pour in the soup and garnish with chives, croutons and pepper.

1 cup mixed dried cannellini, borlotti beans and chickpeas

1 cup *cicerchia*

1 cup combined celery, carrot and onion

Extra virgin olive oil

2 cups vegetable stock

2 cloves garlic

10 chives, chopped

Toasted bread croutons

Pepper

PUREA DI CICERCHIA CON ERBE AMARE

Cicerchia purée with bitter greens

The Marchegiani would use wild chicory, we could use wilted arugula, or wilted arugula and spinach.

Serves 6

Prepare the *cicerchia* as in the previous recipe. Cook for 40 minutes in unsalted water. Leave in the cooking liquid.

Purée the *cicerchia* in a blender with enough of the cooking liquid to give the consistency of thick cream. Add the chopped chives. Clean the chicory thoroughly. Boil for 5 minutes in salted water. Drain, and toss in a little olive oil. Serve the *cicerchia* purée on hot plates with the greens on top. Sprinkle with salt and pepper and add a splash of olive oil.

1 1/4 cups cicerchia
2 tablespoons chives, chopped
1 lb chicory
Extra virgin olive oil
Salt and pepper, to taste

CONIGLIO IN PORCHETTA

Rabbit prepared in the same way as pork

The wild fennel in the rabbit's stuffing grows prolifically in this region, and reaches a state of intensity that the murky stuff of the English garden doesn't begin to approach. It adds a punchy belt to the dish. I ate various versions of this dish all the way through Le Marche. This one belongs to Signor Mancini.

Serves 4

Turn on the oven to 400°. Bone the body of the rabbit, reserving the legs for another dish. Finely chop the pancetta and prosciutto and the rabbit liver. Chop the fennel and crush the garlic. Season the inside of the rabbit. Line it with pancetta slices. Place the chopped pancetta, prosciutto, liver, fennel and crushed garlic on top. Wrap the rabbit around the stuffing and sew into a sausage shape. Put the rabbit into a roasting pan with a drizzle of oil. Add the wine and 1-1¹⁄₃ cups of water. Put the rabbit into the oven and roast until golden brown and tender, 30-45 minutes.

1 rabbit

6 oz pancetta and
    prosciutto crudo, mixed

2 sprigs wild fennel

3 cloves garlic

Slices of pancetta

Extra virgin olive oil

1-1½ cups of white wine

Salt and pepper, to taste

FRUSTINGO

Frustingo cake

Aka frustenga, frostenga, pistingo, *this is a pudding of the poor, a way of using up bits and pieces. This recipe, from Eating in the Marches, published by the Department of Tourism, seems as authentic as any. It was devised by inventive shepherds as a way of varying their monotonous polenta-based diet.*
Serves 12

Wash the figs in warm water, put into a pan with the wine and add water to cover. Simmer for 20 minutes. Leave to cool in the liquid, preferably overnight. Take them out (reserving the liquid) and chop coarsely.

Dry the almonds in the oven, then chop them roughly, along with the walnuts and the candied lemon.

Put all the ingredients (except the bread crumbs) into a bowl and mix thoroughly. Moisten the mixture with several tablespoons of the fig liquid. The mixture must not be dry.

Oil a tray and scatter bread crumbs all over it. Pour in the mixture and bake at 350° for about 1 hour. Cool before cutting and eating.

$2_{1/2}$ lb dried figs
1 glass of dry white wine
$1_{1/4}$ cups blanched almonds
$1_{3/4}$ cups shelled walnuts
2/3 cup candied lemon
1/4 cup sugar
1/4 cup honey
3/4 cup grated chocolate
$2_{3/4}$ cups wholewheat flour
1 small cup (4oz) rum
3 small cups (8oz) of coffee
4 tablespoons plus 1 teaspoon cocoa powder
Grated zest and juice of 1 orange
Grated zest of 1 lemon
2/3 cup golden raisins
1 glass (6oz) of extra virgin olive oil
Pinch of pepper
1 teaspoon ground cinnamon
Pinch of grated nutmeg
1 glass (6oz)of grape juice
Bread crumbs

9
'SARA UN SI AMENO GIORNO PROPIZIO AI VIAGGIATOR'

ANCONA – CERVIA COMACCHIO

Ciarimbolo

The filigree of fat taken from the outside of a pig's intestine was cooked a padella *– on a hot flat pan – so that it had become as delicate as a crisp spider's web, and slightly burnt; and when I bit into it, warm fat, subtly flavoured with pork, salt, pepper and rosemary, ran exquisitely down my throat.*

We sat around a table in the Antiche Fonti della Romita in Cupramontana in the hills inland from Ancona – Laura, Silvia, Luca, Andrea, Franco, il contadino and me.

It was September, and Silvia was the proprietor of the Antiche Fonti della Romita, which she ran with her husband. Luca was an instructor at the *scuola alberghiera* at Cingoli. Andrea was one of the new hot-shot Verdicchio producers. *Il contadino* was the man whose refined, burgundy-red prosciutto we were eating. Laura, journalist, fundraiser, mother of two and wife to a paediatrician to the offspring of sporting stars at Loreto, was the catalyst. We were all friends of Laura. I had known her for only a few hours, but I was a friend of Laura's, too.

We ate a selection of *salumi,* some from a smart *alimentari* in Ancona, more from a butcher's in Staffolo and yet more from the larder of the restaurant. There was *ciauscolo, lonza, coppa di testa,* seven different salamis and *il contadino's* prosciutto. There was some sausage which we ate raw, squeezing the contents of a single fat skin on to grilled bread like toothpaste. There were cheese,s *formaggio di fossa, casciotta di Urbino* and *pecorino.* There was a *pizza al formaggio* – a tall cake like a brioche, only drier and crumblier and cheesy.

Then we had *gnocchi di patate,* with a sauce of wild boar. And then *coniglio in porchetta; fegatini* – pig's liver wrapped in caul with a single bay leaf for company, and then fried; and *ciarimboli.* The filigree of fat taken from the outside of a pig's intestine was cooked *a padella* – on a hot flat pan – so that it had become as delicate as a crisp spider's web, and slightly burnt; and when I bit into it, warm fat, subtly flavoured with pork, salt, pepper and rosemary, ran exquisitely down my throat. The food was classic Marchegiana tucker, ample, rounded, full-throated and full-frontally flavoured. We drank Andrea's voluptuous, fruity Verdicchio, and then his rich, astringent red, and talked, about food. We talked about food, and wine, for three hours without cease.

We talked about the desirability of using real corks rather than plastic ones, about the pricing of olive oil and the pricing of wine, about how difficult it was to get Italians to pay a realistic price for artisanal produce, about individual taste, about cheese and cheese makers. We talked about the provenance of the wild boar, the rarity of *ciarimbolo*, *il contadino's* prosciuttos, of which he made only four a year, the gradual industrialisation of farming, the survival of artisanal producers, and the failure of the young to want to continue the cooking and eating traditions of their parents.

And we talked about the food and cooking of the Marche, of the way in which the Marche is divided horizontally, as it were, into the coastal strip, the fertile rolling hills and the mountains, and then divided again vertically by the rivers that flow down from the mountains — the Tronto, the Tonna, the Potenza, the Esino, the Metauro and the Aso, the valley of each having quite different food from the next. But my companions could not agree on the exact characteristics of each.

The more the conversation circled round the complexities of local cooking, the more impossible it became, it seemed to me, to make meaningful generalisations about the character of regional food cultures. Tiny distances made huge differences to ingredients and the manner in which they were treated. Views as to the suitability of this ingredient for that dish were held with absolute conviction, and were contradicted by the next person who spoke. When I tried to say that the Marche seemed to mark the end of the empire of chili, I was politely put in my place. When I tried to suggest that *orecchiette* weren't necessarily particular to Puglia, I was firmly corrected.

Indeed, it struck me that the true, universal food of Italy is not pasta but pizza. Pasta has so many forms, each of which provoke fierce local loyalty. On the other hand, pizza, whether *margherita or caprese, quattro formaggi or boscaiolo, bianca or napoletana*, is found everywhere, from Melito to Milan, from Taranto to Turin. It reflects the routes taken by southern Italians as they emigrated from their homelands in the search for work, during the 1960s in particular, colonising as they went. Its roots may be in southern poverty, but it has become the universal staple of modern urban society.

We ate some more cheese with honey and some round biscuits with aniseed in them, some *lonzino di fico* (the sausage made of dried figs, almonds, fennel and aniseed – some said, darkly, too much aniseed), and *cantucci* (small crunchy biscuits); and we drank *vino cotto* and then some *visciolato*, a digestif made of wild cherries. And we kept on talking until Luca had to go to college and Andrea back to his vineyard and Laura to pick up her children from school. I felt so full I wasn't sure that I would ever eat again.

'Never, never, never, never, never. Pray you, undo this button,' as King Lear said.

Button undone, that evening I found myself standing in front of a little stall selling shellfish dishes in the Corso Giuseppe Mazzini in Ancona, a little way along from the Fonte del Calano, a public drinking fountain with thirteen spouts. The little display cabinet held neat trays of oysters, *ragusa in porchetta, ragusa letta, bombo, vongole, cannello, cannocchie, insalata di frutti di mare* and *cozze ripiene*. There were two men working their way steadily through a dish of a few oysters, and another of stuffed mussels, and then they called for some *insalata di frutti di mare*.

I ordered three stuffed mussels and a glass of white wine. The wine was cool and sharp. The stall was manned by Signora Sabbatini – 'two bs, one t', she said firmly. She said that they bought the fish at the market and cooked it themselves. 'With my sons, that makes four generations that have worked here.' She carefully cut the string binding off the shells of the mussels, and forced them open with a knife. Each was stuffed with chopped mussel flesh flavoured with herbs, a substantial mouthful. The tomato sauce in which they had been cooked carried the seaweed and iodine flavour of mussel juice.

It was another of those small enterprises that survived on entrepreneurial modesty and the integrity of the family, adding another tiny, but glittering, facet to the variety of human pleasure.

'*Grazie, signora,*' I said.

'*Arrivederla,*' she smiled as I turned away and made my way to the Trattoria Moretta.

The Trattoria Moretta was at the other end of the gastro-nomic spectrum from the Sabbatini fish stall, but clearly part of the same culture. It had all the sobriety and gravitas of a tradi-tional bourgeois watering hole honoured by time and service, it had been serving traditional *piatti anconetani* to city worthies since 1897. The dining room was a fugue in brown. The walls were panelled in narrow tongue-and-groove the colour of amber; the floor was of reddish-brown tiles; the furniture was deep mahogany chocolate and heavy enough to build a house on; the orange wall lights added an autumnal glow. Even the bright, airy townscapes of the chocolate-box school of art did little to leaven the air of carefully orderly sobriety.

But these were the right conditions in which to eat the clas-sics of Ancona cooking, *seppioline con piselli* and *stoccafisso all'an-conetana*. No matter that the *seppioline* were past their high sea-son, and peas were not in season at all. The little curls of squid had been cooked so long that they had become as tender as warmed fat. The tomato-based juices in which they came had become suffused with distilled marine intensity, decorated with the little peas. This was a dish that faced two ways: out to sea, from which the squid came, and to the rich agricultural plain behind Ancona, which provided the peas and tomatoes.

The provenance of *stoccafisso all'anconetana* is rather more fanciful. Stockfish is cod, or some cod-like fish, which is hung out to dry in the seer winds of Norway until it is stiff as a board. It is a technique developed by the Vikings as a means of pre-serving fish in times of glut for eating in times when diet was a bit restricted. One theory credits the aristocratic fifteenth-cen-tury explorer Piero Querini with its introduction to Italy as a means of feeding the poor. However, there is evidence of a trade with southern Europe and Africa going back to the tenth century. It is part of the great cod diaspora, which drove trade, industry and culinary progress, and on the back of which for-tunes were made and lost. In the eighteenth century, Louis de Béchamel, Marquis de Nointel, came up with béchamel sauce as a means of trying to get people to eat the dried cod he had shipped across from Newfoundland, having sunk the family fortunes into the cod fisheries there. Not content with one classic sauce, Béchamel also invented soubise and mornay sauces.

In the fifteenth and sixteenth centuries the fish came to Ancona via the Baltic states and now serves as a reminder of the importance that the Baltic once played in the trade with the port. Curiously, history is now repeating itself, because Ancona has become the port of choice once again for many of the Eastern European countries that were formerly part of the USSR. *Stoccafisso* still comes from Norway, but it has moved upmarket and become something of a pricey gourmet delight. So pricey, indeed, that it has become a prime target for hijackers, to the extent that several Norwegian insurance companies refuse to provide cover for the lorries taking it south.

In that splendidly confusing fashion in which Italy seems to delight, *lo stoccafisso* is known as *baccalà* in the northern cities of Vicenza and Venice, while the rest of Italy knows that *baccalà* is salt cod, a very different kettle of fish. *Stoccafisso* has none of salt cod's salinity, flavour of boiled wool or disgusting smell.

And, according to Silvia Cappello, the sage of Reggio di Calabria, the excellence of a dish of stoccafisso will depend upon the particular quality of the water in which the fish is soaked before being cooked.

But if the origin of the main ingredient is very much Scandinavian, the treatment at the Trattoria Moretta was wholly Adriatic. Chunks of stockfish sat in a colossal mulch of potatoes, tomatoes, olives, chili and olive oil. It was a heroic dish, rich, robust, full of powerful asides. It was difficult to isolate specific flavours. It was a monument constructed out of natural substances, as opulent as a Bernini sculpture.

In the middle of dinner it rained heavily. I had a melancholy sense of foreboding.

My foreboding was not misplaced. In my absence, Bud had been tuned to new levels of purring power, but it was raining again as I left Ancona. It wasn't just raining; it was cold, too. Within ten minutes I was chilled as well as wet. Within half an hour I was numb and sodden. The SS16 from Ancona to Padua runs parallel to the coast. I followed it with determination fortified by the urge to survive. It was patrolled by an unbroken convoy of heavy lorries and speeding cars, each throwing up a miasma of spray, and lined on either side by factories, furniture shops, car agencies, megastores and all the commerical chaff of the modern commercial state. When I stopped for lunch at a roadside snack bar, I shook uncontrollably with cold as I ate a *piadina* filled with sausage and beetroot tops.

The *piadina* was ubiquitous here, delicious, healthy and versatile. In essence it is a pancake of unleavened bread, not unlike Persian *naan* or other Arab flat breads, about a centimetre thick and stiff. In this case it was cooked as a single round about thirty centimetres across, and then sliced in half, the sausage, which had itself been halved along its length for cooking, placed on one half, along with the dark green spinach leaves, and the other half placed on top. It was wrapped in paper and then in foil so that it could be eaten there and then. It was fast food *par excellence*; simple, tasty and cheering.

It may have been a coincidence, but at about that time the rain stopped. The mass of ragged grey cloud began to break up. A patch of blue appeared. I wasn't exactly cheerful yet but I was further from being miserable. My spirits lifted still more as I passed Pesaro, birthplace of Rossini. It wasn't simply Rossini's exuberant gift for sunny melodies or his innate laziness that appealed to me. It wasn't even his passion for higher gastronomy – he once confessed to having cried three times in his life: when his first opera was booed; when he first heard Paganini play; and when a truffled turkey fell overboard during a boat trip. No, it was his habit of wearing wigs, two of them, one on top of the other, to keep his head warm in winter.

Shortly afterwards I crossed from the Marche into Emilia-Romagna. Doing so, I passed out of the no-man's land of the non-existent middle of Italy and into the unquestionable north, where fresh pasta took over from dry, butter ranked alongside oil, where stews were staples and where cheeses were made from cows' milk rather than sheeps' milk.

Emilia-Romagna is the composite region formed in 1947. The Emiliani, from the area north and west of Bologna, have the reputation of being more sophisticated than the rustic Romagnoli, but both are recognised as having a passion for food and life remarkable even by Italian standards. Perhaps as a consequence, the area has played a unique part in the political life of Italy, giving the country both Benito Mussolini and Italy's longest-serving, and most successful, Communist town council in Bologna – aka La Grassa, the Fat One, in 1945 the only city to free itself from Nazi occupation without help from the Allied forces. Emilia-Romagna has long been a breeding ground of radical politics, inseparable from the tradition of the *mezzadri*, the sharecroppers, who worked the land here and in the Marche right up until the agrarian reforms of the 1950s and '60s.

At the beginning of the twenty-first century, it is almost impossible to understand how such a feudal system of land ownership and agriculture could have operated in a European country until so recently. Outright ownership of land was relatively rare. Extreme poverty was widespread. The struggle to change these inequalities led to a deeply politicised people that prosperity has done little to lessen.

The sun began to take hold, and as I hit the beginning of the vast plain of La Pianura Padana – the Po valley – north of Rimini, the birthplace of Federico Fellini, I was suffused with the full warmth of a fine autumn afternoon. Smallholdings began to find spaces between the factories, lighting shops, car dealerships and building yards, and I noticed that the zucchini, tomatoes, carrots and pale green lettuces of summer had given way to lines of cabbages, fennel, the long, dark green, reticulated leaves of chicory and the tight, purple-blotched heads of *grumello*, a hardy winter lettuce. There were fields, too, of cannellini beans, in their red-striped pods, looking mud-spattered and bedraggled on plants that sat low on the sodden ground. By the time I turned off the interminable stretches of the SS16 to Cervia, I was dried out, if not quite thawed out.

Cervia was the first place that I ever visited in Italy, in 1958. I was eleven then. We – four brothers ranging from seven to thirteen and two parents – stayed in the Hotel Mare e Pineta, which was notable as much for the slightly bewildered tolerance with which it coped with the unpredictable behaviour of small boys as it was for the Lucullan magnificence of its Thursday lunchtime buffets.

Contemporary Cervia bore little resemblance to the Cervia of memory. In place of the charming, dusty, scruffy resort of the 1950s was a well-ordered grid of roads shaded by mature plane trees, a prosperous town centre, and hotel upon hotel upon hotel – Gambrinus, Astor, Wally, July, Italy, K2, Bristol, Concordia – stretching along the front. I docked at the Grand Hotel Cervia, a delicious, pink 1930s confection, standing in splendid isolation on the edge of the endless beach, and set about finding the monuments of my past.

In fact Cervia had a great deal more to offer than memory allowed, or, indeed, than I had ever been aware of – a marina, a canal harbour along which were moored fishing boats supporting a small canal-side market, a handsome sixteenth-century square tower, eighteenth-century warehouses and those charming squares that even the most uncompromisingly tawdry, resort-driven Adriatic town seems to keep tucked secretly about itself.

But of the Hotel Mare e Pineta I could find no trace. It was like trying to reconstruct some past event from a torn-up photograph. I wasn't even sure that I had all the pieces of the picture. Was this the street down which we walked to the gelateria each evening? Could this have been the path down to the beach? Was this the square where the humming-bird hawkmoths came to sip from the flowers of scrubby acacia? Each line of plane trees, each stand of umbrella pines seemed to have something suggestive about it and tugged at the memory, but was it recognition?

Wrapped in the seductive melancholy of the out-of-season resort, I wandered past the shuttered houses, the darkened hotels, the shops with half-hearted displays of the dead summer's beach gear and games, their owners looking out with stoic hope from their doorways, the first fall of leaves on the pavement.

The beach on which I had played as a boy glowed with the

afternoon light. A few hardy souls basted their bodies in the rays, and several even hardier ones bounced in the sea. The occasional younger jogger came puffing past. A handful of young parents lugged pushchairs on the strand, outnumbered by dogs – poodles, schnauzers, Dobermanns, mongrels. But mostly there were sunset people in a sunset mood – a cardy and cream crimplene trousers for her, blue, short-sleeved shirt, visible vest and pale grey cotton trousers for him – taking advantage of end-of-season prices, walking well back from where one modest wave after another approached the shore in neat, parallel, broken lines and expired with a polite sigh on the sand. And out at sea there was a vast mass of triangular white sails moving slowly from right to left, like an army of pristine tents.

It was a short hop in fine weather from Cervia to Comacchio, the next point on the map that I wanted to visit. Comacchio is not the first city of Emilia-Romagna, or, indeed, the ninth or tenth, but it is unique. My brother Tom had excited my interest in this curious, watery corner of the world, and had written evocatively about it in his *The Book of Eels*, for Comacchio is a town built upon eels and salt.

The profits from these curious trades had enriched the Benedictine brothers who built the dramatic Abbazia di Pomposa near by, the elegant tower of which dominates the flatlands about, and where Guido d'Arezzo invented the modern musical scale in the eleventh century. Later, the wealth generated by the lakes, canals and rivers was put to less spiritual uses, to judge by the many handsome houses built along the five or six canals that run through Comacchio, and round it, which help give the town a calm and spacious air. The effect was less like Venice in miniature than Bourton-on-the-Water, designed by an Italian Clough Williams-Ellis in Portmeirion mood.

Here I met Giacomo Benelli, who was working with Il Parco del Delta del Po, a quango devoted to the interests of the vast reserve formed by the Po delta. He immediately took me under his wing and off to lunch, of eels, naturally, one dish of them stewed in vinegar, onions and water, which was gently sour, and another of them grilled crisp, succulent and rich. He was a delightful fellow, curious about everything, with an excellent sense of humour and passionate about the environment, but very diffident in his manner.

His grandparents had been *mezzadri* who had bettered themselves to become *contadini*, rural smallholders, carefully building up their farm from five to twenty-five hectares. One generation later, no one in the family farmed any more, though both he and his parents still lived with his grandparents in the old family house. Giacomo's father worked for Fiat. His mother sold computers. Giacomo himself was a naturalist.

He insisted that we would have dinner with his uncle and aunt, Giancarlo and Ilde, who lived at Godo not far away, so that I could get a feel of how the Romagnoli eat, and that I should stay with his family at Piangipane, near Ravenna. Not for the first time, I felt a surge of gratitude and embarrassment at the generosity of strangers.

Giancarlo and Ilde seemed completely undisturbed by the sudden addition of a stranger to their dinner table. They were warm, courteous, welcoming and endlessly talkative. We sat in the kitchen, which was as neat and trim as a captain's cabin, and chattered while they pottered about. Giancarlo supervised the grilling of a grey mullet on a most ingenious, wood-fired, indoor barbecue, which was, effectively, an eye-level fireplace, while Ilde made ready the pasta and the salad. Everything spoke of frugality, modesty and decency. The food was very simple, but very good, really typical Romagnolo, Giacomo kept on telling me. The pasta, *sedanini,* a variation on *maccheroni,* was dried.

'I usually make my own,' said Ilde. Like her husband, she had once been a teacher; now both were retired. Her eyes, beneath a helmet of grey hair, cut elegant and short, were magnified by large, round spectacles. 'Tagliatelle, fettuccine, and *cappelletti.* But for this, dried is better. It's a good brand. And the vegetables came from the garden. We had a lot of *melanzane* and peppers, so I made some of them into this sauce.'

The grey mullet had been stuffed with rosemary and salt, and then served with lemon squeezed over it. Perhaps it was just that I was eating in unfamiliar circumstances, but I was struck by the clarity of the tastes, the lightness of the dishes, the quality of the fish. Even the seasoning seemed fresh and precise. I said as much.

'It's a pity you couldn't try my pig's cheek,' said Giancarlo.

'Pig's cheek?' I said. I have long nursed a passion for this, the most delicate and sweetest meat of the pig.

'Pig's cheek,' he said. 'I get fresh pig's cheeks and bury them in a tray of salt for eight days. You must tip the tray at a slight angle so that the water runs away from the meat. After eight days I add fresh salt and leave it for another five days or so. Then I wash off the salt, take off the skin and slice the cheeks like this,' he indicated about two centimetres 'and freeze them until I want them.'

'When I want to eat them, I fry the cheek slices in a little oil until the fat runs. Then I add a glass of white wine and cook it for another twenty minutes or so. Then I add a little vinegar, just a little, bring it to the boil to reduce the liquid a bit, and pour the whole lot over sliced radicchio. And eat it as fast as possible. It was one of the dishes I used to eat as a boy.'

He spoke about how he had been born in the house that Giacomo's parents lived in, and about how hard life had been for the farming people of the Po Valley sixty, seventy years ago, and about how the social structures of farming had changed since the war.

Once there had been a great network of farming families, who had owned perhaps five hectares each. Each family had known the other, visited each other, helped each other out at harvest and married into each other. But there had been times of great hunger and hardship, too. Gradually, farming techniques became more intensive, hedges were cut down and trees pulled up.

'Even now,' said Giacomo, 'My grandparents can't understand why anyone should want hedges on their land or let trees grow. Keeping hedges trimmed means unproductive work, and where trees cast a shadow, crops don't grow so well.' And, of course, said Giancarlo, along with the hedges and the trees, the humans went as well, because they weren't needed. There were machines to do the work more efficiently.

'Would you like some salad now?'

The salad was no fancy affair, simply chopped romaine lettuce and grated carrot, with a dressing of olive oil, vinegar and salt, mixed at the table with some ritual by Giancarlo.

'Are you sure it's all right?' he asked. 'That's the way I like to do it, but you might like some more oil. I don't like too much oil, myself. I prefer the flavour of the vinegar. Or perhaps I didn't use enough salt. Do feel free to add some more salt if you like.'

Ritual or not, there is none of the refinement of the vinaigrette or the vulgarity of the creamy dressing about the way Italians anoint their salad leaves. In the south it was olive oil, lemon and salt. Further north, olive oil, white wine vinegar and salt. Even in restaurants, the customer was expected to mix this to their own specifications at the table. Its simplicity and clarity let the flavour of the leaves shine through.

Next, a slice of cheese – *cimbro da Verano*. No, this wasn't just any old cheese, said Giancarlo. There was still something of the schoolmaster about him, a gentle Mr Chipsian didacticism. The cheese was made from cows' milk and had a sharp, bustling kind of flavour. Finally, we had a slice of cake, *ciambella, fatta in casa* (made in the house), yellow as saffron, light as down.

'How come it's so light?'

'Potato flour,' said Ilde. 'I use potato flour as well as wheat flour. That's the real secret.' Potato flour was a throwback to the *mezzadria* culture, when it was cheaper than wheat flour.

And then we nibbled *giuggiole*, fruit that I had never come across before, although I had seen them in the market in Ancona. They looked like brown olives, and I thought that they might be a kind of crab apple. They were very crisp, with a single small stone at the centre, and had a vaguely appley flavour.

To be honest, I couldn't get terribly excited about them, but Giacomo, Giancarlo and Ilde seemed to reserve the kind of rapture for *giuggiole* that I have for raspberries. Maybe this was because they have such a short season, about two weeks.

'This is the greatest pleasure for me,' said Giancarlo, sitting back, his black-and-white checked shirt swelling over his generous tummy. 'To sit at the table, to eat and enjoy conversation.'

Giacomo and I met *il vecchio pescatore*, the old fisherman, on a backwater just outside Comacchio.

'How old do you think I am?' he asked. He looked as old as the landscape, and that didn't seem to have changed much since time began. 'I am eighty-two.'

Along the banks of the canals, channels and streams that criss-cross the Po valley stood extraordinary fishing stations, one every fifty metres or so. They consisted of a hut standing on a platform built out over the river. In many cases, these huts were quite substantial affairs. Extending out from the hut, suspended between two arms, were huge square nets, perhaps ten metres across. The arms were controlled by a complex series of ropes and pulleys. *Il vecchio pescatore* occupied one of these stations. It was more ramshackle than most, spectacularly dilapidated. Indeed, it seemed something of a wonder that the hut stayed upright at all, particularly when *il vecchio pescatore* started up the shuddering diesel engine housed in a small shed at the back of the platform that he used to raise and lower the enormous net into the turbid waters of the Corso di Comacchio some four or so metres below.

Each time the net rose dripping out of the water, the old man would lean forward with a smaller, fine-meshed net on a rounded stiff wire frame on the end of a pole that must have been fully ten metres long. With it he scooped up anything that happened to have been caught – mostly small crabs – and transferred them to a plastic basin. His real quarry was *aquadelle*, minnows, and any other small fish. There were strict rules about the size of fish these netsmen were allowed to keep, strict rules that were strictly ignored. These were not disciplined, professional fishermen, just people from round about looking for a weekend activity and a cheap source of protein, as they always had. He sorted through his catch like a prospector examining his pan for gold. He transferred the crabs to a bucket, and the tiny silver fish to a box which he covered with a damp cloth. He made a great show of occasionally putting back some minuscule *cefali* (grey mullet) or other fish.

'Very good fried,' he said, pointing at the aquadelle, 'or grilled. Very good.' His rheumy old eyes gleamed.

Giacomo and I left him to his careful harvest. As we passed on down the road, there were several other fishing stations in action, some with entire families engaged in the business.

We headed up beyond Comacchio, deeper into the Po delta where the river split up into several separate broad stretches before it reached the sea. We stopped at Goro on the Golfo di Goro, home to a substantial fleet designated principally for gathering the clams which Italians are so pleased to serve with spaghetti. There is a good deal of clam and mussel farming in the Golfo di Goro. Stakes on which the mollusc-encrusted ropes hung ran in lines out in the bay, producing more than 500 tonnes a year. Clams – *vongole veraci, fasolari* and *tartufi* – are big business. So big, indeed, that the fishermen of Chioggia and Ravenna have fought pitched battles over the beds of wild clams elsewhere in the Adriatic.

From Goro we went north to the Sacca di Scadovari, entering a region as strange as anywhere I have ever been. The land was utterly flat, stretched like a membrane between long, rush-lined fingers of water, held in place by high, dyked banks. The road ran on and on into this desolate landscape. It was dusk. Occasionally we came across a large farm establishment, lights gleaming in the glimmering twilight. Road signs seemed to lead us round in circles. The banks on either side of us closed in. A sense of forlorn isolation enveloped everything. Giacomo quoted from Eugenio Montale's poem 'Delta':

Tutto ignoro di te fuor del messaggio
muto che mi sostenta sulla via:
se forma esisti o ubbia nella fumea
d'un sogno t'alimenta
la riviera che infebbra, torba, e scroscia
incontro alla marea.

I know nothing about you except for the mute message
which sustains me on the way:
whether you exist as a shade
nourishing a dream
or whether the shore turns feverish,
troubled and crashes
with the rising tide.

EATING UP ITALY

Recipes

FEGATINI

Grilled pig's liver

It could be known as fegatelli, *and it could be claimed by several regions as their own. I ate it in the Marche, and that's where it belongs for me.*

Serves 6

Soak the caul in warm water to soften it, then cut it into pieces approximately 4-inch square. Cut the liver into large pieces (but small enough to be wrapped in the caul). Lay the pieces of caul out on a work surface. Place a piece of liver in the centre of each, season generously and top with a bay leaf. Wrap the caul round them. Brush with oil and grill, preferably over a wood barbecue, for about 10 minutes.

1/2 lb caul

1¾ lb pig's liver

Salt and pepper, to taste

Bay leaves

Olive oil

PIADINA ROMAGNOLA

Flat bread from the Romagna

Makes about 18 piadine

Mix together the flour, sugar, salt with *strutto* or olive oil, then add enough milk to produce a soft dough. Knead briefly. Rest in a cool place for 1 hour.

Roll pieces into rounds about 1-11/2 inches thick and about 10 inches across. Grill each piadina without any fat for 2 minutes on each side. Place whatever filling you like – ham, cheese, spinach–on the bread and fold in half to eat.

4½ cups durum flour

3 oz *strutto* (pork fat),

(or 3–4 tablespoons olive oil)

4 teaspoons sugar

Pinch of salt

Milk

STOCCOFISSO
ALL 'ANCONETANA

Stockfish Ancona style

A grand classic of fish cookery, and a dish that is as splendid as it is potent.
It has to be made with stockfish – wind-dried cod – not salt cod

Serves 4–6

Cut the stockfish into four pieces.
Dice the onion, carrot and celery.
Peel and chop the tomatoes, discard
the seeds. Heat some olive oil in a
casserole or large saucepan, add the
onion, carrot, celery and chili, and
brown them, then add the tomatoes,
herbs and stockfish. Pour in the
wine. Add the potatoes and olives,
and cover with water. Bring to a
simmer and cook gently for 2½
hours.

2¼ lbs stockfish, soaked in
    several changes of fresh
    water for several hours

1 onion

1 carrot

1 stick of celery

2 lbs very ripe tomatoes

Olive oil

1 sprig each of rosemary,
    oregano and thyme

1/2-2/3 cup of *Verdicchio*

4 large potatoes, cut into
    chunks

16 black olives

1 red chili pepper, chopped

ANGUILLA IN UMIDO ALLA COMACCHIESE

Stewed eel Comacchio style

Serves 6

Use large eels, and don't remove their skin. Cut into pieces about 2 inches long. Chop up quite a lot of onions and parsley. Heat some oil in a casserole and add the onions and parsley, salt and pepper. Brown the onions. Add the eel, and cook for a few minutes to let it absorb the flavours of the seasonings. Add the vinegar and tomato paste, and enough water to cover the eel. Bring to a simmer, stir, then cover and cook for 40 minutes. Serve with toast, although there is a school of thought that recommends polenta.

2¼ lbs eels

2–3 large onions

Large bunch of flat-leaf parsley

Olive oil

Salt and pepper, to taste

4½ tablespoons red wine

Vinegar

3 tablespoons tomato paste

MINESTRA CON RICOTTA

Ricotta sauce

Serves 4

Chop the parsley very finely, or mince it. Mix all the ingredients together in a bowl and keep on beating them together for about 20 minutes.

When you boil the pasta, scoop off 2–3 spoonfuls of the boiling water and add to the ricotta mixture. Mix well. It should become like cream. Strain the pasta. Pour the ricotta cream over, mix well and serve right away.

Large bunch of parsley
1 cup sheep's milk ricotta
Butter the size of a walnut
5-6 tablespoons grated Parmesan
Salt and pepper, to taste

MINESTRA CON MELANZANE E PEPERONI

Eggplant and sweet pepper sauce

Literally, minestra *means soup – or so my dictionary says – but Ilde and Giancarlo Plazzi, who provided these recipes, use the word to mean sauce. This was one of the dishes they fed me. It has a distinctive lightness that I think is typical of their house style rather than Emiliano cooking in general. It was very good.*

Serves 4

Peel the eggplants, and cut into small pieces. Put into a colander and sprinkle with salt. Leave for an hour before rinsing off the salt in fresh water. Dry thoroughly on paper-towel. Wash the pepper and cut it into small pieces.

Pour some olive oil into a frying pan and add the diced eggplant. Fry for a few minutes before adding the pieces of pepper and seasoning. Cover with a lid and cook over a very low heat, stirring from time to time. Add a little stock, if you fancy.

Cook the pasta, drain and add the sauce to it. Add some finely chopped parsley (as much or as little as you like), and some grated Parmesan (ditto). And if you want to be really fancy or to stretch the sauce further, add a little cream.

3 long, dark-skinned
    eggplants
Salt
1 red or yellow pepper
Olive oil
Pasta
Parsley
Grated Parmesan
A little cream (optional)

CIAMBELLA

Ring-shaped cake

Another charmer from the Plazzi kitchen.

Serves 8

Mix the yeast with 8 tablespoons warm water and wait for it to begin to foam. Put the flours, sugar and butter into a bowl and mix thoroughly. Add the eggs and then the lemon zest and yeast. Mix thoroughly to make a soft dough. Turn into a buttered ring mould (approximately 10 inches) and bake at 375º for 50–60 minutes.

$2_{1/2}$ oz dried yeast

2 cups durum flour

2 cups potato flour

3/4 cup superfine sugar

1 cup unsalted butter

4 eggs

Grated zest of 1 lemon

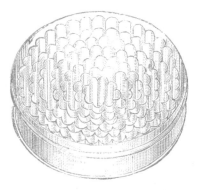

10
THE SUPREME
SAUSAGE

COMACCHIO – FERRARA
MANTUA – CREMONA

La salama da sugo

*The thick slices of sausage were a dark, purply brown. Their tex-
ture was compact and dense. Each exploded in my mouth with a
flavour of enormous power, very deep and full, with a keen salty
edge. Small chunks of fat greased each mouthful. The bland,
unsalted mashed potato acted as a perfect foil, absorbing the fat, a
neutral antidote to the intensity of the meat.*

It was cool, golden and misty on the road to Ferrara across the immense flatness of the agricultural heartland of Emilia-Romagna. The land spoke of agro-industrial money. It was depressingly monocultural, with sugar beet stacked in mounds like rubble of muddy chalk, blasted stalks of maize, and blocks of apple, peach and nectarine trees in mathematically precise lines. There seemed to be fewer little plots of vegetables beside the road, either because the land was too valuable to be turned over to domestic production, or because there were no pensioners near by to cultivate them. Barns and farmhouses stood out, moored like ships in a vast brown sea.

Some of the older buildings were imposingly handsome, or would have been had they not been showing such signs of decay. These were the *cascine*, the symbols of the power of past farming barons, their present-day dereliction a potent symbol of the passing of power, and of new priorities. They looked like fortresses, or small villages under a single roof, and that's more or less what they had been. Once, they would have housed the landowners, farm workers and their families, a school, canteen, wine press, even a chapel, as well as animals, and their feed, hay
and abattoir. Landowners, animals and their feed still had their place in the landscape, but the armies of labourers and their communities had all gone. Machines had taken over from men, chemicals from care.

According to Paul Ginsborg in *Italy and its Discontents*, an intimidatingly scholarly, but eminently lucid, exposition of Italian politics and society since 1980, between 1951 and 1993 the number of agricultural workers as a percentage of the total working population fell from 12 per cent to 3 per cent, and peasant proprietors fell from 31 per cent to 6 per cent. At the heart of this transformation, according to Ginsborg, was the invasion of multinational companies, such as Nestlé-Italia, Kraft-Italia, Unilever-Italia and BSN. In 1980, multinationals accounted for 4.9 per cent of turnover and 3.6 per cent of employees of the top 100 Italian food companies. By 1992 these figures had become 32.2 per cent and 42.2 per cent

EATING UP ITALY

respectively. 'The multinationals had been attracted to Italy by the increasing popularity of Italian food products throughout the world, and by the large number of medium-sized farms which could be bought up at reasonable prices.' Of course, multinationals hadn't been the only agricultural and food predators around. Italy had produced a number of its own. Barilla, Parmalat and Ciro could be counted up there with the best.

Ferrara declared itself to be the 'City of Bicycles', and so it was. As it was quite flat, I could see that cycling was an ideal way for the environmentally conscious citizens to get about. Indeed, if you drained the colour from the average street scene so that it became black and white, Ferrara would have looked like one of those verismo films, such as *The Bicycle Thief*, or an early Antonioni documentary. In fact, Antonioni came from Ferrara.

The consequences of bicycle culture for the unwary tourist were less happy. The Ferraresi rode bicycles as if they were motorbikes, with the same fierce disregard for order and strangers. The streets became stages for a kind of mechanised ballet, with riders weaving in and out, seemingly never clattering to the ground. Unlike scooters, however, which you can hear some way off, bicycles are silent, and silence is deadly to the pedestrian.

I lost count of the times I was in the process of stepping off a pavement only to become suddenly aware of a cyclist, or several cyclists, a metre or so away, bearing down on me. On several occasions I had got halfway across a street, leapt back out of the way of some speedster, only to find myself in the path of another unheard menace going in the opposite direction. The cyclists would stop, wobble, smile tolerantly and continue, sped on their way by my embarrassed smiles and apologies.

These caveats aside, Ferrara was immensely likeable; handsome, bourgeois, prosperous. In the evening everyone gathered in the streets. The lights shone in the windows of the *panetterie* and *alimentari*. At 6:30 p.m. butcher, baker, deli, greengrocer and cheese shop were doing brisk business. Folk were stocking up with *salama da sugo, ciccioli, polpettone, scaloppine alla milanese, cappellacci di zucca, torta salata con spinaci e cotto, torta di mele, torta di noci, Parmigiano stagionata, Fior di latte di Molise* and *Montasio stagionato,* all to be carried home by bicycle.

It was as if the city had always been like this. The old centre was still largely composed of well-set-up houses and palazzi of distinctive narrow red bricks, which the sun gilded so that they glowed. Its present prosperity allowed it to sit easily with its distinguished past. It exuded a kind of civilised humanity, which was misleading. As the novels and stories of Giorgio Bassani testify, the Jews in Ferrara were shamefully abandoned by their fellow citizens during the Second World War. Of the Jewish community that thrived here until 1939, hardly any trace remains.

Almost every city of the Po valley – Ferrara, Mantua, Cremona, Bologna, Pavia, Casale Monferrato, Turin – once had had a substantial Jewish population. There was a degree of religious tolerance in the fourteenth and fifteenth centuries, particularly under the Este family in Ferrara and the Gonzagas in Mantua, that encouraged Jews to settle and flourish. (This tolerance extended to John Calvin, who lived in Ferrara under the name of Charles Heppeville.) Even in the less generous centuries that followed, the presence of Jews was accepted. Even when Ferrara became part of the Papal States in 1598, they weren't seriously troubled. It seemed that they had become a constant part of the wider Italian urban society. The Fascist *leggi razziali,* or race laws, showed that this was not the case.

There seemed to be little physical evidence to indicate the size of the Jewish communities. I searched restaurant menus for signs of culinary traces. I had been told that it was possible to enjoy a fusion of both Sephardic and Ashkenazi traditions, with an element of local Emilian gluttony thrown in for good measure. Aside from *oca* (goose) here and there, which was used by Jewish cooks in place of pork, I could find nothing.

It was another glowing autumn day. The sun loomed like a hazy sunflower through the traces of mist that hung over the fields and lines of apples and pears. I took the road to Quartesana, and wound my way – not all the roads were dead straight – to the fruit farm of Sergio Natali.

A thickset young man, with an open face and wide brown eyes, Sergio was tidying up the strawberry beds with his wife. Strawberries were a new departure for them, he said, like peaches and nectarines. Conventionally, they grew apples and pears – 'Golden Delicious', 'Melagala', 'Imperatore', and a few of the newer varieties, such as 'Fuji' and 'Pink Lady'.

'But I am a traditionalist. We grow a few of the new varieties because that's what the market wants. Some of the big farms grow just one variety. It may be more economical, but what if they get some disease and the whole lot are wiped out, or people decide they don't like them anymore – what happens then? No, I prefer the old varieties, 'Abate' pears most of all. I feel comfortable with them, and this area is particularly suited to them. The humidity helps bring out the best.'

Generally he was pessimistic about the future of farms the size of theirs – about thirty-five hectares, which he managed with his wife and his father and mother. Small farms like theirs could not survive in the long term producing in the way they had for years. The farm simply wasn't big enough to afford the investment needed to compete in a market that bought food globally. He employed one worker other than his wife. He had to pay her five times as much as a labourer in, say, Chile, he said.

Little by little, he was converting the farm back to a mixed system his grandparents would have recognised. Multifunctional, he called it. It was a neat updating of the traditional concept. They had chickens, which ranged freely about the yard and property, and a few cows for home consumption, and pigs, twenty plump black-and-white Large Whites, snorting and snuffling happily in their sty. These were the raw material for the legendary *salama da sugo*, the great boiling sausage of Ferrara, traditionally eaten at Christmas and Easter.

Making the *salama da sugo,* or *salamina* – the names seemed to be interchangeable – was a relatively recent departure for the family. Sergio was persuaded to start making it only a couple of years ago by his wife after they had visited the Salone del Gusto organised by Slow Food in Turin with a group of local young farmers. They had talked to Slow Food, an international organisation set up to protect and promote indigenous food products and cultures, about local produce that needed artisanal production, and worked with the organisation's experts to draw up a code of production.

The pigs lived a happy and carefree life for thirteen or fourteen months in their sty, feeding on maize, bran, barley, soya and any fruit that didn't make it to the distributors. Sergio's father looked after them. He had grown up on a mixed farm, where his parents had kept pigs, and had learnt about their ways. He loved his pigs, he said. He named them, fed them, washed them, mucked out their sty and nursed them when they got sick, staying up all night with them, if necessary.

However, each November and December – the *salama* can be made only during those months, when the weather is cold enough, according to Slow Food regulations – at fourteen months that was it: off they went to the abattoir thirty kilometres away. Even that relatively short journey disturbed Sergio's father. 'If it wasn't for the hygiene regulations and the EU rules, I would slaughter them here. It would be much less stressful for the animals,' he said.

The carcasses were brought back to the farm, where they were butchered. The choicest cuts, such as the leg and loin, were made into *salame all'aglio.* The lesser but tastier cuts, such as shoulder, neck, belly and cheek, went into the *salama da sugo,* along with tongue, a small amount of liver and fat. Some of the meat was cut by hand, a smaller proportion by machine. The sausage mix was thoroughly soaked in a great deal of wine – '*Buon vino.* Sangiovese di Romagna. Some makers add rum, or *nocino* [nut liqueur] or cinnamon,' said Sergio, 'but I don't think that that's a good idea. I just want to taste the meat and the wine. If the meat is good enough, that's what you want.' Then it's all packed into *la vescica*, the bladder.

'But it has been thoroughly cleaned,' Sergio assured me, in case I found the notion of using the bladder offensive.

'But why the bladder?'

Because it is the last bit of the pig left.' I did not ask if Eurocrats had got round to bladder specifications yet. Or perhaps bladders were exempt from Eurocratic consideration.

We were standing in the room where these wonders of the sausage world were made. It was a medium-sized space, clean and white. A child's model car stood on a stainless-steel table among mincing machines and other tools of the trade. The walls were tiled in the approved EU manner, but the table, on which the butchery was carried out, was a plain, wooden farmhouse table. There was a fireplace at one end of the room, with a large pot suspended from a moving arm.

'We make *ciccioli* in it with any bits left over,' explained Sergio. *Ciccioli* are a kind of Emilian pork scratchings. 'We don't waste anything,' he said, repeating the mantra of Candido Passamonti in the Marche.

Once the skins of the *salame all'aglio* and bladders of the *salame da sugo* were safely packed, they were taken to the maturing room, which had been converted from another farm building next door, where they were strung up from metal rods and left to age for at least a year. There did not appear to be any form of refrigeration, other than the natural, airy cool of the room, and the only form of protection that I could make out was the floor-to-ceiling flyproof mesh mounted on a distinctly home-made wooden frame.

The *salame* looked like large, furry gourds. They were dark and slightly knobbly inside their string nets. Each had a label attached to it, with the name of the customer written on it and the date when they were made. These were bespoke sausages.

'People come along and choose their *salamina*, and we keep them here until they want them, at Easter or Christmas,' Sergio explained. Some were two years old. 'Occasionally people forget about them or prefer the extra ageing. The older they get, the stronger and sharper the flavour,' he said.

We walked across the yard to the house where his mother and father lived, and ate lunch in the kitchen. We started with another Ferrarese speciality, *cappellacci*, one of the apparently endless varieties of ravioli filled with pumpkin in pork sauce, the mild sweetness of the pumpkin contrasting with the potent, salty condiment.

And then we came to the *salama da sugo*, which was served according to tradition with mashed potato, made with boiling milk, butter and grated Parmesan. 'Usually it is served broken up, like a kind of stew,' she said, 'but we cut ours up. We prefer it that way.'

I helped myself to two pieces, and some potato. When I finished these, I had a third piece, and then a fourth. The thick slices of sausage were a dark, purply brown. Their texture was compact and dense. Each exploded in my mouth with a flavour of enormous power, very deep and full, with a keen salty edge. Small chunks of fat greased each mouthful. The bland, unsalted mashed potato acted as a perfect foil, absorbing the fat, a neutral antibody to the intensity of the meat. I would have eaten the whole thing, had my stomach allowed. It was tremendous, stupendous, monster, prodigious, the definitive boiling sausage, intense, colossal in its depth of flavour, penetrating and pervading every corner of my mouth, spicy, rich, complex, intoxicating.

'What do you think?' asked *la signora* anxiously.

I was stricken by the inadequacy of my Italian to express the full range of my astonishment and pleasure. I considered kissing her hand, and then thought better of it. 'It's very nice,' I said. 'Very, very, very nice.'

While we ate, we talked about pigs and fat, about the decline of the traditional use of *strutto* (pork fat) in baking, and about the pleasures of *ciccioli*. I said that we had our own *ciccioli* in England, called pork scratchings, and that people used to use lard or beef dripping in baking, but hardly anyone did anymore because they didn't think it was healthy. That was ridiculous, they said. Sergio's father said that he was so fond of pork fat that he used the *contadino's* trick of dressing his salad with vinegar and warm pig fat, and then eating it very quickly before the fat had time to congeal.

We spoke, too, about the drift of young people away from farming, about the shape of the farming of the future. The Natalis belonged to a scheme that opened the farm to the public twice a year. We discussed different marketing ideas – websites, farm gates, farmers' markets. It struck me that these people were desperate for outside interest, different points of view, ideas that might give them some kind of economic hope. Making these sausages wasn't a hobby for the family, or a gesture towards doing their bit for Ferrarese culinary culture. It represented a serious form of income for the farm, diversification, another activity that would allow them to continue the way of life that they knew. It seemed very hard to me.

We finished with some of their 'Abate' pears, dripping with sweet juices, and fat flakes of Parmesan, and I left them in the warm afternoon sunshine, ready to go back to the strawberry beds.

Such people have become marginalised in our contemporary culture. Seventy years ago Cesare Pavese wrote novels and short stories about the *mezzadria* of Piedmont. Fifty years ago Michelangelo Antonioni made documentaries about the workers of the Po delta. Films such as *Riso Amaro* and *The Tree of the Wooden Clogs* were declared classics. Now, with agriculture so economically insignificant, farmers and growers and producers have found no place in contemporary literature or the cinema. There is no one to tell their stories.

I left Ferrara, and headed for Mantua. As I crossed from Emilia-Romagna into Lombardy, the landscape seemed to change subtly. It wasn't any less flat or endless, or less intensively farmed come to that, but now there were trees, regimented blocks of ragged-headed willows and plumed poplars silhouetted by the mist on the horizon. The trees gave the landscape scale and contrast. They were vertical, not horizontal. They suggested finitude, not the infinity of the unbroken prairie. Their shapes were more beautiful than factories. Their leaves were turning and beginning to fall.

There were people, too. I passed a field where half a dozen or so workers were picking French beans. There were already several boxes filled with them, crisp, bright and green. Some tractors were chewing up what remained of the maize stubble. Others were already ploughing, tipped over at an impossible angle, the wheels on one side resting on the untilled ground, those on the other churning through the preceding furrow, the dark earth curling away from the plough in glistening, chocolate waves.

The houses in the small villages scattered along the way had smart, flower-bright gardens, with persimmons glowing amber-yellow against dark leaves, pomegranates as bright as Christmas decorations and unobtrusive *giuggiole*. Vegetable gardens were tucked away at the back, to be glimpsed over hedges, through fences or in gaps between the houses. From time to time there were signs of rural neglect, too: deserted, shuttered houses, abandoned farm buildings, tumbledown barns. But, for the most part, the land seemed well managed and well worked, providing substantial benefits for those who stayed.

It was very pleasant riding for the most part, but cold. I had four layers on top (T-shirt, shirt, jersey, jacket) and three below (pants, long johns, trousers). I was grateful for every layer. The mist stayed with me all day, although little by little the world turned a soft gold, and the day was drowsy with warmth by the time I stopped at one of the rare spots where the road ran along the edge of the Po for a short while.

I sat on a bench in the smoky sunlight, watching people fishing off a mud bank on the far side of the river, and dozed. Presently an old man came and sat next to me on the bench. He was smartly dressed in a blue suit and blue shirt, with polished black shoes and a snappy, old-fashioned hat of the kind that Bing Crosby used to wear. He was very tanned, and his face looked as if it had been refined by the wind and the sun. His voice was gentle and hesitant.

He said something, but I couldn't understand a word, so dense was the dialect. As soon as he realised that I couldn't follow what he was saying, he switched to standard Italian, and apologised. He told me that he had once been a professional fisherman on the river.

'Not now. Many years ago. We used to fish *con le rete* [with nets]. *Capisce?*' And he mimed throwing a net. 'Not fishing with a rod. We fished from *una barca* [a boat], and there would be four of us, two to handle the boat and two to handle the net.'

They caught carp, eels and catfish, he said, and other fish, too.

'And pike?'

Yes. And pike.

There weren't any fishermen anymore, not fishermen like him and his friends. 'They are hobby fishermen,' he said, gesturing with his chin at the people on the far bank. 'Not professional fishermen. We fished to eat and to live.'

'What fish did you like to eat best?' I asked.

'Catfish. Catfish was best, just fried in butter.'

'No onion or wine?'

'No. Just butter. Simple is best.'

He wouldn't eat the fish from the river now. It had changed. The water wasn't so good. Anyway, there was this fish, *il pesce siluro*, a kind of giant catfish, in the Po that ate all the other fish. But he still came down to the river.

Every day?

'Most days, in the afternoon. About now.'

He nodded to me, and wished me a good trip, and got into his car and drove off.

Just outside Mantua, there was another secret world, tucked away among the motorways, trunk roads, bypasses, factories, industrial zones, shopping centres and all the other paraphernalia of the modern urban sprawl. It was a world of canals, streams, tributaries, waterways and watercourses, of water trapped, directed, redirected, switched, blocked, sent down this channel or that; of reed beds and rushes, willow and poplar; and, it has to be said, of the overwhelming rank, gamey smell of pig.

Although there were more than a million pigs in the region, I never saw one. They were hidden away in huge units, for reasons, I deduced, of economics. If they were kept in barns, they were easier to look after, and it was easier to control their feed. More to the point, they took up less room than if they were allowed to roam in less intensive, free-range systems. Put them out on to the fields, and the owners wouldn't be able to use that lovely, rich soil to grow profitable sugar beet, maize or rice. And obviously there was a good deal of money circulating hereabouts, to judge by the massive establishments.

The water wasn't there for the pigs. It was there for the rice: *arborio, vialone nano* and *carnaroli*. This small corner of the *zona mantovana*, where the villages had names such as Cadé, Villa Garibaldi and Roncoferraro, wasn't the really big rice-producing area of Italy. That was over towards Pavia, Vercelli and Novara. Rice wasn't even the major cash crop around here, to judge by the maize stubble and sugar beet mountains; but if you want quality rice, this is where you came for it. At least, that's what Signor Vanzini, a tall, trim, bald figure in a pair of bright scarlet shoes, told me at Il Galeotto, a mill near Cadé.

Rice was grown in India and Asia at least 3,500 years before Christ. Quite why it took so long to reach Europe is something of a mystery. The Greeks and Romans knew of it, but treated it as a medicine, as was usual when foodstuffs were prohibitively expensive. There seems to be some dispute as to who should claim the honour of introducing rice to Italy. Some say it was the Arabs, who created paddy fields in Sicily in the thirteenth century. Other authorities argue that rice was brought back to Europe by Alexander the Great in the third century BC, and came to Italy much earlier. As usual, the subject is a minefield of conflicting academic monographs, in which the ingenuous amateur has no place.

Suffice it to say that the fields of rice and their manner of cultivation were well established around Vercelli, further north from Mantua, by 1427, when they began to register on official correspondence and tax receipts. And, as cultivation depended on large amounts of controllable water, which that area has, that's where it continues to be grown. Other localities with similar conditions, such as this corner of the province of Mantua, also turned to it as a cash crop.

Il Galeotto had not been around for so long, but it had been operating on that spot since 1763, when, as a handsome framed document on the wall declared, Francesco Galeotto was licensed by the Empress Maria Theresa – this part of Italy was still part of the Austro-Hungarian empire at the time – to use the waters of the stream to power the wheel that ground the husks from the corn and the rice – and still did.

The mill squatted over the clear, powerfully flowing waters of some nameless brook. Part of the building was converted into the kitchen and dining room needed for an *azienda agricola*. The rest still housed the mill and all its wooden, water-driven workings, which had been lovingly renovated to pristine working condition. At the flick of a switch, Signor Vanzini, grandson of the woman who bought the property from the heirs of Francesco Galeotto, opened a sluice gate to increase the flow of water through a watercourse and on to the wooden paddles of the great mill wheel, housed at one end of the mill. The wheel went from stationary to full, powerful circulation with remarkable speed, the sound it made hardly audible above the rush of water. Next door, in the milling room, wooden cogs began to turn and engage with a gentle rumble, but there was no rice yet for its threshing machinery to work on. The rice wasn't ready yet. Maybe in a week's time, said Signor Vanzini, they would begin harvesting the family's rice fields at Ronconferraro some eight kilometres away.

It had not been an easy year for rice, Signor Vanzini said. They had planted it in May, as normal, because rice needs sunlight and heat almost as much as it needs water to provide nutrients and to regulate the temperature. But the succession of storms that had rolled over northern Italy throughout that summer had sent the temperature rising and falling like a seismic wave. Even so, he was confident that their rice would be up to its normal quality. They only produced about 2,000 quintals a year, but the slow, gentle milling of the traditional water-driven system meant that the finished husked rice, the speciality of the locality, was at its best. Of course it was more expensive, he said. It should be. The method that they used at Il Galeotto was slow and more labour-intensive, but when it came to quality, well, it was the best.

'What about chemicals?' I asked. I had read that growing rice in Italy depended on chemicals, and yet more chemicals, and that pesticide residues had become a serious problem.

This was true up near Vercelli and Novara, said Signor Vanzini, where the rice was grown very intensively, and maybe some of the big rice producers in this area weren't as careful as they might be, but the rice for Il Galeotto had to be the best, so they only used *'un sistema che rispetta l'ambiente'*.

So I sat down in a dining room next to the threshing room, and ate some; a creamy *risotto con la zucca* (pumpkin), which used *carnaroli* rice suitable for sloppy risotti; a *risotto con pesce d'acqua dolce* (freshwater fish), and a *risotto con maiale e salsiccia* (pork and sausage), which both used *vialone nano* because these dishes were dry.

In Britain, *arborio* rice is commonplace in most supermarkets. I had come across *carnaroli* and *vialone nano* in some, as well as in specialist delis, but of *baldo, balilla* and *Sant' Andrea*, let alone *cripto, rubino, rosa marchetti, lido, titanio, monticelli, italico* and *maratelli* and two dozen other varieties, I knew nothing. Still less did I know about the classification of each variety by size and shape of grain into *comuni, semifini, fini* and *superfini*. Needless to say, each had precisely designated uses, although which rice was most suitable for which dish was, as usual, the subject of intense debate.

The chef at Il Galeotto, one of Signor Vanzini's sons, clearly knew his stuff as far as the family's own rice was concerned. The *risotto con la zucca* was delicious in its unctuous smoothness, and this was the season of pumpkin, after all, but the dry risotti were more interesting, because I had never come across them before. They involved a technique that required absolute precision in how much water – you only ever used water for these dishes, apparently – and rice you used. The water was brought to the boil, and all the rice poured in at once. The lid was put on the top of the saucepan, the heat turned off, and the rice left for twenty minutes or so. The rice absorbed all the water, leaving each grain perfectly cooked but separate from its fellow.

The result was delicious, dry and nutty, particularly when served with tiny little fish – minuscule carp and minnows, and the smallest shrimps I had ever seen, smaller than the nail on my little finger, fried crisp, and *croccanti*, which were like whitebait. They were caught, according Signor Vanzini, in the rice fields, which sounded delightfully holistic, but I was not sure that I believed him. More likely they came out of the innumerable watercourses. I wondered who caught them; it was something of a mystery.

When I left Mantua for Cremona, thick fog blanketed everything. Through it, unseen, hurtled vast sixteen-wheeler articulated lorries, causing Bud to wobble alarmingly as the turbulence they caused threatened to suck us beneath their great tyres, or send us spinning into who-knew-what gulf beyond the edge of the road. I made my habitual modest speed more modest still, and was very glad of the various layers of protection, particularly my long johns, in spite of their irritating habit of sliding inexorably and uncomfortably down my bum until they came to rest at the top of my thighs.

Then I got lost. And lost again. The thinning of the fog did little to illuminate my lostness. I was getting a little tired of the flat, fecund immensity of the Pianura Padana before I got to Mantua. It was made no more appealing by the sudden mushrooming of enormous factories beside the road. And then there was the matter of lunch. The prospect of reaching my designated trattoria faded and then vanished. Pangs of notional hunger began to flutter in my brain.

In desperation I pulled over at a scruffy-looking trattoria just outside a scruffy village. When I went into the dining room, my spirits soared. It was packed. There was linoleum on the floor and cheap tongue-and-groove panelling on the walls. There were two hard-working, hard-faced waitresses clattering among the tables. This is it, I thought. One of those places kept secret from restaurant inspectors and tourists, where real people tuck into the real food of the area.

I proceeded to eat one of the nastiest meals I had had in a long time. First came a plate of *maccheroni* in a puddle of water with a swathe of gritty low-caste *ragù* slopped on top. And then a chicken leg of Frankensteinian proportions swimming in grease, which managed to be both tasteless and dry, in spite of the grease. With it I had *patate al forno*, potatoes which, if they had seen as much of the inside of the oven as they had of the tin from which they indubitably came, might possibly have just been edible. And they swum in grease, too. It's funny what you'll eat if you're desperate.

EATING UP ITALY

Recipes

CAPPELLACCI DI ZUCCA CON SUGO DI MAIALE

Pumpkin-filled cappellacci with pork sauce

Serves 4

Pour the flour onto a work surface and make a well in the centre. Break an egg into the well. Using a fork or fingertips, draw the flour into the egg and mix in. Repeat the process with each of the eggs. Knead vigorously. It will be pretty stiff to begin with, but gradually – after about 15 minutes – it will become soft and pliant. Roll into a ball and leave to rest while you cook the pumpkin.

Heat the oven to 375°. Wash the pumpkin, cut off the top and scoop out the seeds. Place the pumpkin on a baking tray. Bake for 90 minutes, or until the flesh can be pierced easily with a knife. Cool, peel and chop finely. Season with salt and pepper and grated nutmeg. Mix with the Parmesan.

ASSEMBLY

Divide the dough and roll out into thin sheets. Cut out rounds approximately 3 inches across. Plop a teaspoon of pumpkin mixture on each round. Fold the circle of dough in half, over the filling. Pull the ends of the semicircle together round your index finger. The two ends should

For the pasta

4 1/4 cups durum flour

5 eggs

For the filling

3 1/2 lbs pumpkin

Salt and pepper, to taste

Nutmeg

2 1/4 cups grated Parmesan

For the sauce

1 onion

1 carrot

1 stick of celery

3 oz pancetta

4 oz *strutto* (pork fat)

12 oz minced pork

1/2 cup red wine

1/2 cup stock

overlap slightly. Press them firmly together.

Finely dice the onion, carrot, celery and pancetta. Fry in the pork
fat until soft – about 10 minutes.
Add the pork and fry gently until
brown. Add the wine and boil
until evaporated. Add the stock
and cook gently for 90 minutes.
Turn up the heat and boil until
most of the liquid has reduced.
The flavour of the pork should
be quite intense.

Boil the cappellacci in salted
water for 5 minutes. Serve immediately, with the pork sauce.

PURÉ DI PATATE

Mashed potato

The classic accompaniment for the great salama da sugo

Serves 4

Wash the potatoes. Do not peel. Put them into a saucepan and cover with cold water. Bring to the boil. Simmer until cooked, 20–30 minutes, depending on their size and age. When cooked, drain and allow to cool slightly. Peel while still warm. Mash or, even better, put through a food mill or potato ricer. Beat in the butter. Heat the milk in a saucepan. Do not let it boil. As soon as little bubbles begin to show around the edge of the milk, pour into the mashed potato. Beat in thoroughly. Add the grated Parmesan and beat some more. Taste and season accordingly. Serve immediately with the sublime sausage, which has been gently simmered for at least 2 hours, either broken up as a sauce or in slices. Would also go very well with top quality U.S. sausage.

1 lb starchy potatoes
1/4 cup butter
2/3 cup milk
1 1/4 cups grated Parmesan
Salt and pepper, to taste

CICCIOLI AND CICCIOLI D'OCA

Pork scratchings and goose scratchings

In Italy no part of the pig is wasted. Even the fat is put to a number of different uses. The purest fat – strutto – is used in cooking, baking in particular. Back fat is cured to make the famous lardo di Collonata. Lardo, made from the cheek, is a delicacy from Parma. The fatty membrane on the outside of the intestine turns up as ciaramboli in the Marche. However, as anyone who has ever rendered down pork fat knows, there is always a kind of crunchy structure left at the end, sometimes with shards of meat still attached or a fragment of crackled skin. These are ciccioli. They are found all over the country (cicoli in Campania, sfrizzoli in Lazio). The same principle applies to goose fat, and ciccioli d'oca is a speciality of Mortara in Lombardy, near which I passed on my scooter. Not surprisingly, it was appreciated by the Jewish communities of northern Italy, being the local version of the gribenes of Ashkenazi tradition.

Ciccioli are usually cooked in bulk, and very slowly – in Salumi d'Italia, the Slow Food authors recommend six hours for 67½ pounds. The home cook does not deal in such quantities. Simply place the cut-up bits of pork or goose to be rendered in a heavy-bottomed pan, place over a low heat or in a low oven and leave there for 3–4 hours. When you judge that all the available fat has been extracted by heat, take the pan off/out of the heat. Pour off the liquid fat, gently pressing the *ciccioli* to extract the last drop. You can eat the crisp, golden bits warm, sprinkled with salt and pepper, with bread as an antipasto, or sprinkled over a salad dressed with pork fat and vinegar. Or keep them and reheat for later use.

RISOTTO CON LA ZUCCA
Pumpkin risotto

In spite of endless expertise regarding which rice is suitable for soups, antipasti, risotti and puddings, it seems that the Piemontese and Lombardi prefer carnaroli *and* vialone nano *from around Mantua, Verona and Venice. So where* arborio *and all the other varieties come in, heaven only knows. Whatever I write is likely to offend someone. Both these recipes come from around Mantua, and so use* vialone nano. *Incidentally, the wheat-like head of a rice plant forms part of the pattern on wallpaper in the Palazzo Gonzaga in the city.*

Serves 6

Melt the butter in the pan in which you are going to cook the risotto. Bring the stock or water to the boil in another pan. Finely dice the onion and celery and saute in the melted butter. Add the pumpkin, cut into chunks, and the rice. Turn in the butter for 4–5 minutes. Pour the boiling stock into the rice and pumpkin pan all at once. Lower the heat to cook the rice slowly. Do not stir. Cover with the lid and cook for 15 minutes. Remove the lid. The contents should be perfectly cooked, and quite dry. Beat in plenty of grated Parmesan.

1/4 cup butter

4 cups vegetable, chicken or veal stock, or water

1 small onion

1 stick of celery

1 lb pumpkin meat, seeded and cubed

2 cups *vialone nano* rice

Grated Parmesan

RISOTTO ALLA PILOTA MAILE E SALSICCIA

Risotto pilota style with pork and sausage meat

Many years ago, rice was husked by hand, by men known as piloti or pilarini. They were also put in charge of cooking rice dishes for the mondine, the rice pickers. Nowadays, the power of the piloti lives on in the claims of various resturants and aziende agricole. Actually, the recipe uses a technique for cooking the rice that I had never come across before. As it involves absolutely no effort, it should appeal to those who balk at the constant stirring risotti require. Oh yes, and according to Signor Vanzini, no stock or wine, just water.

Serves 4–6

Melt the butter in a pan. Fry the sausage meat, pork and onion until they are cooked and the pork is tender.

In another pot, bring the water to the boil. Pour the rice into the boiling water all at once to form a pyramid with its top just below the surface of the water. Shake the pan gently to collapse the pyramid. Add a little salt. Put the top on the pan, and cook very gently for 10 minutes. Turn off the heat and let it stand for another 10 minutes. The rice should have absorbed all the water and be quite dry. Stir in a good deal of grated Parmesan and then the pork. Serve immediately.

1/4 cup butter

1/2 lb Italian sausage meat

1/2 lb pork, cut into small cubes

1 onion, finely chopped

Water – the locals will tell you that you need the same quantity of rice to water, plus half a cup for the pot

1 3/4 cups *Vialone Nano* rice

Salt

Grated Parmesan

11
THE MOZART OF
MUSHROOMS

CREMONA – CASALE
MONFERRATO – ASTI
BRA – TURIN

Tartuffi bianchi

The proprietor brought something that looked like a large cigar box to the table, and opened it. Immediately the air was full of the unmistakable, bosky, musky, primordial, sexy odour of white truffles.

I came to Cremona through the usual *cordon insanitaire* of industrial zones.

I went to the hotel where I had booked a room two days before. No, said the old biddy at the reception desk, we have no booking in that name here. Are you sure? I said. I rang two days ago. Quite sure, she said. We're fully booked. Then began a theatrical display of bad temper, as the old biddy blamed her husband, slouched in a chair behind her, for his incompetence, while he blamed her for I cared not what. The efficient young woman in the tourist office explained that local hoteliers hereabouts operate on the same basis as airlines: they double book, take the early arrivals and plead ignorance to the rest.

However, the lady in the tourist office eventually found me a room, in the most depressing hotel I had stayed in since I was a teenager. The room was below ground level, and gloomy. The soundproofing was such that every other guest seemed to be occupying some corner, even though I couldn't see them. Once again a great wave of depression and hopelessness and home-sickness swept over me. It's possible to laugh at such trials when there is someone to laugh with. On my own, they seemed to lose their humour. What was it that the poet said about the darkest hour coming just before the dawn? The poet was an ass.

I went back into the Piazza del Duomo that evening, and sauntered about in front of the wonderful façade of the Duomo, with its spectacular campanile, the highest in Italy, and treated myself to a Campari soda in one of the several cafés. I watched a black man trying to sell tiny carved animals to the café's patrons. He went over to a table around which sat six well-dressed men and women and put one of his wares on it. He stood there but they did not acknowledge his presence in any way. They went on chatting and playing with their mobile phones. He didn't exist for them.

While sipping and pondering, I rang the highly rated restaurant La Sosta. The conversation went like this:

'Do you have a table for dinner tonight?'

'Certainly. For how many?'

'For one person.'

'For one?'

'Yes.'

'We have no tables.'

'What, not —' Click.

Cremona might be the town of Monteverdi, Ponchielli, Amati father and son, Stradivarius and Guarneri, it might be prosperous and pleased with itself and its women among the most beautiful in the land, but there was something wrong with the attitude of its citizens. They lacked charity. They lacked generosity. For all their celebrated virtues of thrift and hard work, the Cremonese seemed to be equally thrifty with charm and unacceptably hard-faced in matters of commercial self-interest.

But then, round the corner, in the Piazza Stradivari, I found a rally in support of a national strike called by the CGIL, the former-Communist trade union, just getting under way. There were red flags, stilt walkers, jugglers with flaming brands, up-beat saccharine pop music, food and whole families out for the evening, wrapped up against the chill and chattering away. It was an endearingly sociable scene, more family picnic than mass protest, more group outing than storming the barricades. It was odd to think that, just a few yards away, the Cremonese entrepreneurs, industrialists and rich farmers sat sipping their fizzy, pink Lambrusco or Campari.

The slightly otherworldly atmosphere was enhanced by an impromptu concert given among the tables by a woman in medieval dress playing a hurdy-gurdy, with a strenuous guitarist/vocalist, a chap bashing a drum and another rattling a tambourine. It all went rather well with the social aspect of the evening.

For a few Euros I got a plate of *salumi (salami, coppa* and *prosciutto cotto)*, a fat slice of frittata with zucchini and onions on it, a slice of apple tart, all of good quality, a lot of bread and a glass of wine, and waited while the comrades gathered. I wondered what a similar gathering in Britain would come up with by way of food. In the unlikely event of my ever joining a Communist party (unlikely because I have a pathological dislike of joining groups that call for collective belief and action), then it would be the Italian DS or Democratici di Sinistra as it has been rebranded. At least they make sure you get fed properly, even if their sense of timekeeping is flexible. According to the timetable of the *festa*, the main speaker was billed at 9 a.m. At 9:15, there was still no sign of him. There was no sign of anybody.

The secretary of the local CGIL eventually turned up at 9:20. He wasn't quite Demosthenes. He wasn't even forceful enough to silence the lively chatter of the crowd of party faithful that was going on around me, fuelled by two hours of gentle drinking and comradeship. However, when he finished there was prolonged and stormy applause, as they used to say in *Pravda*, and I went back to my dreary hotel much restored.

I was utterly weary of the eternal monotony of the Pianura Padana. The roads were so straight for kilometre after kilometre that they began to induce the hallucinatory illusion that I was remaining static. Only a check at my watch would confirm the passing of time, or the occasional signpost establish the sensation of movement. An endless succession of rice fields – tidy rectangles, stretching away into infinity, a dull, reddish gold through the fog – was quite as boring as an endless succession of sugar beet and maize fields. In summer the weather would have made the region into a vast steamer, sultry, sticky and sweltering, and infested with mosquitoes. Presently, it would turn grey and freezing. Right then it was just grey and cold. Locked away inside my helmet, I tried to ponder on what Jack Kerouac had meant by 'the purity of the road', but I simply became obsessed with keeping warm, wondering if I had made some major map-reading error, when I would eat next, how I was going to organise a clothes wash and other like matters of international significance.

The chilly tedium was broken briefly when I was hauled in by the police, one of the innumerable branches of the constabulary. The pretext was that I did not have my headlight on.

'Where are you going?' asked the principal interrogator, who sported a moustache of startling size, like trophy horns on a buffalo.

'Turin.'

'Turin! On a Vespa? Where have you come from?'

'Ancona.'

'Ancona!'

'Well, I'm doing this tour of Italy.'

'On a Vespa!?'

This generated a great deal of moustache chewing as he consulted his companion, who was as smooth as he was hairy. I got the impression that they would have liked to have had a long chat about my adventures, but the gravity of their office got the better of them, and they sent me on my way.

'You're lucky it was us,' called out the moustached one. 'If it had been the Polizia Statale, you would have been in real trouble.'

After this, I was pleased to putter into Casale Monferrato in time for lunch. The seasonal Sardinian and Sicilian chestnut roasters were busy in the square in front of the Castello dei Paleologi, clouds of smoke rising from their braziers into the chill morning air. I was even more pleased to meet Augusto Lana, a retired printer who bore more than a passing resemblance to the Walrus in *Alice in Wonderland*, and, like the Walrus, was very keen on his food and wine.

I parked Bud and off we went for lunch at a trattoria in Serralunga di Crea, in the hills outside Casale. I was immensely cheered by the sight of land that wasn't as flat as a skillet. Even through the curtain of rain that had now set in, the countryside was very beautiful, rounded hill folding into rounded hill, winding valleys, this slope laid out in the neat order of a vineyard, that lined with poplars or walnuts or elm, their leaves turning and falling. There were the inevitable blocks of maize, but also garden patches stuffed with lines of cardoons trussed up in brown paper, feathery with fennel and bustling with cabbages.

We had a splendid lunch distinguished by the best risotto that I had ever eaten, flavoured simply with stock and Parmesan, and served in a hollowed-out half-cheese. It was one of those dishes, the flavour of which was so profound, so all-enveloping, so penetrating that it seemed to permeate my entire body. There was a subtle carpaccio of veal; some *agnolotti* – yet another ravioli variant; and a number of other dishes as well that I forgot to write down because I was listening to the chef, who went simply by the name of Balin, and Augusto duetting on matters of rice, wine, local food, politics and the culinary traditions of the area.

Augusto reported that he had recently got into trouble by suggesting that rice culture and tourism might be incompatible. 'The trouble is,' he said, 'that you need water to grow rice, and mosquitoes breed in the water and feed on the tourists. I said that I didn't think the area would ever be a great tourist destination while the mosquitoes were here. This didn't go down very well. Of course, they could get rid of the mosquitoes with pesticide, but these days everyone is so concerned about the environment that they don't dare.'

Soon, however, the conversation drifted back into the culinary mainstream. Balin said, quite rightly, that treating recipes as the result of some kind of carefully graduated, rational process was obviously nonsense.

'Cooking is a matter of practicality. The housewife cooks with whatever she has. If she wants to make *agnolotti*, she doesn't carefully measure out 100 grams of chicken and 100 grams of veal. She takes whatever she has left over, meat and vegetables, minces it up, and makes the filling out of that. 'It is the same with *fritto misto*. Originally *fritto misto* was a way of using up the bits of meat that weren't used in the kitchens of the local landowner. That's why it consisted of coxcombs, calf's spinal column, brains, sweetbreads and all the rest. These were the leftovers. Of course, these days it's become the food of the rich. But that's because the people who were poor, the contadini, moved to the cities and became better off. They could afford the expensive cuts of meat but still wanted to eat the food that reminded them of their roots. And so these dishes became rich dishes. It just goes to show, we shouldn't be too precious about recipes.'

Augusto pointed out that history changed food cultures, anyway. 'When I was a boy, there really weren't that many vegetables to choose from. Cabbage, cardoons, carrots, celery, stuff like that. Things changed in the markets when the southerners came north. They brought their taste for tomatoes, chili, *cime di rapa*, broccoli, *broccoletti* and chicories with them, and that transformed choice in the markets for the rest of us.'

As I had travelled up the Po valley, I had kept coming across tantalising glimpses of the Jewish communities whose culture had once enriched the great towns, Ferrara and Mantua in particular. There was little or nothing left of these communities now, but in Casale Monferrato there was a particularly charming eighteenth-century synagogue, its blue, cream and gold interior graceful with rococo mouldings that might have been more at home in Vienna or Prague than in a small town in northern Italy; but of course this area had been part of the Austro-Hungarian empire for 200 years until the Risorgimento precipitated by Garibaldi had led to the Habsburg dynasty being driven out of Italy.

Until 1938 there had been 2,000 Jews living in Casale, with a history stretching back to 1492, when they had fled from Spain to escape the pogroms of Ferdinand and Isabella. They flourished under the Gonzagas, who showed a religious tolerance that has been rare in Europe since, particularly in the century just past.

'Now there are eight of us,' said Signora Ottolenghi, sitting in her spartan office at the back of the synagogue in Casale Monferrato. She was a short, handsome woman with charm and energy like a forcefield. 'The sad thing is that most Jews were reported to the authorities by their neighbours. I prefer to think that they did not know that the Jews were going to concentration camps and their deaths,' she added with a degree of humanity that was remarkable.

There was still a rich tradition of Jewish/Italian food, she said, such as *salame d'oca* (a sausage of goose wrapped in the skin of the neck), *ciccioli d'oca* (crisp goose fat), *prosciutto d'oca* (goose prosciutto), *polpettone di pollo* (chicken meat balls), *involtini di tacchino* (roll of turkey), *nidi di uova e carciofi* (nests of eggs and artichokes), *testina di spinaci* (little head of spinach), *torta puntura d'api* (literally bee-sting cake – the stings perhaps a poetic image for the shards of almonds), to name but a few.

She confirmed that the Sephardic and Ashkenazi cooking traditions had mingled freely in Italy and become entangled inextricably with Italy's own non-Jewish dishes. Luckily there had been much about Italian food culture that sat easily with Jewish dietary regulations. In fact, Signora Ottolenghi claimed that the celebrated Casalese biscuit, the *krumiro*, which, legend has it, was formed in the shape of the moustache of some Austro-Hungarian emperor, was in fact based on the Jewish *masod nasirod*. 'The ingredients are virtually identical,' she pointed out.

In spite of the decline in the numbers of her community, she and other members of the congregation actively continued the former traditions of inter-community tolerance. 'The other day,' she said as we walked along the passage that led to the heavy door that opened on to a quiet back street, 'we held a joint celebration in Casale with the Christian church and the Muslims. We each brought along the food of our faith, so that we could eat together afterwards. Food is a great bridge between people.'

The sun shone with the warmth of high summer. The sky was as blue as aquamarine. The hills between Casale and Asti were still in the golden autumnal heat. They reminded me of the open and rolling Colli del Verdicchio of the Marche. There were the same blocks of regimented vines, their leaves now greeny gold or the colour of crushed red grape skins, laid out like the squares of infantry drawn up in eighteenth-century prints of the battle of Dettingen or Waterloo. But the trees were quite different. Whereas in the Marche there were cypresses and pines, here there were oaks, poplars, walnuts and groves of hazelnuts. The occasional medieval tower and fortified manor house aside, the houses seemed more modern, painted with white stucco. It was a civilised landscape, cultured as well as cultivated.

Asti is the city of fizzy wine and the poet Vittorio Alfieri, who ran off with the wife of a late Stuart Pretender. By the picturesque standards of Cremona, Mantua or Ferrara, or even Casale Monferrato, it was not much to look at. As I toured it in a gingerly fashion, some parts struck me as quite pleasant, but much of it was remarkably dreary, and just about the dreariest bit was around the station, which was where I found the Saclà factory head office and Giuseppe Ercole, brimming with youthful energy and world-weary charm.

Saclà is a successful medium-sized company specialising in certain pasta sauces, such as pesto, bottled vegetables and sundry other *condimenti* for the table. It is well known in Britain, and also exported to Germany, France, Switzerland, Japan and America, where it has established itself as a high-quality brand of Italian tracklements.

The company is an interesting example of a modern phenomenon of Italian food culture. It had been started about eighty years before by Giuseppe's grandfather, Armando Ercole, an entrepreneurial *contadino*, who bought vegetables from his fellow growers and bottled them to sell on. As well as being known for its fizzy wine, Asti is also the centre for the rich fruit and vegetable lands around; there was an excellent small public market, and a gigantic Mercato Ortofrutta, a glowering concrete construction in monolithic, neo-Stalinist style that housed a commercial fruit and vegetable market.

Saclà was still owned by the family, and, in its familial dynamism, outlook, and entrepreneurial agility, has much in common with many Asian companies in Britain, while at the same time being just as much a part of Italian food culture as the most horny-handed sheeps' cheese producer in the Monte Matese or the Sabbatini fish stall in Ancona.

Giuseppe, one of the third generation, had been responsible for a strategy that had seen the company's exports grow from nothing to 45 per cent of Saclà's profits in ten years. Exports, he predicted, should overtake Italian sales within a year or two.

'The Italian market is still very fragmented,' he explained.

'We are the market leader in pesto and other sauces, but we have a long way to go before we have the supermarket culture that you have in Britain. Some companies – Famila and Auchan, for example – are growing, but still the bulk of the food market is broken up between individual shops and small local chains. That's one of the reasons we have to look abroad for growth.'

Giuseppe took me to lunch at a rather elegant trattoria outside Asti. Before we set about choosing our dishes, he summoned the proprietor, who brought something that looked like a large cigar box to the table, and opened it. Immediately the air was full of the unmistakable, bosky, musky, primordial, sexy odour of white truffles. There must have been thousands of pounds' worth of them. I seemed to remember Gertrude Stein saying that one should only ever eat truffles when you can eat them as if they were potatoes. Such vulgarity. Director of exports or not, there was something warming about a chap who picked up and sniffed a dozen truffles one after the other, before selecting the one he wanted, and grated it on to his veal tartare and then on to his plate of *agnolotti* stuffed with *fonduta* (melted cheese).

Giuseppe sat back with a smile of hedonistic satisfaction.

'This is the moment I most look forward to in the year,' he said. 'The first truffle! The season has only just started, and they haven't developed their full flavour yet. They won't be at their best until November or December. Then the perfume is incredible. But these are good already. It is going to be a good year for truffles.'

'How can you tell?'

'They say that it's always a good year for truffles when it's a bad year for wine. And this year is not a good year for wine.'

So we ate the veal tartare and the *agnolotti*, separated by a helping of cardoon baked with cheese and *insalata russa* – Russian salad. Why Russian salad? It seemed to crop up with remarkable regularity in Piedmont, but I wasn't sure why, and no one was able to offer a reasonable explanation. Maybe it was a bizarre legacy from the days of French influences. It used to be a staple of the buffet table in Britain, albeit in a considerably more plebeian form than the refined version we ate.

Giuseppe spoke about Saclà's business possibilities; about supplying 7,000 new hotels in China; about the rigours of the Japanese market; the difficulties of maintaining absolute consistency when the raw materials vary in intensity from season to season; about the pressures of competing with the giant Italian food companies which were beginning to enter the markets that Saclà had pioneered; about the strains and stresses of a family business, the management of which embraced two generations who had different perspectives; and about the local passion for donkey meat.

These days, the British shy away from the very idea of eating horse or donkey, forgetting that horse was a regular part of our diet, in Yorkshire in particular, up until the 1930s. The Piedmontese have never lost their taste for it or donkey. I had come across donkey before, at L'Umbreleèr, a restaurant between Mantua and Cremona. It had been cooked to a kind of paste, *stracotto d'asino*, and served as a sauce with *maccheroncini*, short, plump pasta tubes slippery with butter. It had a distinctive but immensely subtle flavour. If I hadn't been told it was donkey, I rather doubt that I would have guessed.

The taste for donkey and horse goes back to the days when these animals were part of everyday agricultural life. In the frugal, unsentimental manner of agricultural communities, all the animals were looked on as a source of protein. Waste was not an option. And, in spite of the wholesale flight from the countryside to the cities, the taste obviously still flourished.

According to Giuseppe, horse was more to the taste of the lowland areas, where the animals had been more common on the farms, while donkey was a dainty of the mountains.

Donkeys had been used extensively in farming in the high regions, and not just in farming, either. Until recently, each man in the Mountain Fusiliers, a unit in the Italian army, had had a donkey assigned to him. As Giuseppe pointed out, the advantages for the Fusiliers were the same as they had been for the mountain farmers: 'Donkeys are very economical. They can carry heavy loads. They can go anywhere. They can eat anything. And you can eat them.'

In spite of the international thrust of his business, and his ceaseless world travel, business-school training and new-man attitude to child care, it was curious how sensitive he still seemed to be to the familial agricultural roots of the business. On the one hand, the family and the business had come immense distances in two generations, so that, on the surface, there seemed to be precious little in common with Armando Ercole's original venture. On the other, Giuseppe manifested, quite naturally, a sense of being connected to the past, in terms of feel for the quality of the products, understanding of the processes needed to produce the raw materials and connection with the underlying patterns of agricultural society from which they came.

We went back to his office. I mounted Bud and prepared for a lordly exit. Then Giuseppe pointed out that I had a flat back tyre. Oh, the shame of it. Almost 5,500 kilometres, and my first disaster.

As it turned out, if I had to have a puncture, it couldn't have happened anywhere better. People poured out of offices to lend a hand. Giuseppe stuck a baseball cap on his head and took command. A fork-lift truck was commandeered to take the Vespa to a tyre centre. The full weight of Saclà was used to help me jump the queue of people waiting to be served and get the tyre changed, and an hour or so later I headed out into Asti's rush-hour traffic and a greasy drizzle, in the direction of the Langhe hills, hotel, hearth and bed.

In 1996 I had been to a food show in Turin at which the sheer scale, diversity and quality of the foods on display had reduced me to a delirium of excitement. For anyone who had had their world view of food formed by the BBC *Good Food Show*, this was a revelation. Small was beautiful. Tiny was king. Craft skills and not manufacturing processes were celebrated. Quality not quantity was the defining criterion. Vast commercial food enterprises had no place in this. Supermarkets could not dominate the open spaces of the Lingotto, the former Fiat factory on the fringes of Turin, which had been converted into an exhibition centre. Here was the man who made the *lardo di Colonnata*, the woman who baked the *buccellato di fichi in Castellamare del Golfo*, and the keepers of the flame for *mustardela delle Valli Valdesi, fagioli Zolfino and agnello di Alpago*.

And here were the people who had paid to come in conversing with the producers, engaging in a debate in a way that was unimaginable in the National Conference Centre in Birmingham. They wanted to know what was the breed of cow that produced the milk for this cheese, when the cheese had been made, what the cattle had been grazing on, how long this salami had been hung for, why it was different from that other one, where had the sunflowers been growing on which the bees had feasted before making their honey. It was intoxicating stuff for anyone interested in food.

That was the first Salone del Gusto organised by Slow Food. This organisation had grown out of Arcigola, an agricultural pressure group set up by a group of friends with common left-of-centre political views. Slow Food started out as a visceral reaction to fast food, and the threat of the destruction of the national culinary culture by global commercial interests. Those basic premises developed into a much more radical philosophy designed to protect culinary diversity and biodiversity, promote sustainable agriculture and resist the commercial and political pressures that result in the globalisation and homogenisation of food cultures. In eighteen years, Slow Food has grown to be a substantial and formidable organisation, involving 80,000 members in forty countries, employing 100 or more very bright and mostly young people in Bra. It has developed an immensely sophisticated programme of membership activities, awards and publications, with a showcase for artisanal food producers, the Salone del Gusto, held every two years in Turin.

The founder, visionary and moving force behind all this was Carlo Petrini, now the president of Slow Food. I had admired him since I had heard him speak at a press conference during the Salone. He dealt with awkward questions of sponsorship with disarming candour and intelligence. But it was when he was asked to define his own passion for food that I really sat up and took notice. He had replied, 'When I wear a pair of Armani underpants, they do not become a part of Carlo Petrini. When I eat a slice of ham it becomes a part of Carlo Petrini. That is why I care about food.' It is rare, I remember thinking, to have a philosophy defined so pithily, wittily and exactly.

Now I had come to Bra to see Signor Petrini. I knew that he had recently been extremely ill. Although recovered, he was a much-reduced figure physically when I met him in his office cluttered with snails in almost every form and material, in keeping with the emblem of Slow Food. His face had been sculpted by illness, giving it a purified, intellectual asceticism, his neck did not fill his shirt and his fingers had a skeletal elegance. But his eyes were clear, his intellectual grasp undiminished, his energy abundant.

He held court not simply to me, but also to various groups of courtiers and supplicants. His discourse was mesmerising. Charm and words came from him in such a sparkling stream, and he expressed his views, on subjects both physical and metaphysical, with such lucidity and fluency, that to be the object of his monologue was deeply pleasurable. He had the ability to see his subject not only with a fundamental clarity but also in its entirety, cultural, social and historical.

'There are only two activities', he said, 'without which the human race would disappear, and they are both connected to pleasure. They are eating and making love. In spite of the individual efforts of people such as Grimaud de la Reynière and Brillat-

Savarin, gastronomy has never been analysed and codified in the way that other aspects of human experience have been, nor accorded the dignity of academic respect. We want to change all this. We should understand the importance of pleasure, in its anthropological, ethnic, agricultural, technological and cultural contexts. This is the reason that we are founding the University of Gastronomy.'

The university was his latest brainwave. The physical structure was taking shape at Pollenzo, a few kilometres south of Bra, in what had been a summer palace of the House of Savoy. It was a splendid, ornate nineteenth-century affair in vivid rufous brick.

As usual with Slow Food, the project had been financed with considerable sophistication. According to Petrini, the university would be run as a limited company, with three hundred shareholders. Part of the huge premises had been given over to a hotel group to turn into a luxury hotel. Part was going to be run as a top-class restaurant by two of Italy's most highly rated chefs, who were closing their own restaurants to do so. Part was being turned into a wine bank of Lago di Como proportions, where the ageing and tasting processes of wine could be scientifically studied and financed by some other group. This left one part of the complex for teaching purposes and a library.

There were to be two academic faculties, the legitimacy of each of which Petrini had persuaded the authorities to accept. The first would deal simply with matters of gastronomy, to establish and promote a basic understanding of how we eat, what we eat, and the connections between ingredients and cooking, and between cooking and tasting. The second faculty was to be devoted to *la conoscenza della materia prima* – environmental and agricultural considerations. The problem, as Petrini saw it, is that the science of agriculture is biased towards the simplified and intensified systems favoured by the agro-industrial giants, because they pay for the research. More environmentally friendly systems will have to develop a parallel base of scientifically acceptable data if they are to fight their corner effectively.

'The real danger of genetically modified foods is that they will lead not only to uncontrolled ecological change but also, even more seriously, to a loss of knowledge and wisdom,' he said. 'It is ludicrous that international agricultural trade agreements are designed to protect the interests of a tiny minority of producers in developed countries – 3 per cent in England and the US. We don't give the *contadini* and traditional producers the recognition and dignity they deserve. We really need to change the way we think about agriculture and the impact we are having on third-world nations. And we can't do that without data, without research. That's what the university will do.'

I found it difficult to resist the force of Petrini's argument, although it might be more truthful to say the force of his personality. It would be cheering to think that his vision is widely shared, but the truth is that the forces of commercial greed and institutional self-interest simply cannot recognise these points. It is not in their nature to do so. They could no more adjust their operations to take into account a more complex, and potentially less profitable, perspective than a great white shark could turn vegetarian. But, according to Joseph Conrad, the only cause worth supporting is a lost one. I tend to agree with him.

Filled with Carlo Petrini's missionary zeal, I headed out of Bra for Turin, on the very last stage of my journey. The road, by way of Carmagnola, was flat once again, as I was back in the Pianura Padana, but, refreshed by the hills of Casale Monferrato and Asti, I felt quite at ease. All I had to do was survive a few more kilometres, and that would be it.

I rode at a steady sixty kilometres per hour, past browny-grey thickets of desiccated maize; past stalls piled high with glossy red and yellow *peperoni quadrati* (sweet peppers), the speciality of the area and the season, and the polytunnels in which they grew; past small factories and then more fields, tilled, already showing the fresh green of new growth of who knew what; past lines of poplars and stands of pollarded willows; down avenues of lime trees, their leaves yellow and falling; past a man forking manure on to his patch of land in the smoky, golden glow of the late autumn afternoon, towards the end of my journey.

EATING UP ITALY

Recipes

TONNO DI CONIGLIO
Rabbit like tuna

Neither this dish, nor the one after it, Capitone marinato, *appear in chapter 11, but so delicious were they that I want to include them. I ate both at Cascina Martini, a restaurant of the highest quality.*

Tonno di Coniglio *is the inland version of tuna in oil. Fresh sea fish would have been unobtainable and tinned tuna expensive.*

The rabbit is poached until tender, taken off the bone, and then marinated in olive oil, garlic and sage. The meat takes on that particular firm, flaky texture of tuna, and absorbs the flavour of the herbs and garlic, too.

Serves 10

Cut the rabbit into pieces. Put in a pan and cover with salted water. Bring to a simmer and cook gently until the meat is ready to fall off the bones, about 45 minutes. Drain the rabbit. Pull the flesh off the bones while still warm. Put it into an earthenware container in layers, with a layer of sage leaves and garlic cloves between each, seasoning each layer as you build. You should have at least three layers of rabbit. Cover with oil. Put in the fridge and leave for at least a night, preferably two or three. At the Cascina Martini it was served on a bed of rice, another local ingredient, but slightly bitter chicory leaves do very well.

1 rabbit

20–30 sage leaves

20 cloves garlic

Salt and pepper, to taste

4 cups extra virgin olive oil

CAPITONE MARINATO

Marinated eel

Serves 10

Divide the eel into fillets, having first removed the skin. Dust the fillets with a mixture of chopped aromatic herbs (thyme, marjoram and fennel) and salt and pepper. Reassemble the fillets into an eel shape, and roll round and round like a coiled hose. Tie the fillets and leave to rest for 30 minutes.

Bring the wine and balsamic vinegar to the boil in a saucepan along with the onion and garlic. When it comes to the boil, gently immerse the eel in the boiling liquid and cook for 5 minutes. Remove the pan from the heat and leave to cool.

The eel is served cold, cut into sections and arranged on a nest of salad which has been dressed with a drizzle of extra virgin olive oil and balsamic vinegar.

2¼ lbs eel

1 bunch of mixed thyme, marjoram and fennel, chopped

Salt and pepper, to taste

2/3 cup of white wine

1/2-2/3 cup of balsamic vinegar

1 onion, chopped

1 clove garlic, diced

L'AGNOLOTTO CASALESE

Agnolotto Casalese

This is a recipe from Augusto Lana, the sage of Casale Monferrato. I give it in his own words: 'Agnolotti are commonly served in our hills and the recipe varies from village to village, from restaurant to restaurant and from family to family. The composition of the filling changes, as does the shape. In order to establish whether the agnolotti are hand made, it is important to analyse the edges – if there are only three edges cut by the agnolotto roller, then they are certainly hand made and not produced using a commercial mould. The components of the filling are generally various meats and vegetables boiled until soft, plus eggs and Parmesan cheese. As a representative recipe of a local agnolotto, I have chosen one from the book La Cucina Monferrina by Francesco Caire. He obtained the recipe after long research. It dates from the beginning of the twentieth century and was used in the kitchen of many Casalesi families. Unusual and in a class of its own is the use of white truffle in the filling, and the non-use of eggs in the pasta. However, I am presenting it to you as it is presented in the book, which is the only available book on the cuisine of Monferrina.'

Serves 10

Poach the beef and the veal in water, along with the slice of ham and the 'kitchen flavourings', i.e. celery, onion and carrot. When the meat is cooked, add the cabbage to the broth and cook it also. Put the meat and cabbage through a mincer along with the stock.

In a separate pan gently fry in butter the finely chopped parsley and the cloves of garlic, add the minced meat mixture and four spoons of stock, which should be thickened with 2 tablespoons flour which has

3½ lbs beef

3/4 lb veal

1/2 lb ham in a single slice

A stick of celery, diced

Half an onion, diced

A small carrot, diced

Half a cabbage

A small bunch of parsley

2 cloves of garlic, diced

3 cups white flour

Parmesan cheese, grated

Pepper

been lightly toasted in the oven. Bring this mixture to the boil and then remove it from the heat, add 4 tablespoons of grated Parmesan, pepper, 5 eggs and a grating of white truffle (this last may be substituted with *funghi porcini*).

6 eggs

1 tablespoon white truffle

2/3 cup of white wine

Salt

THE PASTA FOR THE AGNOLOTTI

Mix 2 cups white flour with tepid water until you have a smooth thick paste. Place this on a board and knead it well, adding more flour until the mixture becomes a manageable unsticky ball. Roll this out into a thin sheet and wet the surface of the pasta with a mixture of beaten egg and water. Dot onto one half of the pasta small heaps of the filling (the size of a hazelnut), in lines. Cover the whole with the remaining half of the pasta. Press all the edges down well and cut the *agnolotti* with the roller.

Remember that *agnolotti* are esteemed if they are small and tender and it is recommended that eggless white pasta should be cooked immediately.

Place the raw *agnolotti* on floured cloths and, 10 minutes before serving, toss them into boiling lightly salted water. When they float, drain them and serve them with butter, cheese and meat sauce. In some families the cabbage is substituted with *scarola* (salad) or spinach; in this case, care should be taken that the filling is not too green.

HAROSET

Haroset

Haroset is a fruit paste eaten during the Passover ritual. This recipe is taken from La Cucina della Memoria, *a book of family recipes from the Jewish community of Casale Monferrato. It comes from Adriana Ottolenghi.*

For 20–25 people

Grind all of the nuts and fruits along with 4–5 tablespoons of sugar, and mix to form a paste. Before serving, moisten it all with orange juice, or white wine or marsala.

1 3/4 cups blanched sweet almonds

1 scant cup skinned hazelnuts

2 1/4 cups pitted dates

2 cups boiled white chestnuts

4 hard-boiled egg yolks or 3 whole hard-boiled eggs

1 cooking apple

1 large pear

1 orange

1 cup plain matzo flour

1 cup sweet matzo flour

SALSICCIA DI BRA

Bra sausage

In Piedmont the production of sausages is fairly widespread and varied according to the local traditions and eating habits. One of the most highly prized and unusual is the sausage from Bra, often wrongly called a veal sausage. In fact it is made from veal and pork fat. In the past, the sausage was made using only beef for the Jewish community in the nearby town of Cherscao. Not wishing to be excluded from the national passion for sausages, they asked butchers to come up with pork-free sausage. It seems this tradition was made official with a royal decree authorizing the butchers of Bra to use beef in the preparation of fresh sausages, the only case in Italy. When numbers in the Jewish community diminished, pork fat was substituted for beef fat, which becomes rancid more quickly.

The sausage is prepared by finely grinding 70–80 per cent of lean Piemontese veal and 20–30 per cent pork fat and belly. The mixture, which should be soft and moist, is packed into small sausage skins made from sheep's gut. All the butchers add sea salt (2/3 cup to every 25 lbs of meat) and their own mixtures of ground spices – usually white pepper, cinnamon, nutmeg and mace in varying amounts depending on the butcher's whim. Each butcher then personalises his sausage by adding garlic, fennel, leek, grated Parmesan cheese and white wine (Arneis or Favorita). Although the recipes are all similar, they are all different and secret. The butchers feed the mystery by only divulging their own sausage recipe to the person who will continue their business.

Bra sausage is preferably eaten raw and as fresh as possible. In fact, the recipe does not contain any additives or preservatives and the sausage mixture tends to go dark very quickly.

12
MIXING MEMORY AND DESIRE

TURIN

Le Fratiglie

There were brains – pig brains, calf brains, sheep brains, horse brains. There were tongues, livers, hearts, kidneys and sweetbreads. There were testicles, lungs, tripe, oesophagi and parts of animals' insides, coiled, flaccid, purple and creamy and glistening, that I couldn't begin to identify. All were being chopped and sold to a crowd of enthusiastic, cheery Ghanaian women dressed in polychromatic brilliance.

The next day in Turin, I turned Bud over to his rightful owners. It was a brisk, unsentimental parting. I walked off up the road, with a slight sense of relief that I did not have to worry about theft, punctures, mechanical failure or personal absurdity any more. Both Vespas had been wonderfully dependable means of transport for almost 5,000 kilometres, travelling at just the right speed for me, undeterred by zigzag mountain tracks or the dead flat roads of the Po valley, resilient and remarkably comfortable. Two months was a long time to spend in another's company, but there had never been a cross word between us.

I sat down on a bench beside the Dora Riparia, a gushing little tributary of the Po that cuts through the city, and watched the water sluicing over a low weir. The dead leaves of autumn lay about my feet. From time to time they were joined by another from the elm trees about me, fluttering down through the grey air. I had accomplished what I had set out to do. The journey was no longer in front of me, but behind me. It was not something to anticipate, but to look back on, not a force of excitement and adventure but a source of anecdote and nostalgia. I felt a great sense of sadness, of loss.

It was right that I ended here in Turin. This was, in reality, where the process of unifying Italy had begun and ended, manipulated in an extraordinary fashion by Count Camillo di Cavour, prime minister to the kingdom of Savoy and then of Italy. He had died before the final act of incorporating the Papal States into the newly unified country, quite possibly as a result of his not inconsiderable greed and his passion for *bicerin*, the artery-clogging Torinese drink of coffee and chocolate.

It was here in Turin that the first parliament of the unified kingdom of Italy had sat in 1861; here that Garibaldi had made a brief stab at subjecting his intemperate spirit to the disciplines of political life before going off in search of further adventures (including leading French armies against the Prussians in the Franco-Prussian war of 1870 at the age of sixty-three).

So was Italy unified in any meaningful sense of the word? There were still deep divisions, between north and south, between region and region, between state and people. There were parts of the country where the inhabitants could not understand what those from another part were saying, so mutually incomprehensible were their dialects. Football reflected the divisive loyalties that in former centuries had been expressed through war. They couldn't even agree on matters such as the correct saucing of *cappellaci*, for heaven's sake.

But, for all its social, linguistic and culinary diversity, Italy, it seemed to me, is indeed united, perhaps more than it recognises. It is united not by notional politics or culture or language, or even by prosciutto, pizza or pasta. It is the passion to grow things to eat, and the casual, commonplace, everyday passion displayed in cooking and eating them, that forms the true, common individual and social currency that fuses the country together.

More than that, food is both the key to understanding Italian life, and a metaphor for Italian politics. The truth takes on a fluid, even nebulous quality where either are concerned. It is possible to trace a recipe or a story back to a certain point, but beyond that point what had seemed incontrovertible becomes curiously controvertible. What is claimed as fact by one authority will be undermined by subtle inference by another, with the suggestion that you, as a foreigner, cannot possibly understand what is really going on. And, just as it is impossible to get agreement on what should go into *salame di fegato* in Sulmona or *pasta e fagioli* in Naples, so it is impossible to get to the bottom of the kidnapping of Aldo Moro, the Gladio affair, the collapse of the Banco Ambrosiano or who planted the bomb that killed sixteen people in the Banco dell' Agricoltura in Milan in 1969. Truth, in the factual sense that I understood it, simply sinks in the sands of many competing, individual interests.

Presently I roused myself and went off to see Guido Gobino, the *giandujotto* king.

The *giandujotto* is the definitive Torinese sweet, made from crushed hazelnuts and chocolate. The Torinesi have the British to thank for it, for in the eighteenth century the British fleet blockaded the Mediterranean in an attempt to bring the France of Napoleon Bonaparte to its knees. As a consequence, no cocoa got into the Mediterranean. In order to make their meagre supplies of chocolate go further, the ingenious sweet makers of Turin began experimenting with various additives. One thing that was in plentiful supply was hazelnuts, which flourish in the hills of the Langhe and around Monferrato. They roasted and crushed them, and added the oily, fragrant mass to milk chocolate. Thus the *gianduja* was born – *giandujotto* meaning a scamp or rascal in the local dialect.

From the outside, 15B Via Cagliari, the court of the *giandujotto* king, was an unremarkable building in an unremarkable street, but entering it, I found myself in the sweet shop equivalent of Emporio Armani. It was chic, with clean lines, slinky lighting, beautiful stacks of coolly packaged chocolate, *giandujotti* and other products, and nice ladies in white coats to take the stack of goodies no reasonably sensible person could fail to buy. At the centre of the shop was a sculptural stand with an immense glass bowl, filled with Gobino products to which any right-thinking person could not but help themselves. Temptation and commercial canniness went hand to mouth, as it were, and around this chocolate-as-fashion-accessory playground eased the *bel mondo* of Turin, fastidious, elegant and greedy.

Behind the immaculate chocolate boutique was the production area, the chocolate factory of Guido Gobino, far removed from the cheery fantasies of Willie Wonka. True, when I stepped into the production area I was immediately wrapped in a sweet coating of the warm, comforting smell of melted chocolate and crushed hazelnuts, but the area was divided up into temperature-regulated zones, and was full of state-of-the-art machinery built to Signor Gobino's specifications – rotating wheels of granite grinding the roasted hazelnuts and paddles steadily churning the *giandujotto* mix to precisely the right texture, before passing it on to another machine that clomped rhythmically as it deposited little peaked mounds – *giandujotto classico, tourinot* or *tourinot maximo* according to the production schedule – on conveyor belts, ready for cooling and for wrapping.

It was quite reassuring, after the temperature zones and computer-controlled machinery, to see the man in charge of roasting the hazelnuts, a process that has to be as precise as splitting the atom, testing the nuts to see if they were ready for grinding. He extracted something that looked like a tiny shovel from its slot in the giant roaster, and tipped the nuts it held into his cupped hand. He held them up to his ear and listened to them for a second or two, before breaking one open with his nail. If the nut was brown enough all the way through, the consignment was ready for crushing.

The workshop, as the company's promotional leaflet describes the establishment, was founded by *'Commendator'* Musso to make chocolates and candles. In 1964, Giuseppe Gobino, already a *chocolatier*, took over chocolate production, becoming the sole owner in 1980. In 1985 his son Guido Gobino joined the firm and set about revolutionising the company's practices and standards.

Guido Gobino did not look like a radical. He was as immaculate as his shop, with a neatly clipped head of hair the colour of a badger-hair shaving brush and a moustache so impeccable that it looked as if it had been drawn in charcoal. In his white coat he had the air of a research chemist, and he spoke about chocolate and nuts with the same degree of exactitude.

The classic *giandujotto* was only one of the products. In his creative zeal, Signor Gobino had pushed back the boundaries of chocolate and hazelnut technology by creating a smaller *giandujotto* of five grams, as opposed to the normal one of ten grams. He called it the *tourinot*.

'The bigger *giandujotto* is quite rich. They coat the mouth,' he said, 'and so people tend to eat only one of them. But they will eat three *tourinots*.'

Then came the *tourinot maximo*, a *giandujotto* made without milk, containing just chocolate, hazelnut and sugar, which had a much purer flavour.

But these were only the beginnings of the results of his experiments with chocolate, nuts and other ingredients. There were pure chocolate discs, slabs of different chocolate with coarsely crushed hazelnuts, and chocolates dosed with cinnamon oil and ginger and mint – each the product of painstaking research and combining very precise amounts of exactly the right chocolate to the necessary proportion of flavouring, and to be accompanied by a specific drink.

Making chocolates may have been for Signor Gobino a passion amounting to an obsession, but it was based on scientific analysis and a precise understanding of the qualities of his chosen medium. He used only single-variety chocolate, a different one with a different flavour profile for each product. He used Piedmontese hazelnuts because only they had the right kind of oil for his purposes.

'Each chocolate presents a different problem, because the balance of the end product has to be exactly right. I source the different chocolates from different small producers in Java, Ghana, Venezuela and Ecuador. Then I have problems finding a refiner I can trust to get the chocolate consistently as I want it. And then the characteristics of the hazelnuts vary from season to season. So it goes on. You can never take anything for granted. It took me five years to develop the chocolate with cinnamon, to find the Venezuelan chocolate with the right degree of bitterness and then to work out that we should use cinnamon essence and not ground cinnamon. Now we use cinnamon essence from Sri Lanka. It has a wonderful delicacy, but it lasts in the mouth, on and on. Do you see?'

I did. I stocked up with enough of the exquisite little boxes of this and that to keep my family going to Christmas – or at least they would have done, had I not made severe inroads on them almost immediately.

'*Che seppie, che seppie. Dai-i. Daaaii-i!*' chanted a large man with a blue chin and a shiny apron standing by a fish stall.

The great market of Porta Palazzo in Turin, where the Via Milano meets the Piazza della Repubblica, could scarely be further removed from the chic niceties of Guido Gobino. It seethed with humanity. It pullulated with noise.

Turin has at least one other market on this huge scale, and several smaller ones serving particular neighbourhoods; but the market at Porta Palazzo is the grandest, the one nearest the centre. This was the one that drew the white-collar workers, blue-collar workers, nursing mothers, provisioning grannies, men, women, Ghanaian and Tunisian immigrants and Romanian gypsies, lovers of horsemeat, tripe and lungs, epicures looking for *funghi porcini*, men from Sardinia, Sicily and Calabria who needed the ingredients to recreate the dishes of the villages of their birth, women who wanted—

'*Due etti di acquadelle.*'

'*Acquadelle buonissime, signora,*' said the man with the blue chin.

There were, what, nine, ten stalls, each banked high with fish. Take your choice of *seppie, polpo, calamari, moscardini* or *ciuffi*, all different kinds of squid or octopus, heaps of shiny, limp limbs. Or boxes of *triglie, branzini, orate* and *pagelli*, neatly lined up in rows. Or hummocks of *gamberetti, gamberi, gamberoni* and *cicale di mare* waving their legs, crabs blowing bubbles, lobsters blue and passive. There were bags of mussels, bags of *ragusa*, bags of razor clams, bags of *vongole*.

'*Tre etti di vongole.*'

'*Tre etti! Tre etti! Per quante persone, signora?*'

'*Per tre.*'

'*Va bene. Vongole freschissime!*'

There were *cernie, sarde, alici, molli, sgombri, naselli, boghe, sogliole, gronchi, razze, costadelle* and *spatole*, silvery, gilt, metallic as gunmetal, red-finned, dark-eyed, barred, striped, tinted with blue, glittering, gleaming, shiny, lambent, lucent scales. There were fillets of perch, white as ivory, with a seam of coral pink running through them, and carp, bronzy-gold like small barrels.

'*Hiy-ou!*'

'*'Namo, 'namo.*'

The smell was piscine, marine, tinged with ammonia.

'*Ciao, ragazze, cozze bellissime!*'

'*Signore, forza, che gamberi, che gamberi.*'

On the other side of the Via Milano was the professionally run fruit and vegetable section, stall upon stall upon stall so lined up that I had to squeeze between them, bumped and banged by shoppers and their bags and their containers on wheels and their baby buggies and their partners, their friends, their families. I was assailed by the smell of pears here and fennel there, and persimmons, celery, tomatoes, salt cod, olives, cigarette smoke and grapes.

'Dai, dai, dai, uvauvauva!'
'Dai, uva bellissima, due euro il chilo.'
'Un euro il chilo.'
'Dai, dai, dai.'

The voices were pitched at a plangent, sing-song level. The singers were Algerians and Moroccans, as well as Sardinians, Sicilians and Calabresi. This was how and where all Italians, of whatever pedigree or provenance, met and melded, brought together, briefly, by the humdrum love of food. Swirling, whirling, bartering, buying, they shared the common cause that was the foundation of the nation's character and sense of community, eating.

'Signore, melone, melone, assaggi il melone!'
'Porcini freschissimi!'
'Fagioli belli!'
'Peperoni nostrani!'
'Insalata mista, colta a mano.'
'Un chilo di pere, signora? Certo.'
'Due cinquanta, signore.'
'Melanzane, forza, forza, melanzane!'
'Due chili? Va bene.'

Tucked away behind a large glass and wrought-iron building that housed some of the butchers' stands and *alimentari*, there was another fruit and vegetable section. This was a quieter, more sedate affair. The sales people were the growers, bringing in their produce from smallholdings on the outskirts of the city. There was little of the hubbub of the main market. Customers were inquisitive, conversational, familiar. They wanted to know about the tomatoes, the celery, the mushrooms, where they came from, how they were grown, when they were picked.

'Everything comes from my garden,' said one old biddy, who looked like the witch in *Snow White*. 'It's grown just ten minutes from here. And it's completely organic. It's important to me, selling here. I have bills to pay. I have a household to feed.'

There was a thin but steady stream of customers, most of whom were women, a small percentage of them elderly men. By contrast, the professional stallholders were mostly in their late twenties and thirties, while the smallholders were middle-aged or older.

Here were the last of the figs; a box or two of dusty, dark blue *uva fragola* – small, strawberry-flavoured grapes; large crescents of brilliant orange pumpkin; clumps of spiky, blanched cardoons; greens for salad – *insalatina, sarsèt, ruga, cicorietta, cicoria, radicchio, catalogna*; and beans, green beens, yellow beans and borlotti beans in white pods fired with pinky/red stripes. One stall had seven varieties of chili. Another was piled with 'Romanesco' broccoli. There were thickets of *cime di rapa,* spinach and chard.

'We are usually busier than this,' grumbled a bald, tanned fellow in a brilliant red jersey. 'But there's the threat of a transport strike. As if we don't have enough troubles. The markets aren't what they were. People live further away from the centre than they used to. They don't have enough time to shop or cook properly. And then there are the supermarkets. And now a strike. Things should be busier tomorrow. I hope.'

One man was selling ducks, chickens, rabbits and pigeons. 'To eat or to lay eggs.'

Another sold just ricotta, another salamis, *cotechini* (boiling sausages) and pancetta, all *'fatti in casa'*. There was even a stall where a Chinese woman stood patiently waiting for takers for pak choi, cylindrical white mooli radishes and winter melons the size of Zeppelins.

Inside the hall behind them the air was filled with the snicker of knives on steel, the fleshy thumps of escalopes being flatted, the thwacks of blades crunching through bone and the hum of chiller cabinets.

And inside those chiller cabinets, lit up brightly so that you could register the exact colour of the flesh inside was an array and diversity of meats – pinky grey veal, grey-pink rabbit, burgundy horse, creamy yellow chicken, coral lamb, claret beef, rosy pork – baffling for even the most experienced carnivore. Rabbits came whole, or half, or just the saddles or just the legs or boned and stuffed. There were quails and turkeys. There were chickens complete with heads and combs, scrawny *nostrani* ('our own') or battery products as round as balloons. There were chickens dissected into any combination of joints you might want.

There were horse butchers, whose cuts vied with those of the veal butcher across the aisle – fillet, rib, cutlet, tongue, tail, burger, sausage. There was *porceδδu* (suckling pig) and *capretto* (kid) from Sardinia. Whole pigs' heads peered with placid solemnity, mouths agape, at the passing trade. Half pigs' heads lay stacked neatly beside piles of trotters and ears. There were brains – pig brains, calf brains, sheep brains, horse brains. There were tongues, livers, hearts, kidneys and sweetbreads. There were testicles, lungs, tripe, oesophagi and parts of animals' insides, coiled, flaccid, purple and creamy and glistening, that I couldn't begin to identify. All were being chopped and sold to a crowd of enthusiastic, cheery Ghanaian women dressed in polychromatic brilliance.

Many of the butchers were young, men and women, which suggested that these were family businesses. One came from Tuscany, another from Sardinia, another from Sicily, another from the Marche. Much of the meat was sourced from their original regions, which meant that it carried the taste of those parts, and was butchered so that the traditional dishes could be cooked by homesick emigrants.

Sausages told their own story of local identity. There wasn't a butcher who didn't do his own. These weren't the chubby links I was used to, but long, thin, sinuous, continuous coils. Nor did the butchers aspire to the exotic combinations with which British butchers seek to excite their jaded customers. Most of the sausages in the market in the Via Roma were simply described as *'puro suino'* – pure pork. Look a little closer and there were a few *'con prezzemolo'* (with parsley) and others *'con finocchietto'* (with fennel). There was a little stack of *cotechini*, some black pudding, *sanguinaccio*, something labelled *'salame di Turgia'*, and something else labelled *'Siciliano'*.

And there was plenty of banter between butcher and customer.

'Ma, sei sempre in vacanze, tu?'

'Vacanze! Che vacanze? Sono sempre al lavoro.'

And then it was down to business, as the meat was ordered bit by bit.

First the lamb. 'Five chops.'

The five chops were carefully cut, laid out on the paper, shown to the *signora*, and then wrapped.

'Anything else?'

'Oh, I'll have four kidneys.'

The lady and the butcher went through the ritual again.

'Anything else?'

'Do you have any *spezzatino*?'

'Of course, signora. How much?'

She conferred with her husband.

'Tre etti e mezzo. No, make that half a kilo.' And so on and so on for twenty minutes.

And all about the same process was going on.

'How much Parmesan, *signora*?'

'What's the fontina like?'

'Ten slices of *prosciutto crudo*, and another of *prosciutto cotto*.'

'The mortadella is *bella, bella*. Shall we get some pancetta, darling? No, perhaps not.'

And so it went, six days a week, fifty-two weeks of the year. Saturday was the big day. *'Favoloso!'* said one man to me. *'Ci sono tutti gli antichi prodotti il sabato. Tutto il giorno.'* There are all these traditional products each Saturday. The market is open all day.

But not that day. Come 2:30 p.m. it was all gone, as if it had never been. Every market day except Saturday, all the fruit and vegetable stalls disappeared at 1 p.m., the unsold produce was boxed up, loaded back in the vans and carted off to the chill rooms, and the stalls were folded up and stacked somewhere, while the street cleaners came in, complete with bulldozer and pressure hoses, and the whole area was suddenly transformed into a car park, except for the fishmongers, butchers and *alimentari* in the sturdy, functional glass and wrought-iron buildings. They continued dishing out the liver and lites, rabbit legs and horse steaks and wafer-thin escalopes of veal and lumps of pecorino and Parmesan until seven thirty in the evening.

And in the streets around, halal butchers, delis selling vines leaves, orange blossom water, yoghurt and the Middle Eastern spice and hut mixture *dukkah*, and *pasticcerie* piled high with baklava and the syrup-sodden pastries of Lebanon and Tunisia, marked the latest Moorish invasion, and latest wave of food cultures washing through Italy.

It was my last evening. Already I felt off duty. I went to dinner with the Larizza family, who lived in a modest but smart house, one of a number on a modern development in Grugliasco, a suburb of Turin. They were friends of John Irving, an Englishman of much individuality, intelligence and expertise in all aspects of Italian culture, who had become a friend of mine on an earlier visit to Turin. He had come to the city from Carlisle in his twenties, drawn by the irresistible lure of the Juventus football team. I have never been able to understand this visceral tribal passion, but there you go, and there John Irving went. The fact that his friend, Nicola Larizza, was a supporter of Inter Milan brought a frisson to their relationship, much as chili livens up the food of Calabria and the Abruzzo.

Nicola ran a tobacconist's shop, which meant that he got up at five every morning, and closed at seven thirty every night. He was known as '*il mago di Matera*', the wizard of Matera, his home town in Basilicata, because the old women of the neighbourhood, to whom he sold lottery tickets, credited him with powers of numerology, and whenever they won even the paltriest sums, assigned their good fortune to his amazing forecasts.

Nicola had a smooth, pouchy face, thinning hair and eyes full of good humour. He radiated commanding vigour and affection. Like so many others, he had originally come to Turin to find work. He had met and married Maura, who came from Ferrara and had a lively, laughing face. They had three children: Elisabetta, the eldest, who was seventeen; Francesco, fifteen, a footballer; and Enrica, aged nine, also known as *'la regina di Spagna'*, the Queen of Spain, for complicated family reasons.

They were one of those families whose friendly energy immediately embraces anyone who comes through their door. There was an easy flow between them and me. The children did not seem inhibited in any way by having a complete stranger in their midst, crowded into the small kitchen where we ate – salami and olives; *pasta al forno; tasca ripiena di spinaci e Parmigiano* (stuffed shoulder of pork); cheese; and ice cream.

This meal was, explained Maura, 'Nothing special, what we would normally eat, more or less, though we like to make a bit of a show when John comes. He needs feeding up, as you can see. It's *la cucina di Basilicata fatta alla maniera di* – in the style of – Ferrara. I could never cook real dishes from Matera, because I have never lived there. You have to grow up with dishes, live with them, to be able to cook them properly.'

She shopped two or three times a week, she said, in the local market, which was a very good one. No, there wasn't much she wanted from a supermarket, and you never knew where the food in them came from, did you?

I commented on the excellence of the bread.

'Ah, but it's really not a patch on the bread of the south,' said Nicola, which was true.

The children talked about food with the same matter-of-fact intelligence as all Italians.

'I prefer the salamis of the north,' said Elisabetta. 'I find the ones that Dad likes to bring back from Basilicata too *piccanti.'*

'Oh, I don't mind the chili. It's quite nice, really,' said her brother.

'And I like olives,' said Enrica.

'I rather thought you did,' I said, having watched her work her way steadily through a bowl of them on the table.

'Only the black ones,' she added.

'They eat what we eat,' said their mother. 'If they don't like it, I won't make a fuss, but I'm not going to cook a separate meal for them. But they're very good. They'll eat most things – *pasta e fagioli,* green vegetables, salad, tripe–'

'Tripe?!'

'Yes, tripe.'

'Do you really like tripe?' I asked Elisabetta.

'Oh, yes,' she said. 'Why not?'

I explained that even adults in England had trouble with tripe. As for children, well, forget it.

'But it's good,' she said. 'And it's very easy to digest.'

They spoke about a recent holiday they had taken in Spain.

'It was very interesting,' said Maura, 'but we didn't really think much of the food. Paella wasn't a patch on a good risotto.'

I suggested that Italians don't really like eating anything other than Italian food, and preferably the food from the locality where they grew up.

'That's true. But that's because it's better,' said Maura simply.

Because it's better: that seemed to sum up everything.

As we shuddered back to Turin in John Irving's rackety Fiat, I savoured the memory of the Larizza family's generosity to me and their affection towards each other and to John. It brought to mind all the other kindnesses and open-handed liberality that I had received, from the Capellos, Gaetanos, Cicchis and the Benellis, and from Giancarlo and Ilde and Augusto Lana and dozens of others, and I wondered for how much longer their kind of unquestioning hospitality would survive, and whether traditional social values based on family responsibilities could exist in a political and commercial environment, which holds that individual choice is the supreme principle.

Many Italians, male and female, still live at home until they are in their thirties. This is even more marked in the south than in the north, because unemployment levels are much higher. If it is hard for men to find work, it is even harder for women. If you aren't working, it is cheaper to stay at home, particularly if you are well fed there. This means that children are exposed to parental domestic influences, including gastronomic ones, to a degree we have forgotten in Britain.

This form of domestic indoctrination is utterly depressing or a source of traditional wisdom, depending on your point of view. On the one hand, it leads to the restriction, not to say repression, of individual liberty and choice, which runs counter to the general course of Western values of the last 500 years, and it has resulted in a conformist society with essentially conservative values. On the other hand, this involuntary restraint means that Italians benefit from a degree of inter-generational civilising and gastronomic continuity that the rest of the developed nations have abandoned. They maintain a sense of social responsibility within their own community. And that is why the food in Italy is so good, and the behaviour generally courteous. It is one of the abiding ironies that the conservative, conformist values of Italian society have fashioned the most stout-hearted of defences of culinary independence.

The tidal wave of unadulterated consumerism that the Berlusconi era has unleashed in Italy, as Margaret Thatcher released it in Britain, and the economic priorities it embraces, threatens to destroy the fine fabric of Italian social and eating habits within one or two generations. If life is treated as a shopping opportunity, in which we have the right to choose from an almost infinite number of possibilities without having to accept any concomitant responsibilities, if the desires of the individual triumph over responsibilities to collective society, even if society is only defined in terms of the family, the traditional values of community experience, of which eating together is one, will vanish.

On the other hand, throughout my trip I saw evidence that this has not yet happened. I kept being told that things were changing, that you couldn't find this sausage or that bread any longer, that agriculture was becoming increasingly industrialised, that more women were working, that fewer people had the time for the rituals of shopping locally and cooking the time-consuming dishes of their region, that the younger generation did not have the same respect for their native food culture that the speaker had. Yet in many cases the speaker was no older than those whose lack of knowledge they were lamenting, and the gloomy assessment was offered in the course of a meal that celebrated the very values they claimed were being lost.

Everywhere I went, I came across foods and dishes so rooted in a specific place and season – the spring tuna in Reggio di Calabria, *taralli* in Naples, *ricotta* in Abruzzo, *coniglio* in *porchetta* in the Marche, *salama da sugo* in Ferrara – that their essential nature was inextricably woven into the sense of identity of the people who produced them and the people who ate them.

Nevertheless, the fact is that Italy does not stand outside the rest of the world, no matter how much we, and many Italians, might wish it to do so. It is subject to the same tides of international commerce, bureaucracy and political duress as all countries.

In spite of so much evidence to the contrary, I found it difficult to escape the conclusion that even Italians are slowly yielding to ferocious, inexorable, incessant external pressures. The streets of many Italian towns are already losing the rich mix of shops that you used to find everywhere, with their narrow fronts and unexpectedly deep interiors, and with them have gone the social services they brought to the neighbourhood. Away from their immediate localities and the inherent loyalties of those markets, small, artisanal producers struggle with the concept of conventional competitiveness. Price, delivery, consistency and regulation all serve to undermine them. How can you compare the price of a salami made by hand from pigs that have slowly grown from piglet to maturity a few yards from the home in which the salami maker lives to even a medium-sized commercial operation? And as the loyal small, local communities slowly vanish, so will the specialist producers who serve and depend on them, to be replaced by economies of scale that compromise quality and individuality.

But if, inevitably, things are changing, the pace of change is far slower than that of other Western countries. This doughty resistance to the shibboleths of modern commerce and society can be interpreted as conservatism or obstinacy or independence. Whichever, it requires cooperation between producers and consumers. And it requires various levels of officialdom and bureaucracy to fail to enforce state and EU diktat. In effect, it requires the conspiracy of a whole people to close their eyes to commercial and political pressures, to GATT agreements, EU regulations and the freebooting antics of international commercial interests designed to restrict, control, exploit and homogenise.

On my way to the airport the next day, I fell into conversation with the taxi driver.

'Food, eh?' he said. 'So you're writing a book about Italian food. That's a big subject.'

I agreed.

'Very complicated.'

I agreed.

'The trouble with Italians,' he said, 'is that they speak in dialect and they eat in dialect.'

I agreed that was how it seemed to me, too.

'And what about Sicilian food?' he said. 'I'm not Sicilian, but I think Sicilian cooking is the best of all. The tomatoes, the *melanzane*, the fish, they're really great, so healthy and the flavours are so intense . . . Do you know about *limoncello*?'

I said that I did, and that the best that I had tasted was in Calabria, in Marina di Maratea.

'Do you have a good recipe for *limoncello*?' he asked.

I admitted that I did not.

'You need one, to remind you of your journey. I like to make my own. You've got to start with really good lemons. The best come from Amalfi. And then—' and away he went, describing how to make the liqueur from lemon peel, sugar and alcohol.

When we got to the airport, I paid him and asked him for a receipt. He scribbled for a moment, and then handed me a piece of paper on which was written:

Limoncello
10 lemons (leave one whole)
1 lb sugar (melted)
1 1/2 quarts of water
1 quart of alcohol
1 month, maximum [sic]
MASSIMO

He stuck his head out of the window of his cab. 'You've got to leave it for at least a month before you drink it. Understand? Not before. Fantastic!'

Fantastic? That hadn't been the half of it.

INDEX

INDEX